COLLINS
COBUILD

ENGLISH GUIDES
1: PREPOSITIONS

KT-487-731

A21229

HarperCollins Publishers
77-85 Fulham Palace Road
London W6 8JB

COBUILD is a trademark of William Collins Sons & Co Ltd

© HarperCollins Publishers Ltd 1991
First published 1991

Reprinted 1991, 1992, 1993, 1994, 1995, 1996

10 9 8 7

All rights reserved. No part of this book may be
reproduced, stored in a retrieval system, or transmitted in
any form or by any means, electronic, mechanical,
photocopying or otherwise, without the prior
permission in writing of the Publisher.

ISBN 0 00 370520 X

Computer typeset by Promenade Graphics, Cheltenham

Printed and bound in Great Britain by
Caledonian International Book Manufacturing Ltd,
Glasgow, G4

NOTE Entered words that we have reason to believe
constitute trademarks have ben designated as such.
However, neither the presence nor absence of such
designation should be regarded as affecting the legal
status of any trademark.

A21229
EALING TERTIARY COLLEGE
ACTON CENTRE LIBRARY

423 col

Editorial Team

Editor in Chief   John Sinclair

Managing Editor   Gwyneth Fox

Senior Editor   Stephen Bullon

Editor   Elizabeth Manning

Assistant Editor   Deborah Yuill

Editorial Assistance   Helen Bruce
Michael Murphy

Computer Staff   Zoe James
Tim Lane

Secretarial Staff   Sue Smith
Sue Crawley

HarperCollins Publishers
Annette Capel, Lorna Heaslip, Marina Maher,
Douglas Williamson

We would like to thank Rosamund Moon for her valuable contribution in the early stages of the project. We would also like to thank Janet Hilsdon, who did much of the research for Part One of the book, and Jane Bradbury and John Todd for their editorial assistance.

COBUILD **Publications**

Collins COBUILD English Dictionary
Collins COBUILD Learner's Dictionary
Collins COBUILD Essential English Dictionary
Collins COBUILD Student's Dictionary
Collins COBUILD Dictionary of Idioms
Collins COBUILD Dictionary of Phrasal Verbs

Collins COBUILD English Grammar
Collins COBUILD Grammar Patterns 1: Verbs
Collins COBUILD Student's Grammar
Collins COBUILD Basic Grammar

Collins COBUILD English Usage
Collins COBUILD Student's Usage

Collins COBUILD English Guides 1: Prepositions
Collins COBUILD English Guides 2: Word Formation
Collins COBUILD English Guides 3: Articles
Collins COBUILD English Guides 4: Confusable Words
Collins COBUILD English Guides 5: Reporting
Collins COBUILD English Guides 6: Homophones
Collins COBUILD English Guides 7: Metaphor
Collins COBUILD English Guides 8: Spelling
Collins COBUILD English Guides 9: Linking Words
Collins COBUILD English Guides 10: Determiners and Quantifiers

Collins COBUILD Keywords in the Media
Collins COBUILD Keywords in Business

Collins COBUILD Vocabulary Builders: Books 1-4

Collins COBUILD Concordance Samplers 1: Prepositions
Collins COBUILD Concordance Samplers 2: Phrasal Verbs
Collins COBUILD Concordance Samplers 3: Reporting
Collins COBUILD Concordance Samplers 4: Tenses

Collins COBUILD English Course: Levels 1-3
Collins COBUILD English Course: Tests
Collins COBUILD English Course: First Lessons

Looking up
The Lexical Syllabus

Foreword

The COBUILD GUIDES each deal with a key area of English. In addition to our general dictionaries and Grammar we have been planning for some time to add smaller but more detailed handbooks dealing with important aspects of grammar and usage.

Each book is specially designed for a specific job. Most have a reference-book style, and some include practice material as well. They are all based on real examples drawn from the 20 million words of the Birmingham Collection of English Text and a further 5 million words from the *Times* newspapers which now form a part of The Bank of English.

The advantages of a Guide which deals with one particular part of English are that there is room for more information than in a big general dictionary, and that this information is easier to find.

This book provides information about the combination of words and prepositions in English, something you need to know for almost every sentence you write or speak. In many cases there is one particular preposition that regularly occurs in relation to a meaning of a word, and it is not always easy to work out which preposition is the appropriate one.

Using this Guide should make this area of English clearer to you. Each preposition has a characteristic range of meaning, and many uses of prepositions are quite regular. Their normal patterns are found in Part One of the book. There are 124 prepositions and 556 different uses.

However, in addition to this, there are a large number of words in English that typically occur with particular prepositions, and these present problems for most learners. Part Two of the book lists these words, with examples. There are over 2,000 entries.

I hope that we have selected useful information and made it easy for you to find what you want, to understand it, and to use it with confidence. Please write to me with any comments or suggestions about how to improve COBUILD publications.

John Sinclair
Editor in Chief
Professor of Modern English Language
University of Birmingham

Introduction

There are over 100 prepositions in English. This is a very small number compared with the vast number of nouns, adjectives, and verbs which English has. Most sentences that people produce contain at least one preposition; indeed, three out of the ten most frequent words of English are prepositions: *of*, *to*, and *in*. This means that the number of times you need to use a particular preposition is much higher than for an ordinary word such as a noun, adjective, or verb.

Prepositions are used as the first word in a **prepositional group**, which provides information about place or time, or in a more abstract way, about relationships between people or things. Prepositions have a function in language rather than a clear meaning of their own. In some cases, the meaning of a sentence can still be understood even if the prepositions are taken out:

Many ... them are used to provide information ... place or time, or, ... a more abstract way, ... relationships ... people or things.

In other cases, the preposition provides essential information:

He put it back ... the desk.

In this example, the missing preposition could be *on*, *behind*, *next to*, *under*, or any of several other prepositions, and the choice here is important for the meaning of the sentence.

In order to produce acceptable and natural English, you need to be able to select the right preposition.

Sometimes the preposition is associated with a verb. For example:

*... if you can't **distinguish between** good and bad.*

Sometimes it is associated with an adjective, for example:

*I know he's **clever at** political debate.*

And in other cases it is associated with a noun, for example:

*My real **friendship with** him began in Rome.*

Like transitive verbs, prepositions take an object, called a **prepositional object**. The object is normally a **noun group**. The noun group can be simply one word, for **example**:

*She looked at **me**.*

or it can be a complex noun group:

You may be surprised at **the range of services it can provide**.

The object can also be a clause built round the '-ing' form of a verb. In these cases, the '-ing' clause acts like a noun group:

They have become expert at **drawing up maps**.

See also the entry for *as*, which can have an adjective after it.

When the object is a personal pronoun, the **object form** of the pronoun must be used. The object forms of personal pronouns are: *me*, *you*, *her*, *him*, *it*, *us*, and *them*. For example, you would say:

We spent ages waiting for **them**.

In this sentence, *we* is a subject pronoun and *them* is the object pronoun which follows the preposition *for*.

One of the most common errors that people learning English make is to use the wrong preposition. This book is intended to help you choose the right preposition at the right time.

How to use the book

This book is divided into two parts, so there are two possible ways of finding out more information about prepositions.

Part One explains the prepositions themselves, and Part Two is an alphabetical list of nouns, verbs, and adjectives which are typically followed by a preposition.

Part One: The Prepositions

The first part contains an alphabetical listing of 124 prepositions. Their meanings and uses are described in separate paragraphs, and an indication is given of where they typically occur in sentences. Examples illustrate the various meanings and grammatical structures that the prepositions occur in. These examples are all drawn from the 20 million words of the Birmingham Collection of English Text and from a corpus of 5 million words of the *Times* newspapers.

Finding the Preposition

The prepositions are listed alphabetically. Where a preposition consists of two words, the alphabetical order is that of the letters, and the space between the words is ignored, so that the order of prepositions starting from *against* is:

against
ahead of
along
alongside
along with
amid

Where a preposition has two possible forms, this is shown in a note after the headword line, often with a comment that tells you whether the alternative form is more formal or literary:

among
The form **amongst** is also used, but is a more literary word.

The Explanations

The explanations of the prepositions are written in full sentences. They give you information about whether the preposition is associated with a verb, noun, or adjective, and also about the sort of prepositional object that is likely to occur:

If something happens before a time or event, it happens earlier than that time or event.

When there is more than one sense, there will be more than one explanation, and the explanations are numbered.

The Grammar Notes

Each sense gives you information about where in a sentence the preposition typically occurs.

1 The preposition is often part of an **adjunct**, which means that it tends to come after a verb. The grammar note will say:

In an adjunct:

If the verb is intransitive, then the preposition is likely to be the next word:

It belongs to me.

If the verb is transitive, the preposition is likely to come after the object of the verb:

He didn't compare himself with other men.

Sometimes, the structure of a sentence involves putting the prepositional object in front of a verb, for example if you want to emphasize the object, or when you are using a verb in the passive. When this happens, the preposition can come after the verb:

They were quite difficult to deal with.
Babies like to be talked to.

When you use a relative clause, there are two possible positions for the preposition. It can come at the end of the clause:

These were the ones I waited for.

Note that some speakers of English believe that it is ungrammatical to have a preposition at the end of a sentence, but it happens very frequently, especially in informal and spoken English.

Alternatively, the preposition can come in front of the relative pronoun:

These were the ones for which I waited.

Putting the preposition in front of a relative pronoun is very formal.

2 Prepositions also come after the link verb *be* or other link verbs such as *seem* or *appear*. If the link verb is typically only *be*, for example in the sentence:

He's from the BBC.

the grammar note will say:

After 'be':

If the preposition can typically go with other link verbs as well, for example:

He looked like a sheepdog.

the grammar note will say:

After a link verb:

3 Prepositions can also be used after a noun to introduce information about the noun rather than about the action described by the verb. For example in the sentence

He had received an invitation to Julie's wedding.

the prepositional phrase tells you more about the invitation than about the fact that he received it. In these cases, the grammar note will say:

After a noun:

4 Finally, some prepositions give you information about adjectives. For example, in the sentence

I was keen on politics.

the prepositional phrase gives more precise information about the adjective and what it relates to. In these cases, the grammar note will say:

After an adjective:

Very occasionally, the grammar note will be slightly longer in order to provide a more detailed piece of information. For example, the grammar note at *except* says:

After an indefinite pronoun or a noun:

The Examples

Each sense is illustrated by several examples drawn from the Birmingham Collection of English Text, showing you how writers and speakers of modern English use prepositions. The examples are in *italic* and follow immediately after the grammar note.

The Lists

Where it is appropriate, a number of related words are grouped together and presented in a list. These lists contain words which typically occur with the preposition. The lists do not contain all the words that are possible, but they do include those that are frequent, and they are intended to give you an idea of the range of words that can go with the preposition in that sense.

Part Two: The Combinations

The second part of this book consists of an alphabetical list of words which are not prepositions. These are nouns, verbs, and adjectives which typically occur with just one or two prepositions, and you can use this part as a quick reference list to check which preposition you need. This section contains over 2,000 entries and more than 4,000 combinations of word and preposition.

There are, of course, a lot of 'free' combinations of words and prepositions. In these cases, the choice of preposition depends on the meaning that you want to express, and it is the preposition that contributes to the meaning. For example, in the sentence:

She works in London.

the preposition *in* has been selected because it gives precise information about the place; but other prepositions could have been chosen, for example *near* or *outside*. So here the choice of preposition is quite wide and combinations such as these are not included in this section.

However, in the sentence:

He always works in oil paints.

the choice of preposition is restricted and not necessarily predictable, and so this combination is included.

The Entries

The entries consist of the headword; a short phrase which shows you which preposition is typically used; and a typical prepositional object. The wording of this phrase tells you what part of speech the word is. If the word is a verb, the phrase begins with the infinitive with *to*:

to **hope for** something.

If the word is a count noun, a determiner is generally used:

an **interest in** something.

If the word is an uncount noun, there is usually no determiner:

freedom from something unpleasant or unwanted.

If the word is an adjective, the phrase starts with the word *be*:

be **enthusiastic about** something.

If more than one preposition is possible, this is shown in the introductory phrase:

to **benefit from** something or **by** something.
be **adamant about** something or **on** something; be **adamant in**
opposing or refusing something.

Where an alternative combination is given in full, the two structures are separated by a semi-colon (;) as in the example above for *adamant*.

The phrase is then followed by one or more examples. If more than one preposition is possible, then an example is given for each preposition.

Often, a word which has more than one sense uses the same preposition in all or many of its senses. Where this happens, we do not list all the senses of the word separately, unless there is likely to be confusion with other senses.

Some words can be pronounced in two different ways, depending on their meaning. When this happens, an indication of the pronunciation is given, following the conventions of the International Phonetic Alphabet. A key to this alphabet is given at the end of this section.

In those cases where the meaning of the combination is unlikely to be clear or might be confused with another combination, a short explanation of the meaning is given after a colon (:).

Note: the most frequent preposition in English is the word *of*. (It occurs over half a million times in the 20 million words of the Birmingham Collection of English Text.) The main uses of *of* are given in Part One. Many of these uses are so common and predictable that they are not included in Part Two.

For example, look at the following sentence:

His arrival transformed the company.

Here, *the company* is the object of the transitive verb *transform*.

Now look at this sentence:

We were amazed at the sudden transformation of the company.

Here, the noun *transformation* is derived from the verb *transform* and *the company* is now in a prepositional phrase headed by *of* and coming after the noun.

Now look at this sentence, which contains an intransitive verb:

The delegation arrived.

Here, *the delegation* is the subject of the verb. But when you replace *arrived* with the noun *arrival*, you can say:

... the arrival of the delegation.

The basic meaning has not changed but *the delegation* now comes in a prepositional phrase headed by *of* after the noun.

This is a standard and very frequent use of the preposition *of*, and it is therefore not recorded in the second part of this book. Only those combinations with *of* that are unpredictable are given here.

Phrases

Prepositions often occur before or after words in phrases. These are listed under the appropriate word in the list, so you will find the phrase *in accordance with* in the entry for *accordance*. If there is more than one phrase, a short definition is provided after a colon (:) so that you can see the difference in meaning:

by accident: not deliberately.
in an accident: in a violent crash or collision.

Pronunciation

Here is a list of the International Phonetic Alphabet symbols for English:

vowel sounds

ɑː	heart, start, calm.
æ	act, mass, lap.
aɪ	dive, cry, mind.
aɪə	fire, tyre, buyer.
aʊ	out, down, loud.
aʊə	flour, tower, sour.
eɪ	say, main, weight.
eə	fair, care, wear.
ɪ	fit, win, list.
iː	feed, me, beat.
ɪə	near, beard, clear.
ɒ	lot, lost, spot.
əʊ	note, phone, coat.
ɔː	more, cord, claw.
ɔɪ	boy, coin, joint.
ʊ	could, stood, hood.
uː	you, use, choose.
ʊə	sure, poor, cure.
ɜː	turn, third, word.
ʌ	but, fund, must.
ə	the weak vowel in butter, about, forgotten.

consonant sounds

b	bed	t	talk
d	done	v	van
f	fit	w	win
g	good	x	loch
h	hat	z	zoo
j	yellow	ʃ	ship
k	king	ʒ	measure
l	lip	ŋ	sing
m	mat	tʃ	cheap
n	nine	θ	thin
p	pay	ð	then
r	run	dʒ	joy
s	soon		

Stressed syllables are indicated by an <u>underline</u> under the vowel symbol for the stressed syllable.

Corpus Acknowledgements

We wish to thank the following, who have kindly given permission for the use of copyright material in the Birmingham Collection of English Texts.

Associated Business Programmes Ltd for: *The Next 200 Years* by Herman Kahn with William Brown and Leon Martel first published in Great Britain by Associated Business Programmes Ltd 1977 · Hudson Institute 1976. David Attenborough and William Collins Sons & Co Ltd for: *Life on Earth* by David Attenborough first published by William Collins Sons & Co Ltd 1979 · David Attenborough Productions Ltd 1979. James Baldwin for: *The Fire Next Time* by James Baldwin published in Great Britain by Michael Joseph Ltd 1963 · James Baldwin 1963. B T Batsford Ltd for: *Witchcraft in England* by Christina Hole first published by B T Batsford Ltd 1945 · Christina Hole 1945. Michael Billington Ltd for: 'Lust at First Sight' by Michael Billington in the *Illustrated London News* July 1981 and 'Truffaut's Tolerance' by Michael Billington in the *Illustrated London News* August 1981. Birmingham International Council For Overseas Students' Aid for: BICOSA Information Leaflets 1981. Basil Blackwell Publishers Ltd for: *Breaking the Mould? The Birth and Prospects of the Social Democratic Party* by Ian Bradley first published by Martin Robertson & Co Ltd 1981 · Ian Bradley 1981. *Seeing Green (The Politics of Ecology Explained)* by Jonathon Porritt first published by Basil Blackwell Publisher Ltd 1984 · Jonathon Porritt 1984. Blond & Briggs Ltd for: *Small is Beautiful* by E F Schumacher first published in Great Britain by Blond & Briggs Ltd 1973 · E F Schumacher 1973. The Bodley Head Ltd for: *The Americans (Letters from America 1969-1979)* by Alistair Cooke first published by Bodley Head Ltd 1979 · Alistair Cooke 1979. *Baby and Child Care* by Dr Benjamin Spock published in Great Britain by The Bodley Head Ltd 1955 · Benjamin Spock MD 1945, 1946, 1957, 1968, 1976, 1979. *What's Wrong With The Modern World?* by Michael Shanks first published by The Bodley Head Ltd 1978 · Michael Shanks 1978. *Future Shock* by Alvin Toffler first published in Great Britain by The Bodley Head Ltd 1970 · Alvin Toffler 1970. *Zen and the Art of Motorcycle Maintenance* by Robert M Pirsig first published in Great Britain by The Bodley Head Ltd 1974 · Robert M Pirsig 1974. *Marnie* by Winston Graham first published by the Bodley Head Ltd 1961 · Winston Graham 1961. *You Can Get There From Here* by Shirley MacLaine first published in Great Britain by The Bodley Head Ltd 1975 · Shirley MacLaine 1975. *It's An Odd Thing, But ...* by Paul Jennings first published by Max Reinhardt Ltd 1971 · Paul Jennings 1971. *King of the Castle (Choice and Responsibility in the Modern World)* by Gai Eaton first published by the Bodley Head Ltd 1977 · Gai Eaton 1977. *Revolutionaries in Modern Britain* by Peter Shipley first published by The Bodley Head Ltd 1976 · Peter Shipley 1976. *The Prerogative of the Harlot (Press Barons and Power)* by Hugh Cudlipp first published by The Bodley Head Ltd 1980 · Hugh Cudlipp 1980. *But What About The Children (A Working Parents' Guide to Child Care)* by Judith Hann first published by The Bodley Head Ltd 1976 · Judith Hann 1976. *Learning to Read* by Margaret Meek first published by The Bodley Head Ltd 1982 · Margaret Meek 1982. Bolt & Watson for: *Two is Lonely* by Lynne Reid Banks first published by Chatto & Windus 1974 · Lynne Reid Banks 1974. The British and Foreign Bible Society with William Collins Sons & Co Ltd for: *Good News Bible (with Deuterocanonical Books/Apocrypha)* first published by The British and Foreign Bible Society with William Collins Sons & Co Ltd 1979 · American Bible Society: Old Testament 1976, Deuterocanonical Books/Apocrypha 1979, New Testament 1966, 1971, 1976 · Maps, British and Foreign Bible Society 1976, 1979. The British Council for: *How to Live in Britain (The British Council's Guide for Overseas Students and Visitors)* first published by The British Council 1952 · The British Council 1984. Mrs R Bronowski for: *The Ascent of Man* by J Bronowski published by Book Club Associates by arrangement with The British Broadcasting Corporation 1977 · J Bronowski 1973. Alison Busby for: *The Death of Trees* by Nigel Dudley first published by Pluto Press Ltd 1985 · Nigel Dudley 1985. Tony Buzan for: *Make The Most of your Mind* by Tony Buzan first published by Colt Books Ltd 1977 · Tony Buzan 1977. Campbell Thomson & McLaughlin Ltd for: *Ring of Bright Water* by Gavin Maxwell first published by Longmans Green & Co 1960, published in Penguin Books Ltd 1976 · The Estate of Gavin Maxwell 1960. Jonathan Cape Ltd for: *Manwatching (A Field Guide to Human Behaviour)* by Desmond Morris first published in Great Britain by Jonathan Cape Ltd 1977 · Text, Desmond Morris 1977 · Compilation, Elsevier Publishing Projects SA, Lausanne, and Jonathan Cape Ltd, London 1977. *Tracks* by Robyn Davidson first published by Jonathan Cape Ltd 1980 · Robyn Davidson 1980. *In the Name of Love* by Jill Tweedie first published by Jonathan Cape Ltd 1979 · Jill Tweedie 1979. *The Use of Lateral Thinking* by Edward de Bono first published by Jonathan Cape 1967 · Edward de Bono 1967. *Trout Fishing in America* by Richard Brautigan first published in Great Britain by Jonathan Cape Ltd 1970 · Richard Brautigan 1967. *The Pendulum Years: Britain and the Sixties* by Bernard Levin first published by Jonathan Cape Ltd 1970 · Bernard Levin 1970. *The Summer Before The Dark* by Doris Lessing first published in Great Britain by Jonathan Cape Ltd 1973 · Doris Lessing 1973. *The Boston Strangler* by Gerold Frank first published in Great Britain by Jonathan Cape Ltd 1967 · Gerold Frank 1966. *I'm OK - You're OK* by Thomas A Harris MD first published in Great Britain as The Book of Choice by Jonathan Cape Ltd 1970 · Thomas A Harris MD, 1967, 1968, 1969. *The Vivisector* by Patrick White first published by Jonathan Cape Ltd 1970 · Patrick White 1970. *The Future of Socialism* by Anthony Crosland first published by Jonathan Cape Ltd 1956 · C A R Crosland 1963. *Funeral in Berlin* by Len Deighton first published by Jonathan Cape Ltd 1964 · Len Deighton 1964. Chatto & Windus Ltd for: *A Postillion Struck by Lightning* by Dirk Bogarde first published by Chatto & Windus Ltd 1977 · Dirk Bogarde 1977. *Nuns and Soldiers* by Iris Murdoch published by Chatto & Windus Ltd 1980 · Iris Murdoch 1980. *Wounded Knee (An Indian History of the American West)* by Dee Brown published by Chatto & Windus Ltd 1978 · Dee Brown 1970. *The Virgin in the Garden* by A S Byatt published by Chatto & Windus Ltd 1978 · A S Byatt 1978. *A Story Like The Wind* by Laurens van der Post published by Clarke Irwin & Co Ltd in association with The Hogarth Press Ltd 1972 · Laurens van der Post 1972. *Brave New World* by Aldous Huxley published by Chatto & Windus Ltd 1932 · Aldous Huxley and Mrs Laura Huxley 1932, 1960. *The Reivers* by William Faulkner first published by Chatto & Windus Ltd 1962 · William Faulkner 1962. *Cider With Rosie* by Laurie Lee published by The Hogarth Press 1959 · Laurie Lee 1959 *The Tenants* by Bernard Malamud first published in Great Britain by Chatto & Windus Ltd 1972 · Bernard Malamud 1971. *Kinflicks* by Lisa Alther first published in Great Britain by Chatto & Windus Ltd 1976 · Lisa Alther 1975. William Collins Sons & Co Ltd for: *The Companion Guide to London* by David Piper published by William Collins Sons & Co Ltd 1964 · David Piper 1964. *The Bedside Guardian 29* edited by

W L Webb published by William Collins & Sons Ltd 1980 Guardian Newspapers Ltd 1980. Bear Island by Alistair MacLean first published by William Collins Sons & Co Ltd 1971 ' Alistair MacLean 1971. Inequality in Britain: Freedom, Welfare and the State by Frank Field first published by Fontana Paperbacks 1981 ' Frank Field 1981. Social Mobility by Anthony Heath first published by Fontana Paperbacks 1981 ' Anthony Heath 1981. Yours Faithfully by Gerald Priestland first published by Fount Paperbacks 1979 ' British Broadcasting Corporation 1977, 1978. Power Without Responsibility: The Press and Broadcasting in Britain by James Curran and Jean Seaton first published by Fontana Paperbacks 1981 ' James Curran and Jean Seaton 1981. The Times Cookery Book by Katie Stewart first published by William Collins Sons & Co Ltd 1972 ' Times Newspapers Ltd. Friends from the Forest by Joy Adamson by Collins and Harvill Press 1981 ' Elsa Limited 1981. The Media Mob by Barry Fantoni and George Melly first published by William Collins Sons & Co Ltd 1980 ' Text, George Melly 1980 ' Illustrations, Barry Fantoni 1980. Shalom (a collection of Australian and Jewish Stories) compiled by Nancy Keesing first published by William Collins Publishers Pty Ltd 1978 ' William Collins Sons &Co Ltd 1978. The Bedside Guardian 31 edited by W L Webb first published by William Collins Sons & Co Ltd 1982 ' Guardian Newspapers Ltd 1982. The Bedside Guardian 32 edited by W L Webb first published by William Collins Sons & Co Ltd 1983 ' Guardian Newspapers Ltd 1983. Design for the Real World by Victor Papanek first published in Great Britain by Thames & Hudson Ltd 1972 ' Victor Papanek 1971. Food For Free by Richard Mabey first published by William Collins Sons & Co Ltd 1972 ' Richard Mabey 1972. Unended Quest by Karl Popper (first published as Autobiography of Karl Popper in The Philosophy of Karl Popper in The Library of Living Philosophers edited by Paul Arthur Schlipp by the Open Court Publishing Co 1974) published by Fontana Paperbacks 1976 ' The Library of Living Philosophers Inc 1974 ' Karl R Popper 1976. My Mother My Self by Nancy Friday first published in Great Britain by Fontana Paperbacks 1979 ' Nancy Friday 1977. The Captain's Diary by Bob Willis first published by Willow Books/William Collins Sons & Co Ltd 1984 ' Bob Willis and Alan Lee 1984 ' New Zealand Scorecards, Bill Frindall 1984. The Bodywork Book by Esme Newton-Dunn first published in Great Britain by Willow Books/William Collins Sons & Co Ltd 1982 ' TVS Ltd/Esme Newton-Dunn 1982. Collins' Encyclopaedia of Fishing in The British Isles edited by Michael Prichard first published by William Collins Sons & Co Ltd 1976 ' William Collins Sons & Co Ltd 1976. The AAA Runner's Guide edited by Heather Thomas first published by William Collins Sons & Co Ltd 1983 ' Sackville Design Group Ltd 1983. Heroes and Contemporaries by David Gower with Derek Hodgson first published by William Collins Sons & Co Ltd 1983 ' David Gower Promotions Ltd 1983. The Berlin Memorandum by Adam Hall first published by William Collins Sons & Co Ltd 1965 ' Jonquil Trevor 1965. Arlott on Cricket: His Writings on the Game edited by David Rayvern Allen first published by William Collins (Willow Books) 1984 ' John Arlott 1984. A Woman in Custody by Audrey Peckham first published by Fontana Paperbacks 1985 ' Audrey Peckham 1985. Play Golf with Peter Alliss by Peter Alliss published by the British Broadcasting Corporation 1977 ' Peter Alliss and Renton Laidlaw 1977. Curtis Brown Ltd for: The Pearl by John Steinbeck first published by William Heinemann Ltd 1948 ' John Steinbeck 1948. An Unfinished History of the World by Hugh Thomas first published in Great Britain by Hamish Hamilton Ltd 1979 ' Hugh Thomas 1979, 1981. The Winter of our Discontent by John Steinbeck first published in Great Britain by William Heinemann Ltd 1961 ' John Steinbeck 1961. Burr by Gore Vidal first published in Great Britain by William Heinemann Ltd 1974 ' Gore Vidal 1974. Doctor on the Job by Richard Gordon first published by William Heinemann Ltd 1976 ' Richard Gordon Ltd 1976. Andre Deutsch Ltd for: How to be an Alien by George Mikes first published by Andre Deutsch Ltd 1946 ' George Mikes and Nicholas Bentley 1946. Jaws by Peter Benchley first published in Great Britain by Andre Deutsch Ltd 1974 ' Peter Benchley 1974. A Bend in the River by V S Naipaul first published by Andre Deutsch Ltd 1979 ' V S Naipaul 1979. Couples by John Updike first published by Andre Deutsch Ltd 1968 ' John Updike 1968. Games People Play by Eric Berne published in Great Britain by Andre Deutsch Ltd 1966 ' Eric Berne 1964. The Age of Uncertainty by John Kenneth Galbraith first published by The British Broadcasting Corporation and Andre Deutsch Ltd 1977 ' John Kenneth Galbraith 1977. The Economist Newspaper Ltd for: The Economist (9-15 May 1981 and 22-28 August 1981) ' published by The Economist Newspaper Ltd 1981. Faber & Faber Ltd for: Lord of the Flies by William Golding first published by Faber & Faber Ltd 1954 ' William Golding 1954. The Complete Book of Self-Sufficiency by John Seymour first published in Great Britain by Faber & Faber Ltd 1976 ' Text, John Seymour 1976, 1977 ' Dorling Kindersley Ltd 1976, 1977. Conversations with Igor Stravinsky by Igor Stravinsky and Robert Craft first published by Faber & Faber Ltd 1959 ' Igor Stravinsky 1958,1959. John Farquharson Ltd for: The Moon's A Balloon by David Niven published in Great Britain by Hamish Hamilton Ltd 1971 ' David Niven 1971. John Gaselee for: 'Going it Alone' by John Gaselee in the Illustrated London News July 1981 and 'The Other Car's Fault' by John Gaselee in the Illustrated London News August 1981. Glidrose Publications Ltd for: The Man with the Golden Gun by Ian Fleming first published by Jonathan Cape Ltd ' Glidrose Productions Ltd 1965. Victor Gollancz Ltd for: The Next Horizon by Chris Bonnington published by Victor Gollancz Ltd 1976 ' Chris Bonnington 1973. Summerhill: A Radical Approach to Education by A S Neill first published by Victor Gollancz Ltd 1962 ' A S Neill 1926, 1932, 1937, 1953, 1961 (US permission by Hart Publishing Inc). Lucky Jim by Kingsley Amis first published by Victor Gollancz Ltd 1954 ' Kingsley Amis 1953. The Mighty Micro (The Impact of the Computer Revolution) by Christopher Evans first published by Victor Gollancz Ltd 1979 ' Christopher Evans 1979. The Longest Day by Cornelius Ryan published by Victor Gollancz Ltd 1960 ' Cornelius Ryan 1959. Asking for Trouble (Autobiography of a Banned Journalist) by Donald Woods published by Victor Gollancz Ltd 1980 ' Donald Woods 1980. The Turin Shroud by Ian Wilson first published in Great Britain by Victor Gollancz Ltd 1978 ' Ian Wilson 1978. Murdo and Other Stories by Iain Crichton Smith published by Victor Gollancz Ltd 1981 ' Iain Crichton Smith 1981. The Class Struggle in Parliament by Eric S Heffer published by Victor Gollancz Ltd 1973 ' Eric S Heffer 1973. A Presumption of Innocence (The Amazing Case of Patrick Meehan) by Ludovic Kennedy published by Victor Gollancz Ltd 1976 ' Ludovic Kennedy 1976. The Treasure of Sainte Foy by MacDonald Harris published by Victor Gollancz Ltd 1980 ' MacDonald Harris 1980. A Long Way to Shiloh by Lionel Davidson first published by Victor Gollancz Ltd 1966 ' Lionel Davidson 1966. Education After School by Tyrrell Burgess first published by Victor Gollancz Ltd 1977 ' Tyrrell Burgess 1977. The View From Serendip by Arthur C Clarke published by Victor Gollancz Ltd 1978 ' Arthur C Clarke 1967, 1968, 1970, 1972, 1974, 1976, 1977. On Wings of Song by Thomas M Disch published by Victor Gollancz Ltd 1979 ' Thomas M Disch 1979. The World of Violence by Colin Wilson published by Victor Gollancz Ltd 1963 ' Colin Wilson 1963. The Lightning Tree by Joan Aiken published by Victor Gollancz Ltd 1980 ' Joan Aiken

Enterprises 1980. *Russia's Political Hospitals* by Sidney Bloch and Peter Reddaway published by Victor Gollancz Ltd 1977 · Sidney Bloch and Peter Reddaway 1977. *Unholy Loves* by Joyce Carol Oates first published in Great Britain by Victor Gollancz Ltd 1980 · Joyce Carol Oates 1979. *Consenting Adults (or The Duchess will be Furious)* by Peter De Vries published by Victor Gollancz Ltd 1981 · Peter De Vries 1980. *The Passion of New Eve* by Angela Carter published by Victor Gollancz Ltd 1977 · Angela Carter 1977. Gower Publishing Co Ltd for: *Solar Prospects (The Potential for Renewable Energy)* by Michael Flood first published in Great Britain by Wildwood House Ltd in association with Friends of the Earth Ltd 1983 · Michael Flood. *Voiceless Victims* by Rebecca Hall first published in Great Britain by Wildwood House Ltd 1984 · Rebecca Hall 1984. Graham Greene and Laurence Pollinger Ltd for: *The Human Factor* by Graham Greene first published by The Bodley Head Ltd 1978 · Graham Greene 1978. Syndication Manager, The Guardian, for: *The Guardian* (12 May 1981, 17 September 1981 and 15 September 1981) · published by Guardian Newspapers Ltd 1981. Hamlyn for: *How to Play Rugby* by David Norrie published by The Hamlyn Publishing Group Ltd 1981 · The Hamlyn Publishing Group Ltd 1981. *How to Play Badminton* by Pat Davies first published by The Hamlyn Publishing Group Ltd 1979 · The Hamlyn Publishing Group Ltd 1979. Margaret Hanbury for: *Crisis and Conservation: Conflict in the British Countryside* by Charlie Pye-Smith and Chris Rose first published by Pelican/Penguin Books Ltd 1984 · Charlie Pye-Smith and Chris Rose 1984. Paul Harrison for: *Inside the Third World* by Paul Harrison first published in Great Britain by The Harvester Press Ltd 1980 · Paul Harrison 1979. A M Heath & Co Ltd for: *Rembrandt's Hat* by Bernard Malamud published by Chatto & Windus Ltd 1982 · Bernard Malamud 1968, 1972, 1973. William Heinemann Ltd for: *It's an Old Country* by J B Priestley first published in Great Britain by William Heinemann Ltd 1967 · J B Priestley 1967. Heinemann Educational Books Ltd and Gower Publishing Co Ltd for: *The Environmental Crisis (A Handbook for all Friends of the Earth)* edited by Des Wilson first published by Heinemann Educational Books Ltd 1984 · Foreword, David Bellamy 1984 · Individual Chapters, the Author of the Chapter 1984 · In the selection and all other matters Des Wilson 1984. The Controller, Her Majesty's Stationery Office, for: Department of Health and Social Security leaflets published by Her Majesty's Stationery Office 1981 · The Crown. David Higham Associates Ltd for: 'Two Peruvian Projects' by E R Chamberlain in the *Illustrated London News* September 1981. *Akenfield: Portrait of an English Village* by Ronald Blythe first published by Allen Lane, Penguin Books Ltd 1969 · Ronald Blythe 1969. *The Far Pavillions* by M M Kaye first published by Allen Lane/Penguin Books Ltd 1978 · M M Kaye 1978. *Staying On* by Paul Scott first published by William Heinemann Ltd 1977 · Paul Scott 1977. *Let Sleeping Vets Lie* by James Herriot first published by Michael Joseph Ltd 1973 · James Herriot 1973. *The Midwich Cuckoos* by John Wyndham first published in Great Britain by Michael Joseph Ltd 1957 · The Estate of John Wyndham 1957. *The Girl in a Swing* by Richard Adams first published in Great Britain by Allen Lane in Penguin Books Ltd 1980 · Richard Adams 1980. Dr K B Hindley for: 'Hot Spots of the Deep' by Dr K B Hindley in the *Illustrated London News July* 1981. Hodder and Stoughton Ltd for: *Supernature* by Lyall Watson first published by Hodder & Stoughton Ltd 1973 · Lyall Watson 1973. *Tinker Tailor Soldier Spy* by John Le Carre first published by Hodder & Stoughton Ltd 1974 · Le Carre Productions 1974. The Editor, Homes and Gardens, for: *Homes and Gardens* (October 1981) (Number 4 Volume 63) · published by IPC Magazines Ltd 1981. Hughes Massie Ltd for: *Elephants Can Remember* by Agatha Christie first published by William Collins Sons & Co Ltd 1972 · Agatha Christie Mallowan. Hutchinson Publishing Group Ltd for: *An Autobiography* by Angela Davis published in Great Britain by Hutchinson & Co Publishers Ltd by arrangement with Bantam Books Inc 1975 · Angela Davis 1974. *The Day of the Jackal* by Frederick Forsyth published in Great Britian by Hutchinson & Co Publishers Ltd 1971 · Frederick Forsyth 1971. *Roots* by Alex Haley first published in Great Britain by Hutchinson & Co Publishers Ltd 1977 · Alex Haley 1976. *The Climate of Treason* by Andrew Boyle first published by Hutchinson & Co Publishers Ltd 1979 · Andrew Boyle 1979. *The Collapsing Universe: The Story of Black Holes* by Isaac Asimov first published by Hutchinson & Co Publishers Ltd 1977 · Isaac Asimov. *XPD* by Len Deighton published by Book Club Associates by arrangement with Hutchinson & Co Publishers Ltd 1981 · Len Deighton 1981. *Show Jumping with Harvey Smith* by Harvey Smith first published by Stanley Paul & Co Ltd 1979 · Tyne-Tees Television Ltd, A Member of the Trident Group 1979. *2001: A Space Odyssey* by Arthur C Clarke first published by Hutchinson & Co Publishers Ltd 1968 · Arthur C Clarke and Polaris Productions Inc 1968 · Epilogue material, Serendip BV 1982, 1983. The Illustrated London News and Sketch Ltd for: *The Illustrated London News* (July 1981, August 1981 and September 1981) · published by the Illustrated London News and Sketch Ltd 1981. The Editor, International Herald Tribune, for: *International Herald Tribune* (25-26 July 1981) · published by International Herald Tribune with The New York Times and The Washington Post 1981. Michael Joseph Ltd for: *Chronicles of Fairacre: Village School* by Miss Read first published in Great Britain by Michael Joseph Ltd 1964 · Miss Read 1955, 1964. *Fire Fox* by Craig Thomas first published in Great Britain by Michael Joseph Ltd 1977 · Craig Thomas 1977. William Kimber & Co Ltd for: *Exodus* by Leon Uris originally published in Great Britain by Alan Wingate Ltd 1959 · Leon Uris 1958. Kogan Page Ltd for: *How to Save the World (Strategy for World Conservation)* by Robert Allen first published by Kogan Page Ltd 1980 · IUCN-UNEP-WWF 1980. Marketing Department, Lloyds Bank PLC, for: *Lloyds Bank Leaflets* (1981) · published by Lloyds Bank PLC 1981. Macmillan Publishers Ltd for: *Appropriate Technology: Technology with a Human Face* by P D Dunn first published by the Macmillan Press Ltd 1978 · P D Dunn 1978. John Murray Publishers Ltd for: *A Backward Place* by Ruth Prawer Jhabvala first published by John Murray Publishers Ltd 1965 · R Prawer Jhabvala 1965. *Food For All The Family* by Magnus Pyke first published by John Murray Publishers Ltd 1980 · Magnus Pyke 1980. *Simple Movement* by Laura Mitchell and Barbara Dale first published by John Murray Publishers Ltd 1980 · Laura Mitchell and Barbara Dale 1980. *Civilisation: A Personal View* by Kenneth Clark first published by the British Broadcasting Corporation and John Murray Publishers Ltd 1969 · Kenneth Clark 1969. The Editor, National Geographic, for: *National Geographic* January, February and March (1980) · published by the National Geographic Society 1979, 1980. The National Magazine Co Ltd for: *Cosmopolitan* (May 1981 and July 1981) · published by the National Magazine Co Ltd 1981. Neilson Leisure Group Ltd for: *NAT Holidays 'Caravans and Tents in the Sun'* (Summer 1983) holiday brochure. Newsweek Inc for: *Newsweek* (11 May 1981, 27 July 1981 and August 1981) · published by Newsweek Inc 1981. The Associate Editor, Now!, for: *Now!* (14-20 November 1980) · published by Cavenham Communications Ltd 1980. Harold Ober Associates Inc for: *The Boys from Brazil* by Ira Levin first published by Michael Joseph Ltd 1976 · Ira Levin 1976. Edna O'Brien and A M Heath & Co Ltd for: *August is a Wicked Month* by Edna O'Brien first published by Jonathan Cape Ltd 1965 · Edna O'Brien

xvii

1965. Pan Books Ltd for: *Dispatches* by Michael Herr first published in Great Britain by Pan Books Ltd 1978 · Michael Herr 1968, 1969, 1970, 1977. *Health and Safety at Work* by Dave Eva and Ron Oswald first published by Pan Books Ltd 1981 · Dave Eva, Ron Oswald and the Workers' Educational Association 1981. *Democracy at Work* by Patrick Burns and Mel Doyle first published by Pan Books Ltd 1981 · Patrick Burns,Mel Doyle and the Workers' Educational Association 1981. *Diet for Life (A Cookbook for Arthritics)* by Mary Laver and Margaret Smith first published by Pan Books Ltd 1981 · Mary Laver and Margaret Smith 1981. Penguin Books Ltd for: *Inside the Company: CIA Diary* by Philip Agee first published in Allen Lane/Penguin Books Ltd 1975 · Philip Agee 1975. Penguin Books Ltd and Spare Ribs Ltd for: *Spare Rib Reader* edited by Marsha Rowe first published in Penguin Books Ltd 1982 · Spare Ribs Ltd 1982. A D Peters & Co Ltd for: 'The Dark Side of Israel' by Norman Moss in Illustrated London News July 1981, 'Aftermath of Osirak' by Norman Moss in the *Illustrated London News* August 1981 and 'Turning Point for Poland' by Norman Moss in the *Illustrated London News* September 1981. 'Recent Fiction' by Sally Emerson in the *Illustrated London News* July 1981, August 1981 and September 1981. *The Complete Upmanship* by Stephen Potter first published in Great Britain by Rupert Hart-Davis Ltd 1970 · Stephen Potter. Elaine Pollard for: Personal Letters 1981 donated by Elaine Pollard. Laurence Pollinger Ltd for: *A Glastonbury Romance* by John Cowper Powys first published by MacDonald & Co Ltd 1933. Murray Pollinger for: *Kiss Kiss* by Roald Dahl published in Great Britain by Michael Joseph Ltd 1960 · Roald Dahl 1962. *Can You Avoid Cancer?* by Peter Goodwin first published by the British Broadcasting Corporation 1984 · Peter Goodwin 1984. Preston Travel Ltd for: Preston Sunroutes 'Camping and Self-Catering' (April to October 1983) holiday brochure. Punch Publications Ltd for: *Punch* (6 May 1981, 29 July 1981, 12 August 1981, 26 August 1981 and 9 September 1981) · published by Punch Publications Ltd 1981. Radala and associates for: *The Naked Civil Servant* by Quentin Crisp first published by Jonathan Cape Ltd 1968 · Quentin Crisp 1968. The Rainbird Publishing Group Ltd for: *The Making of Mankind* by Richard E Leakey first published in Great Britain by Michael Joseph Ltd 1981 · Sherma BV 1981. Robson Books Ltd for: *The Punch Book of Short Stories 3* selected by Alan Coren first published in Great Britain by Robson Books Ltd in association with Punch Publications Ltd 1981 · Robson Books Ltd 1981.*The Best of Robert Morley* by Robert Morley first published in Great Britain by Robson Books Ltd 1981 · Robert Morley 1981. Deborah Rogers Ltd for: 'Picasso's Late Works' by Edward Lucie-Smith in the *Illustrated London News* July 1981, 'David Jones at the Tate' by Edward Lucie-Smith in the *Illustrated London News* August 1981 and 'Further Light on Spanish Painting' by Edward Lucie-Smith in the *Illustrated London News* September 1981. *The Godfather* by Mario Puzo first published in Great Britain by William Heinemann Ltd 1969 · Mario Puzo 1969. Routledge & Kegan Paul Ltd for: *How To Pass Examinations* by John Erasmus first published by Oriel Press Ltd 1967 · Oriel Press Ltd 1980. *Daisy, Daisy* by Christian Miller first published by Routledge & Kegan Paul Ltd 1980 · Christian Miller 1980. *The National Front* by Nigel Fielding first published by Routledge & Kegan Paul Ltd 1981 · Nigel Fielding 1981. *The Myth of Home Ownership* by Jim Kemeny first published by Routledge & Kegan Paul Ltd 1980 · J Kemeny 1981. *Absent With Cause (Lessons of Truancy)* by Roger White first published by Routledge & Kegan Paul Ltd 1980 · Roger White 1980. *The Powers of Evil (in Western Religion, Magic and Folk Belief)* by Richard Cavendish first published by Routledge & Kegan Paul Ltd 1975 · Richard Cavendish 1975. *Crime and

Personality by H J Eysenck first published by Routledge & Kegan Paul Ltd 1964 · H J Eysenck 1964, 1977. Martin Secker & Warburg Ltd for: *Changing Places* by David Lodge first published in England by Martin Secker & Warburg Ltd 1975 · David Lodge 1975. *The History Man* by Malcolm Bradbury first published by Martin Secker & Warburg 1975 · Malcolm Bradbury 1975. *Humboldt's Gift* by Saul Bellow first published in England by The Alison Press/Martin Secker & Warburg Ltd 1975 · Saul Bellow 1973, 1974, 1975. *Wilt* by Tom Sharpe first published in England by Martin Secker & Warburg Ltd 1976 · Tom Sharpe 1976. *The Last Days of America* by Paul E Erdman first published in England by Martin Secker & Warburg Ltd 1981 · Paul E Erdman 1981. *Autumn Manoeuvres* by Melvyn Bragg first published in England by Martin Secker & Warburg Ltd 1978 · Melvyn Bragg 1978. *The Act of Being* by Charles Marowitz first published in England by Martin Secker & Warburg Ltd 1978 · Charles Marowitz 1978. *As If By Magic* by Angus Wilson first published in England by Martin Secker & Warburg Ltd 1973 · Angus Wilson 1973. *All the President's Men* by Carl Bernstein and Bob Woodward first published in England by Martin Secker & Warburg Ltd 1974 · Carl Bernstein and Bob Woodward 1974. *The Myth of the Nation and the Vision of Revolution* by J L Talmon first published by Martin Secker & Warburg Ltd 1981 · J L Talmon 1980. *Animal Farm* by George Orwell first published by Martin Secker & Warburg 1945 · Eric Blair 1945. Anthony Sheil Associates Ltd for: *Daniel Martin* by John Fowles first published in Great Britain by Jonathan Cape Ltd 1977 · J R Fowles Ltd 1977. *Love Story* by Erich Segal published by Hodder & Stoughton Ltd 1970 · Erich Segal 1970. Sidgwick & Jackson Ltd for: *The Third World War* by General Sir John Hackett and others first published in Great Britain by Sidgwick & Jackson Ltd 1978 · General Sir John Hackett 1978. *Superwoman* by Shirley Conran first published by Sidgwick & Jackson Ltd 1975 · Shirley Conran 1975, 1977. *An Actor and His Time* by John Gielgud first published in Great Britain by Sidgwick & Jackson Ltd 1979 · John Gielgud, John Miller and John Powell 1979 · Biographical Notes, John Miller 1979. Simon & Schuster for: *Our Bodies Ourselves (A Health Book by and for Women)* by the Boston Women's Health Book Collective (British Edition by Angela Phillips and Jill Rakusen) published in Allen Lane and Penguin Books Ltd 1978 · The Boston Women's Health Collective Inc 1971, 1973, 1976 · Material for British Edition, Angela Phillips and Jill Rakusen 1978. Souvenir Press Ltd for: *The Bermuda Triangle* by Charles Berlitz (An Incredible Saga of Unexplained Disappearances) first published in Great Britain by Souvenir Press Ltd 1975 · Charles Berlitz 1974. Souvenir Press Ltd and Michael Joseph Ltd for: *Airport* by Arthur Hailey first published in Great Britain by Michael Joseph Ltd in association with Souvenir Press Ltd 1968 · Arthur Hailey Ltd 1968. Sunmed Holidays Ltd for: 'Go Greek' (Summer 1983) holiday brochure. Maurice Temple Smith Ltd for: *Friends of the Earth Pollution Guide* by Brian Price published by Maurice Temple Smith Ltd 1983 · Brian Price 1983. Maurice Temple Smith and Gower Publishing Co Ltd for: *Working the Land (A New Plan for a Healthy Agriculture)* by Charlie Pye-Smith and Richard North first published by Maurice Temple Smith Ltd 1984 · Charlie Pye-Smith and Richard North 1984. Times Newspapers Ltd for: *The Sunday Times Magazine* (13 January 1980, 20 January 1980 and 11 May 1980) · published by Times Newspapers Ltd 1981. *The Times* (7 September 1981) · published by Times Newspapers Ltd 1981. Twenty's Holidays for: 'The Best 18-33 Holidays' (Winter 1982/83) holiday brochure. University of Birmingham for: Living in Birmingham (1984) · published by The University of Birmingham 1984. Birmingham University Overseas Student Guide · The University of Birmingham. Working with

Industry and Commerce published by The University of Birmingham 1984. University of Birmingham Prospectus (June 1985) published by The University of Birmingham 1985. University of Birmingham Library Guide published by The University of Birmingham. University of Birmingham Institute of Research and Development (1984) published by the University of Birmingham 1984. Biological Sciences at The University of Birmingham (1985) published by The University of Birmingham 1985. History at the University of Birmingham (1985) published by the University of Birmingham 1985. Faculty of Arts Handbook (1984-85) published by The University of Birmingham 1984. Virago Press Ltd for: *Benefits* by Zoe Fairbairns published by Virago Press Ltd 1979 Zoe Fairbairns 1979. *Simple Steps to Public Life* by Pamela Anderson, Mary Stott and Fay Weldon published in Great Britain by Virago Press Ltd 1980 Action Opportunities 1980. *Tell Me A Riddle* by Tillie Olsen published by Virago Press Ltd 1980 this edition Tillie Olsen 1980. A P Watt (& Sons) Ltd for: *The Glittering Prizes* by Frederic Raphael first published in Great Britain by Penguin Books Ltd 1976 Volatic Ltd 1976. *Then and Now* by W Somerset Maugham first published by William Heinemann Ltd 1946 W Somerset Maugham 1946. *The Language of Clothes* by Alison Lurie published by William Heinemann Ltd 1981 Alison Lurie 1981. 'Herschel Commemorative' by Patrick Moore in the *Illustrated London News* July 1981. 'The Outermost Giant' by Patrick Moore in the *Illustrated London News* August 1981. 'Cosmic Bombardment' by Patrick Moore in the *Illustrated London News* September 1981. Weidenfeld & Nicolson Ltd for: 'The Miraculous Toy' by Susan Briggs in the *Illustrated London News* August 1981. *The Needle's Eye* by Margaret Drabble first published by Weidenfeld & Nicolson Ltd 1972 Margaret Drabble 1972. *Success Without Tears: A Woman's Guide to the Top* by Rachel Nelson first published in Great Britain by Weidenfeld & Nicolson Ltd 1979 Rachel Nelson 1979. *Education in the Modern World* by John Vaizey published by Weidenfeld & Nicolson Ltd 1967 John Vaizey 1967. *Rich Man, Poor Man* by Irwin Shaw first published in Great Britain by Weidenfeld & Nicolson Ltd 1970 Irwin Shaw 1969, 1970. *Lolita* by Vladimir Nabokov first published in Great Britain by Weidenfeld & Nicolson Ltd 1959 Vladimir Nabokov 1955, 1959, 1968, G P Putnam's Sons 1963 McGraw-Hill International Inc 1971. *The Third World* by Peter Worsley first published by Weidenfeld & Nicolson Ltd 1964 Peter Worsley 1964, 1967. *Portrait of a Marriage* by Nigel Nicolson published by Weidenfeld & Nicolson Ltd 1973 Nigel Nicolson 1973. *The Dogs Bark: Public People and Private Places* by Truman Capote first published in Great Britain by Weidenfeld & Nicolson Ltd 1974 Truman Capote 1974. *Great Planning Disasters* by Peter Hall first published in Great Britain by George Weidenfeld & Nicolson Ltd 1980 Peter Hall 1980. The Writers and Readers Publishing Co-operative Ltd for: *Working with Words. Literacy Beyond School* by Jane Mace published by The Writers and Readers Publishing Co-operative Ltd 1979 Jane Mace 1979. *The Alienated: Growing Old Today* by Gladys Elder OAP published by The Writers and Readers Publishing Co-operative Ltd 1977 Text, The Estate of Gladys Elder 1977 Photographs, Mike Abrahams 1977. *Beyond the Crisis in Art* by Peter Fuller published by The Writers and Readers Publishing Co-operative Ltd 1980 Peter Fuller 1980. *The War and Peace Book* by Dave Noble published by The Writers and Readers Publishing Co-operative Ltd 1977 Dave Noble 1977. *Tony Benn: A Political Biography* by Robert Jenkins first published by The Writers and Readers Publishing Co-operative Ltd 1980 Robert Jenkins 1980. *Nuclear Power for Beginners* by Stephen Croall and Kaianders Sempler first published by The Writers and Readers Publishing Co-operative Ltd 1978 Text, Stephen Croall 1978, 1980 Illustrations Kaianders Sempler 1978, 1980. Yale University Press for: *Life in the English Country House: A Social and Architectural History* by Mark Girouard published by Yale University Press Ltd, London 1978 Yale University 1978. The British Broadcasting Corporation for transcripts of radio transmissions of 'Kaleidoscope', 'Any Questions', 'Money Box' and 'Arts and Africa' 1981 and 1982. The British Broadcasting Corporation and Mrs Shirley Williams for transcripts of television interviews with Mrs Shirley Williams 1979. Dr B L Smith, School of Mathematics and Physical Sciences, University of Sussex for programmes on Current Affairs, Science and The Arts originally broadcast on Radio Sussex 1979 and 1980 B L Smith. The following people in the University of Birmingham: Professor J McH Sinclair, Department of English, for his tapes of informal conversation (personal collection). Mr R Wallace, formerly Department of Accounting and Finance, and Ms D Houghton, Department of English, for transcripts of his accountancy lectures. Dr B K Gazey, Department of Electrical Engineering and Dr M Montgomery, University of Strathclyde, Department of English, for a transcript of Dr Gazey's lecture. Dr L W Poel, Department of Plant Biology, and Dr M Montgomery, University of Strathclyde, Department of English, for a transcript of Dr Poel's lecture. Professor J G Hawkes, formerly Department of Plant Biology, for recordings of his lectures. Dr M S Snaith, Department of Transportation for recordings of his lectures. Dr M P Hoey, Department of English, and Dr M Cooper, The British Council, for a recording of their discussion on discourse analysis. Ms A Renouf, Department of English, for recordings of job and academic interviews 1977. Mr R H Hubbard, formerly a B Phil (Ed) student, Faculty of Education, for his research recordings of expressions of uncertainty 1978-79. Mr A E Hare, formerly a B Phil (Ed) student, Faculty of Education, for his transcripts of telephone conversations 1978. Dr A Tsui, formerly Department of English, for her recordings of informal conversation. Mr J Couperthwaite, formerly Department of English, for a recording of informal conversation 1981. Ms C Emmott, M Litt student, Department of English, for a recording of informal conversation 1981. Mrs B T Atkins for the transcript of an account of a dream 1981. The British Council for 'Authentic Materials Numbers 1-28' 1981. Professor M Hammerton and Mr K Coghill, Department of Psychology, University of Newcastle-upon-Tyne, for tape recordings of their lectures 1981. Mr G P Graveson, formerly research student, University of Newcastle, for his recordings of teacher discussion 1977. Mr W R Jones, formerly research student, University of Southampton, for his recordings of classroom talk. Mr Ian Fisher, formerly BA student, Newcastle Polytechnic, for his transcripts of interviews on local history 1981. Dr N Coupland, formerly PhD student, Department of English, UWIST, for his transcripts of travel agency talk 1981. Professor D B Bromley, Department of Psychology, University of Liverpool, for his transcript of a research recording. Mr Brian Lawrence, formerly of Saffron Walden County High School, for a tape of his talk on 'The British Education System' 1979.

Thanks are also due to Times Newspapers Ltd for providing machine-readable copies of The Times and The Sunday Times for linguistic analysis.

Every effort has been made to trace the copyright holders, but if any have been inadvertently overlooked the publishers will be pleased to make the necessary acknowledgments at the first opportunity.

Prepositions in Part One

aboard
about
above
according to
across
across from
after
against
ahead of
along
alongside
along with
amid
amidst
among
amongst
apart from
around
as
as for
aside from
as to
astride
at
away from
bar
barring
because of
before
behind
below

beneath
beside
besides
between
beyond
but
by
by means of
close to
concerning
considering
contrary to
depending on
despite
down
due to
during
except
except for
excepting
excluding
following
for
forward of
from
in
in between
including
in favour of
in front of
in lieu of

inside
inside of
in spite of
instead of
into
irrespective of
like
minus
near
near to
next to
notwithstanding
of
off
on
on account of
on board
onto
on top of
opposite
opposite to
other than
out of
outside
outside of
over
owing to
past
pending
per
plus

preparatory to
prior to
regarding
regardless of
round
save
save for
since
than
thanks to
through
throughout
till
to
together with
toward
towards
under
underneath
unlike
until
up
up against
upon
up to
up until
via
with
within
without
worth

Part One

The Prepositions

aboard

If you are **aboard** a ship, aircraft, or spacecraft, you are on it or in it.
In an adjunct or after 'be': *I came aboard the Queen Mary longing to
be impressed... The official said calmly that our luggage was now
aboard a BEA plane due for take-off in seven minutes.
...experiments carried out aboard the U.S. space shuttle.*
After a noun: *More lives could be saved through improved safety
measures aboard aircraft.*
Also used as an adverb: *The DC10 crashed, killing all 346 people
aboard.* ⁇

about

1 If you write, talk, think, or have feelings **about** a particular
thing, your words, thoughts, or feelings concern that thing.
In an adjunct or after 'be', often followed by an '-ing' clause: *Let's
talk about this in the morning... Don't worry about getting killed...
I forgot all about it... This book is about death.*
Here are some verbs which are typically followed by **about**:

agree	care	forget	muse	tell
argue	chat	fret	protest	think
ask	complain	fuss	quibble	warn
bitch	consult	groan	rave	wonder
boast	disagree	grumble	read	worry
brag	dream	inquire	speak	
brood	fantasize	moan	talk	

After a noun: *...a book about fishing... You will have to give them
information about your income.*
Here are some nouns which are typically followed by **about**:

advice	decision	misunderstanding
agreement	fuss	news
anxiety	idea	opinion
book	information	outcry
chat	joke	phobia
complex	judgement	prediction
concern	lecture	quarrel
consultation	letter	question
debate	misgivings	row

After an adjective: *Pembridge is said to be angry about the delay...
Yet how could she have been mistaken about a thing like this?... I*

above

couldn't sleep properly because I was worried about being late in the morning.

Here are some adjectives which are typically followed by **about**:

adamant	enthusiastic	pleased	undecided
angry	fussy	positive	uneasy
annoyed	guilty	scathing	unhappy
anxious	happy	sceptical	unsure
apprehensive	ignorant	sensitive	upset
bothered	indignant	sentimental	vague
certain	miserable	serious	wary
complacent	mistaken	sorry	worried
concerned	nervous	uncertain	
crazy	optimistic	unclear	
embarrassed	passionate	unconcerned	

2 If you do something **about** an unsatisfactory situation, you try to improve it.

In an adjunct following 'do': *We can't do much about heredity... I should do something about those spots, dear, if I were you.*

3 If you say that there is a vague quality **about** someone or something, you mean that they have it.

In an adjunct: *He has a sort of originality about him... There was something frightening about the experience... There is nothing particularly frail about him in the physical sense.*

4 If there are things **about** something, they surround it or exist on every side of it.

After a noun: *The little wrinkles about her eyes were more noticeable now.... Youngsters are receiving maximum exposure to new ideas of the world about them.*

In an adjunct: *He put his arms about her and clung to her... Shells exploded all about them.*

5 If you move **about** a place, you go to several different parts of it.

In an adjunct: *I wandered about the flat, letting the time pass... It wouldn't be safe to have the children running about the grounds.*

Also used as an adverb: *I wandered about, admiring these detailed preparations.*

above

1 If one thing is **above** another, it is higher than the other thing or over the top of it.

In an adjunct or after 'be': *Above the town, the fire was still blazing... I felt sure, now, that the noise was above me.*

After a noun: *Sarah was put in the room above me. ...the hills above the town.*

Also used as an adverb: *The music seemed to be coming from the floor above.*

2 If something is **above** a particular amount or level, it is greater or higher than that amount or level.

In an adjunct or after 'be': *The temperature has not risen much above zero for the past week... Otto's voice was low, just above a whisper.*

3 If someone is **above** you, they are in a higher social position than you or in a position of authority over you.

After a noun: *Well, my mum's a nurse and she has to bow to the matron above her... It did not even work all that well for the gentry above them.*

After 'be' or 'marry': *Guy was above her... She married above herself.*

4 If someone thinks they are **above** a particular activity, they think they are too good or important to do it.

After a link verb: *They were supposed to be above such crude methods of communication. ...even for the minority who consider themselves above such mercenary transactions.*

5 If someone is **above** criticism or suspicion, they cannot be criticized or suspected because they have such good qualities or such a high social position.

After 'be': *...those whose loyalty and morals were above reproach... Martyn was merely an erudite eccentric and entirely above suspicion.*

according to

1 If someone says that something is true **according to** a particular person, book, or other source of information, they are indicating where they got their information.

In an adjunct: *According to Cooke, the amount of pesticides used by farmers could be reduced 1,000 times... According to a recent American study, there has been no increase in the incidence of severe mental illness over the last 100 years.*

2 If something is done **according to** a particular set of principles, it is done using these principles as a basis.

In an adjunct: *Computers are created by humans according to sets of rules... You should care for your car and have it serviced according to the manufacturer's instructions.*

3 If something varies **according to** a changing or variable factor, it varies in a way determined by this factor.

In an adjunct: *Timber yields vary according to the type of tree and the location and soil quality.*

4 If something goes **according to** plan or **according to** schedule, it happens exactly in the way that it was intended to happen.

across

In an adjunct: *But things do not always proceed according to plan... Everything went according to schedule.*

across

1 If someone or something goes **across** a place, they go from one side of it to the other.
In an adjunct: *We went across the street to that restaurant downstairs in the Bahnhof... He rode the longer way home, across the canal bridge... He drew a finger expressively across his throat.*
After a noun: *He hadn't liked the journey across Africa at all.*
Also used as an adverb: *Alice walked across to Dawlish's desk.*
2 If something is situated or stretched **across** something else, it is situated or stretched from one side of it to the other.
In an adjunct: *Printed across the poster in large, broad letters was the word 'Wanted.'... They found Evelyn Corbin sprawled across her bed. ...a banner stretched across the street.*
After a noun: *...the main bridge across the river.*
3 Something that is **across** something such as a street, river, or area is on the other side of it.
After 'be': *My car's just across the street... It's over near Beddingham, across the railway.*
After a noun: *They went into the diner across the street.*
4 You use **across** to say that a particular expression is shown on someone's face, usually for only a moment.
In an adjunct: *Disapproval flickered across her face... He stopped and a quick smile went across his face.*
5 If something happens **across** a place or organization, it happens equally everywhere within it.
In an adjunct: *The habit of male face-shaving is widespread across the globe... Yet this ideology does not apply universally across the membership.*
After a noun: *At party meetings across the country they were choosing delegates.*
6 When something happens **across** a political, religious, or social barrier, it involves people in different groups.
In an adjunct: *Issues tended to cut across party lines.*
After a noun: *They found no trouble in controlling love across colour barriers... We are more used to argument across disciplines.*
7 If you come, run, or stumble **across** something, you find it unexpectedly.
In an adjunct: *The other day I came across a letter from Brunel... The idea is that in the course of their search for something they may stumble across something quite different and of great value... It's very unusual to run across Americans in this part of the world.*

across from

If one person or thing is situated **across from** another, they are opposite them.

In an adjunct or after 'be': *...seeing his mother sitting across from him at table... You must know the Hotel Hirschen; it's right across from the church.*

After a noun: *...the park across from the church.*

after

1 If something happens **after** a time, event, or period, it happens during the period of time that follows that time, event, or period.

In an adjunct, often followed by an '-ing' clause: *Dan came in just after midnight... We'll hear about everything after dinner... She returned after a few minutes... The play closed disastrously after a few performances... Frank Brown was released from prison after serving three years.*

After a noun: *I hate the time after sunset before you come home.*

Also used as an adverb: *We had one girl who left just before Christmas, and one girl who left just after.*

2 You use **after** to indicate a previous event or experience which affects the present situation.

In an adjunct: *...a light that seemed greenish after the brightness outside... After a statement like Mr Howell's you could hardly blame them.*

3 If you do something **after** someone else, you do it when they have already done it.

In an adjunct: *A male member of the staff stood up after me and said he totally agreed with everything I said.*

4 If someone goes **after** a person or thing, they follow that person or thing, usually in an effort to catch up with them.

In an adjunct or after 'be': *He hurried after his men... He turned and went after his brothers... No, my friend, they are not after me... 'After her!' shouted the Captain.*

5 If you are **after** something, you want to get it for yourself.

After 'be' or in an adjunct: *Let's assume that they are really after information and not scandal... Large mining corporations began lusting after Aboriginal Reserve land.*

6 If you call, shout, or stare **after** someone, you call, shout, or stare at them as they move away from you.

In an adjunct: *'And stop drinking!' Doctor Percival called after Castle... As I ran along the wall, voices shouted after me but no one followed... He broke into a run, leaving Belinda to stare after him.*

7 If you do something **after** someone, you do it for them when they have left.

against

In an adjunct: *She liked picking up after him... His wife used to run round after him... Peter went and closed the door after her.*

8 If you write something **after** something else, you write it to the right of the other thing.

In an adjunct: *He wrote on the large yellow pad 'Mohr, August', and put a question mark after it.*

9 If you are named **after** someone, you are given the same name as them.

In an adjunct: *'It's named after one of your famous aviators,' said the agent... My mother had six girls and called them all after flowers... They all had jokey nicknames like 'Heath Robinson' after the 1930s cartoonist.*

10 If you take **after** a relative, you have some of the same characteristics as they have.

In an adjunct: *He took after his grandfather where character was concerned.*

11 If you ask **after** someone or something, you ask for news about them.

In an adjunct: *He asked after his friends in Florence... She enquired after Mrs Carstairs' daughter.*

12 After is also used, usually between identical nouns, to emphasize that a long series of things occur or are encountered.

After a noun: *...when you trudge twenty miles a day, day after day, month after month... We passed through village after village until finally we stopped... This was copied by one illustrator after another.*

against

1 If something is leaning or pressing **against** something else, it is touching it.

In an adjunct or after 'be': *I saw Kruger leaning against a wall in the terminal building... But the man just lay there, propped up against the door... Breslow shrank away and fell against the wall... Rain splashed against the window panes.*

2 If you compete, fight, or take action **against** someone, you try to defeat them or harm them.

In an adjunct: *I played against Ian Botham only twice in three seasons... How would an 8 stone boxer fare against a 14 stone boxer? ...activities designed to rally and organise workers against Wilson.*

Here are some verbs which are typically followed by **against:**

agitate	compete	play
align	conspire	plot
ally	fight	side

After a noun: *Ian Gould was injured during a match against New*

*South Wales... We cannot expect to win a war against seven armies.
...after being accused of conspiracy against the Emperor.*
Here are some nouns which are typically followed by **against**:

aggression	blasphemy	crime	sanctions
ally	boycott	fight	victory
battle	conspiracy	match	war

3 If you take action **against** something, you try to end it, prevent
it, or make its effects less harmful.
In an adjunct: *He fought doggedly against trade restraints... Action
is also taken to protect consumers against misleading
advertisements... The Vice-President warned against the
continuing dangers of compassion.*
Here are some verbs which are typically followed by **against**:

advise	guard	inoculate	militate	warn
counsel	hedge	insulate	protect	
fight	immunize	insure	vaccinate	

After a noun: *The time had come for a full campaign against
vandals. ...his heroic fight against despair. ...a national scheme for
insurance against industrial injuries... One possible defence
against such threats is the possession of private means.*
Here are some nouns which are typically followed by **against**:

bastion	bulwark	fight	safeguard
battle	campaign	insurance	shield
blow	defence	legislation	war

4 If you are **against** something, you think it is a bad thing.
After 'be' or in an adjunct: *The SDP leaders are against unilateral
disarmament... Workers themselves began to protest against their
appalling conditions. ...those MPs who voted against the ban.*
After a noun: *...a public protest against apartheid. ...the arguments
against our current defence strategy.*
After an adjective: *...complaining that the well-educated are
prejudiced against industry.*
Also used as an adverb: *The Belgians were in favour, the Dutch
against.*
5 If there is evidence **against** a theory or person, there are facts
which suggest that the theory is wrong or the person has done
something wrong.
After a noun: *We can get rid of the real evidence against him.*
After 'be': *All the evidence is against the view that we need an elite
system of education... Yet all the evidence was against intelligent
life elsewhere in the Solar System.*
6 If you act **against** someone's wishes, advice, or orders, you do not
do what they want you to do or tell you to do.

ahead of

In an adjunct: *He acted against the wishes of the electors. ...unless you are travelling against your doctor's advice.*
7 If something is **against** the law, there is a law which says you must not do it.
After 'be': *Someone who is insolvent can't be a company director; it's against the law... It was strictly against the rules to unlock prisoners at night.*
8 If you are moving **against** a current or wind, you are moving in the opposite direction to it.
In an adjunct: *The wind was so strong that I could no longer bicycle against it.*
9 If something is seen **against** something else, it is seen in comparison or in contrast to it.
In an adjunct: *...dark brown wood set against white emulsion... The obvious attractions must be weighed against the high financial cost... Presumably this has to be set against an enormous increase in crime?... These factors have to be measured against the dangers and anxiety of pregnancy.*
10 The odds **against** something happening are the chances that it will not happen.
After a noun: *The odds against him losing his job have lengthened.... The chances against successful transmission are a thousand to one.*
Also used as an adverb: *The odds are 2 to 1 against.*

ahead of

1 If something is **ahead of** you, it is directly in front of you.
In an adjunct or after 'be': *Philip trotted ahead of her... Brody was several steps ahead of Cassidy... All at once the lights flickering ahead of him merged together.*
After a noun: *The cabin ahead of him was dark.*
2 If an event or period of time lies **ahead of** you, it is going to happen or take place soon or in the future.
In an adjunct: *Perhaps, after all, the most astonishing changes may still lie ahead of us... We've got a long journey ahead of us, so let's talk to pass the time... You've got the whole day ahead of you.*
3 If you do something **ahead of** someone else, you do it before that person does it.
In an adjunct: *I got here just ahead of you... Portugal applied to join the EEC in March 1977, four months ahead of Spain.*
4 If something happens **ahead of** an event or time, it happens before that event or time.
In an adjunct: *Poles stocked up on sugar, petrol and other items ahead of the price rises. ...concern that Mrs Thatcher might express disagreement ahead of next month's summit.*

5 If something happens **ahead of** schedule, it happens earlier than was planned.
In an adjunct or after 'be': *He had arrived in France slightly ahead of schedule... We are now easily two years ahead of schedule.*
6 If someone is **ahead of** someone else, they have made more progress and are more advanced in what they are doing.
After 'be': *Apparently we are far ahead of the Americans in one range of goods... In the nineteenth century, German university education was considerably ahead of that of the rest of the world.*

along

1 When you go **along** something such as a road, you move towards one end of it.
In an adjunct: *We went on back along the street towards the stable. ...driving his car along a lane in East Surrey. ...riding along a dusty mountain track in Morocco.*
Also used as an adverb: *He trotted along at my side.*
2 If something is situated **along** something such as a road or a corridor, it is situated beside it.
After a noun: *The door, like most of the doors along the corridor, was open... He had some sandwiches in a pub along the road.*
In an adjunct or after 'be': *My room's just along the corridor... Halfway along the road, the trees suddenly stopped.*

alongside

1 If something is **alongside** something else, it is next to it.
In an adjunct or after 'be': *An ambulance pulled up alongside the coach... She hurried to catch me up and walked alongside me... The Chapel is alongside the Students' Union building.*
After a noun: *The road alongside the river was never quiet... He had rented one acre of land alongside a cherry orchard down the valley.*
Also used as an adverb: *The parents ran alongside, screaming farewells.*
2 If you work **alongside** someone else, you work in the same place and in co-operation with them.
In an adjunct: *British and American forces were fighting alongside each other... Montgomery himself worked alongside us, clearing a path.*
3 If one thing exists **alongside** another, the two things exist together in the same situation and at the same time.
In an adjunct: *She has managed to show how commercial farming can take place alongside the conservation of wildlife and landscape... The rising tide of political violence, alongside an*

along with

increase in criminal and social violence, poses a threat to the country's stability.
After a noun: *The energy supply problem is just one problem alongside countless others.*

along with

Along with is used when mentioning someone or something else that is also present or involved.
In an adjunct: *On March 14, she was sworn in, along with eleven other jurors... Along with numbers of other wealthy citizens, he had a fine house on the banks of the river... The eggs were delivered from the farm along with the milk.*

amid

The form **amidst** is also used, but is a more literary word.
1 If something happens **amid** noises or events of some kind, it happens while they are occurring.
In an adjunct: *He sat quietly amid the uproar, drawing... He moved towards the piano amidst a storm of applause... I got the impression, amid all her chatter, that Jane had changed much more than Anthony.*
2 If something is **amid** other things, it is surrounded by them; a literary use.
In an adjunct or after 'be': *White patches radiated brilliantly amid mottled shades of red and orange. ...a dairy farm set amid the woody valleys of Kent... It was a few hundred yards farther down the Cromwell Road, amidst a swarm of hotels.*

among

The form **amongst** is also used, but is a more literary word.
1 Something or someone that is situated or moving **among** a group of things or people is surrounded by them.
In an adjunct: *They found the cat crouching amongst a hoard of cardboard boxes. ...the dangers of flying among high mountains... Potatoes and cabbages were planted at random among foxgloves and roses... There were at least four new wigs found among her things.*
After a noun: *He turned and went back to the shallow cave among the rocks.*
2 If someone is **among** people of a particular kind, they are with them and having contact with them.
In an adjunct or after 'be': *He had lived his short life among adults... I had only imagined that I was among friends.*

3 If someone or something is **among** a group, they are a member of that group.

After 'be': *I was among the happy few who managed to escape... Among his other purchases were several sheets of foam rubber and two paint brushes.*

4 If something applies to a particular person or thing **among** others, it also applies to other people or things.

In an adjunct: *Alistair Sim, among others, always refused to give autographs... The Institute for the Future is, among other things, investigating the effects of advanced communications technology.*

5 If something such as a feeling, opinion, or situation exists **among** a group of people, most of them have it or experience it.

After a noun: *...the resentment among the poor... Though illegal, this was a well-established custom among the prisoners... It has led to a growing preoccupation among trade unionists with 'getting the procedure right'.*

In an adjunct: *And thirdly, even amongst adults, a substantial number of people can't drive.*

After an adjective: *He was never particularly popular among his contemporaries.*

6 If something is shared **among** a number of people, some of it is given to all of them.

In an adjunct: *The proceeds had to be divided up among four hundred people. ...handing out gifts to be distributed among members' families.*

7 If people talk, fight, or agree something **among** themselves, they do it together, without involving anyone else.

In an adjunct: *They took the opportunity to gossip happily among themselves... It is uncertain whether they will be able to agree among themselves on the details.*

apart from

1 You use **apart from** when you are making an exception to a general statement.

In an adjunct: *Father was the only one who knew you thoroughly, apart from me... Apart from that, the Russians said nothing... Apart from the occasional article, he hadn't published anything for years.*

2 You use **apart from** to indicate that you are aware of one aspect of a situation, but that you are going to focus on another aspect.

In an adjunct, often followed by an '-ing' clause: *Even apart from her illness she had been very unhappy... And, quite apart from anything else, how are we going to pay our way?... Apart from making you sick, it can also cause cramp.*

around

See **round**.

as

1 You use **as** when you are indicating what someone or something is or is thought to be, or what function they have.
In an adjunct: *She was regarded as a hero by masses of people. ...a large wage claim, which the financial press condemned as unrealistic... He used the shirt as a rag to clean the lawn mower... The news clearly came as a shock to him. ...a man who worked as a reporter on the local paper.*
Here are some transitive verbs which are typically followed by **as:**

acknowledge	class	designate	mark
address	classify	diagnose	name
adopt	conceive	disguise	nominate
brand	condemn	elect	perceive
cast	consider	employ	project
categorize	construe	establish	regard
certify	count	groom	stamp
characterize	denounce	hail	use
choose	depict	interpret	
cite	describe	label	

Here are some intransitive verbs which are typically followed by **as:**

act	double	pass	work
begin	function	pose	
come	masquerade	serve	

After a noun: *...his reputation as a man of great wisdom. ...the use of her house as headquarters for the resistance movement. ...my ability as a climber.*
2 If you do something **as** a child or a teenager, for example, you do it when you are a child or a teenager.
In an adjunct: *...creatures that she could remember seeing as a child.*
3 You use **as** to introduce the thing that something is being compared with.
In an adjunct, usually after 'as' and an adjective or adverb: *...when the sea is as smooth as glass... Bison can run more than twice as fast as a sprinting man... They were exactly the same as each other.*

as for

You use **as for** at the beginning of a clause to introduce a different subject that is connected with the previous one.
In an adjunct: *I was in the presence of a very great woman; as for*

our predicament, there was never any doubt in my mind that she would rescue us.

aside from

Aside from means the same as **apart from;** used especially in American English.
In an adjunct: *They had to stop twice because Billy felt sick, but aside from that, the trip was a pleasant one... Potatoes are valuable aside from their calories.*

as to

1 You use **as to** when you are indicating the subject of a piece of information, a question, or a debate; used in British English.
After a noun: *The tenant doesn't know who the landlord is and has no information as to their address. ...making decisions as to how much money we spend on sport and recreation.*
After an adjective: *I'm still a bit puzzled as to why this tremendous surge of interest continues.*
In an adjunct: *Mr Pike inquired as to the part-exchange price.*
2 You also use **as to** at the beginning of a clause to introduce a different subject that is connected with the previous one; a formal use.
In an adjunct: *Two years imprisonment was absolutely right, and as to the five-year disqualification, it could well have been longer.*

astride

If you sit or stand **astride** something, you sit or stand with one leg on each side of it.
In an adjunct: *Karen sat astride a large white horse... He drew up a chair and, sitting astride it, began to talk to us.*

at

1 If you are **at** a place, you are there.
In an adjunct or after 'be': *She was at the hairdresser... Margaret Elmer kept a thoroughbred horse at Garrod's Farm near Cirencester... Dan came to the airport to meet me at Los Angeles... Karin was standing at the top of the stairs.*
After a noun: *The incident was indicative of the mood at the factory, where optimism was high... I was a shorthand typist at Kendalls... My mother was a relation of the people at the Hall.*
2 If someone is **at** school or college, or **at** a particular school or college, they go there to study regularly.
After 'be' or in an adjunct: *Sam should be at school... I've been in*

politics since I was at university... He spent four years at the school his father and grandfather had attended before him.

3 If you are **at** something such as a table or desk, a door or window, or someone's side or feet, you are next to it or them.

In an adjunct or after 'be': *My brother-in-law was sitting at a table laid for four... Ellen waited at the door until the last of the cars had pulled out of the driveway... She dropped to her knees at his side.*
After a noun: *...the girls at the enquiry desk.*

4 If something happens **at** an event or a meal, it happens where and when that event or meal is taking place.

In an adjunct or after 'be': *Mr Foot spoke at the rally... On May 8 they were at the concert for Victory Day... That Sunday, at breakfast, Mark greeted me coldly.*

5 You say that something happens **at** a particular time to indicate when it happens.

In an adjunct: *My last train leaves Euston at 11.30... I went back to my daughter and husband at weekends... At Christmas, I'd sent her twenty pounds... He used to come and read to me at bedtime.*

6 If you do something **at** a particular age, you do it when you are that age.

In an adjunct: *Anyone choosing not to retire at 65 is allowed to draw a state pension... Henze began composing at the age of 12... He, at thirty-two, ought to know better.*

7 You use **at** to express a rate, frequency, or price.

In an adjunct: *Then I beat it down the steps at full speed... Rents will rise at a slower rate than mortgage repayments... They are required to check every bird at regular intervals... You can buy them at $87.50 a share. ...roads that they are building at great expense.*

8 When you are describing where someone or something is, you can say that they are **at** a certain distance, or that they are **at** an angle in relation to something else.

In an adjunct or after 'be': *Ash followed at a discreet distance... He awoke to find his nice new car sitting in his drive at a crazy angle with its tyres missing.*

9 You use **at** when giving information about the level of something.
In an adjunct: *Interest rates have to stay at their present high level for some time to come... Its efficiency remains high even when working at a low output level.*

10 If someone or something is **at** their best or **at** their most patient, for example, they have a quality to the highest degree that they ever have it.

After 'be': *The garden is at its best now.... Indeed, he was always at his most patient where some fathers might have ranted. ...in the early eighteenth century, when absolute monarchy was at its most powerful.*

11 If you look **at** someone or something, you look towards them.

In an adjunct: *They stood looking at each other for a long moment... Willie glared at her for a moment, then he burst into laughter too.*

Here are some verbs which are typically followed by **at**:

gape	glance	look	stare
gaze	glare	squint	

After a noun: *'Well, yes,' Ginny said with a quick glance at her mother.*

12 If you shout **at** someone, you say something to them loudly or rudely without necessarily expecting them to reply.

In an adjunct: *I'm sorry I shouted at you... He could hear them swearing at each other... She wanted to scream at him.*

Here are some verbs which are typically followed by **at**:

bark	shout	swear
scream	snap	yell

13 If you smile or wave, for example, **at** someone, you put on an expression or make a gesture that they are meant to see and understand.

In an adjunct: *For the first time since he had been in the villa she smiled at him... Then somebody else waved at me, frantically... Then Kaspar winked at me, as if to an old friend.*

Here are some verbs which are typically followed by **at**:

beam	grin	smile	wave
frown	scowl	sneer	wink

14 If you point or gesture **at** something, you move part of your body in its direction so that it will be noticed by someone you are with.

In an adjunct: *He pointed at her as if he meant her to stand up and answer questions... He gestured at a chair and said: 'Sit.'*

15 You use **at** to indicate what someone is attempting to hit, get, or take hold of.

In an adjunct: *Then he threw a stone at a thin cat in a red collar... He hurled himself to one side and grabbed at the plywood... We can only guess at the number of missiles they have.... I was aiming at reconciliation.*

Here are some verbs which are typically followed by **at**:

aim	grasp	snatch
clutch	guess	strike
grab	shoot	throw

After a noun: *'That must be my man,' she said in an attempt at her normal tone of voice.*

16 You use **at** to indicate what someone is attempting to move.

In an adjunct: *He pulled at his companion's arm... Stuart pushed at the wire fence.*

After a noun: *Tom felt a tug at his sleeve.*

17 You use **at** to indicate what someone or something is repeatedly touching or doing something to.

In an adjunct: *He groaned as he hacked at his desk with a jack-knife... He could see her dabbing at her eyes with a handkerchief... She nibbled away at the cold hard dinner rolls... Now that he was working at this painting, his sleep was always brief and broken.*

Here are some verbs which are typically followed by **at**:

claw	gnaw	nibble	poke	work
dab	hack	pick	tear	

18 You use **at** to indicate an activity or task when saying how well someone does it.

After an adjective, often followed by an '-ing' clause: *Computers are quite good at this sort of thing... He was good at persuading people... I know he's clever at political debate... Players will get most out of it by being proficient at the basic skills.*

After a noun: *Now, Lyndon Johnson was an expert at political second thoughts.*

In an adjunct after 'excel' or 'shine': *This is something at which Handel excels... Mr Ronald Reagan, of course, shone at the business, managing good-natured self-mockery while keeping some dignified distance.*

19 You use **at** to indicate what someone is reacting to.

After an adjective, often followed by an '-ing' clause: *'Just a minute,' Uri said, somewhat bewildered at the rapid turn of events... The Bastille was found to contain only seven old men who were annoyed at being disturbed.*

Here are some adjectives which are typically followed by **at**:

aghast	annoyed	embarrassed	pleased
alarmed	appalled	furious	surprised
amazed	astonished	impatient	unhappy
amused	bewildered	indignant	upset
angry	disappointed	irritated	

After a noun, often followed by an '-ing' clause: *At tonight's meeting, I expressed delight at the performance. ...her pleasure at hearing his voice.*

In an adjunct: *She shuddered at the bitter taste... So we all laughed at his little joke.*

Here are some verbs which are typically followed by **at**:

chafe	jeer	protest	recoil	smile
exclaim	laugh	rail	scoff	sneer
frown	marvel	rave	shudder	wonder

20 If you do something **at** someone's request, you do it because they have asked you to.
In an adjunct: *She went at the invitation of an unknown man... At Sussman's request, both Bernstein and Woodward returned to the office the next morning... Outside the hotel, a taxi will be summoned at your bidding.*

away from

1 If you move **away from** a place, thing, or person, you move so that you are no longer in that place or near that thing or person.
In an adjunct: *Let us go away from here to somewhere where the air is cleaner... Kitty stepped outside and walked away from the building... He pulled away from her and ran down the stairs.*
2 If you are **away from** a place, you are not there.
After 'be' or in an adjunct: *You may be away from home for a period of time... Today my mother lives a thousand miles away from Charleston.*

bar

When it is used as a preposition, **bar** means the same as **except.**
After an indefinite pronoun or a noun: *Almost every woman, bar the very young, can produce tales of this sort... I am perfectly willing to serve under anybody else bar the rest of the present team.*

barring

You use **barring** to show that the person, thing, or situation you are referring to is an exception to your statement.
In an adjunct: *Barring complications, the aircraft will be in operation next year.*
After an indefinite pronoun or a noun: *It is hard to imagine anyone, barring a lunatic, starting a war.*

because of

If an event or situation occurs **because of** something, that thing is the reason or cause.
In an adjunct or after 'be': *Because of the heat, the front door was open... President Gorbachov's visit was postponed because of last month's earthquake in Armenia... The business is certainly doing well and its directors claim this is because of its efficient management.*

before

1 If something happens **before** a time or event, it happens earlier than that time or event.

In an adjunct, often followed by an '-ing' clause: *She arrived just before 7.30 a.m... And I can deliver it before Christmas... We might not emerge from the first phase before the late 1980s... The baby teeth are formed in the gums before birth... Before going to bed, he wrote a letter to his father.*

Also used as an adverb: *The monument had been put up only a few years before.*

2 If you do something **before** someone else, you do it when they have not yet done it.

In an adjunct: *She did have this tendency to start drinking before anyone else.*

3 If a person or thing is **before** something, they are in front of it; a formal use.

In an adjunct or after 'be': *He bowed down before them... Edward the First buried them before the high altar.*

4 If you tell someone that one place is a certain distance **before** another, you mean that they will come to the first place first.

In an adjunct or after 'be': *There's a garage about two hundred yards before the turning.... Just before Warren Farm, turn left through a wooden gate.*

5 If someone or something appears or comes **before** a person or group, they are there to be heard or considered officially by that person or group.

In an adjunct or after 'be': *He clearly was not impressed by the evidence put before him... It was a little like being up before the headmaster.*

After a noun: *President Ronald Reagan's appearance before Congress was a personal triumph.*

6 If you have something such as a journey, a task, or a stage of your life **before** you, you must do it or live through it in the future.

In an adjunct or after 'be': *I have a difficult job before me. ...as if his life were still before him.*

7 When you want to say that one person or thing is more important than another, you can say that they come **before** the other person or thing.

In an adjunct: *Should we place the needs of Europe's working classes before the needs of the masses of Africa and Asia?*

behind

1 If something is **behind** a thing or person, it is on the other side of them from you, or near their back rather than their front.

In an adjunct or after 'be': *The sun had dropped behind the rooftops... He walked back to the village behind his brother... Behind the gramophone there were some records. ...fathers who are hidden behind the paper.*

After a noun: *The man behind the desk watched them register... The driver behind me began hooting.*

Also used as an adverb: *There were twenty more in a truck following behind.*

2 When you shut a door or a gate **behind** you, you shut it after you have gone through it.

In an adjunct: *He looked up as Gant shut the door behind him.*

3 The reason or person **behind** something caused it or is responsible for it.

After a noun: *The mayor attempted to explain the reasons behind the meat shortage. ...one of the strongest drives behind the women's movement... He was the moving spirit behind this venture to the Arctic.*

In an adjunct or after 'be': *Of course, behind the Cabinet decision lay two major political considerations... I knew that she was behind my being victimised.*

4 If you are **behind** someone, you support them.

After 'be' or in an adjunct: *Well, emotionally, I'm very much behind Michael Foot on this... The whole of our organisation is behind you, at every minute... They have funds behind them and can carry on for a while.*

5 If you refer to what is **behind** someone's outside appearance, you are referring to a characteristic which is not immediately visible or apparent, but which you think is there.

In an adjunct: *I guessed that Miss Crabbe, behind that impassive veneer, had a very nasty temper... It was a good indication of the ability that lay behind his deficiency in literacy skills.*

After a noun: *...the reality behind their people-oriented facade.*

6 If you are **behind** someone, you are less successful than them, or have done less or advanced less.

In an adjunct or after 'be': *In the Championship he finished 11 strokes behind Watson... These children are only a matter of weeks behind children of non-working mothers... She had fallen behind the rest of the class.*

Also used as an adverb: *The idea came to me that as a community we had fallen behind.*

7 If an experience is **behind** you, it is in your past and not happening now.

In an adjunct: *He already had one divorce behind him... I wanted desperately to get that part of my academic life behind me... With the first fifteen exercises behind him, he stopped for a rest.*

8 If something is **behind** schedule, it is not as far advanced as people had planned.
In an adjunct or after 'be': *Stage 1 was eventually completed nearly two years behind schedule... We were running behind schedule when we boarded a bus for Suva... We're already well behind schedule.*

below

1 If something is **below** something else, it is in a lower position.
In an adjunct or after 'be': *It lay a mile below the surface of the Pacific Ocean... Below us on our left there was a big river... She touched her bare arm where Arnold's hand had held it, just below the elbow.*
After a noun: *...when man first came to live in the caves below the cliffs.*
Also used as an adverb: *Then we waited to hear it hit the surface of the water far below.*
2 If something is **below** a particular amount, rate, or level, it is less than that amount, rate, or level.
In an adjunct or after a link verb: *Few experts expect their share to dip below 20 per cent... You cannot go below absolute zero... She, for a girl, seemed tall, and he, for a man, just below average height.*
Also used as an adverb: *Keep the room temperature down to 68 or below.*
3 If someone is **below** you in an organization or system of assessment, they are lower in rank.
In an adjunct or after 'be': *These conflicts usually rage well below the level of top management... I believe he is a genius, somewhere above Auden but below Eliot.*

beneath

1 If something is **beneath** something else, it is directly between it and the ground or floor.
In an adjunct or after 'be': *There is a heater beneath the table... She placed a pillow beneath his head... The people shivered beneath their blankets.*
After a noun: *The ground beneath them was a bank covered with grass.*
Also used as an adverb: *...vast regions of smooth ice, where water has welled up from the ocean beneath.*
2 When you want to talk about the aspects of something which are not obvious, you can talk about what lies **beneath** the surface.
In an adjunct or after 'be': *I hope I sounded more convincing than I*

felt beneath the brave front... I never thought that beneath your stolid exterior there was so much fire and fury.

After a noun: *But the traveller does not have to look far to encounter the tensions beneath the surface.*

3 If you say that something or someone is **beneath** you, you mean that you feel they are not good enough for you or not suitable for you.

In an adjunct or after 'be': *'You're a landowner now,' they teased him. 'Work is beneath you.'... Posy found this beneath consideration. They stopped discussing it... He thought it beneath his official dignity to haggle... The Duke married beneath him.*

beside

The form **besides** is also used for paragraph 4.

1 If someone or something is **beside** someone or something else, they are at their side or next to them.

In an adjunct or after 'be': *Michael sat down beside her on the bed... Beside him was a little African boy... I made myself wait, standing beside the car.*

After a noun: *He gestured towards the man beside him.*

2 If you work or fight **beside** someone, you work or fight together in cooperation with each other.

In an adjunct: *I'll fight beside you in Africa, Bovis, not in Europe.*

3 Beside is used to show that you are comparing two things.

In an adjunct: *What is love beside art!... The deficit shot up again to £350,000. That sounds small beside Covent Garden's £3 million pounds deficit.*

4 If you have something **beside** other things or **besides** other things, you have it in addition to those things.

In an adjunct: *Anyway, there was plenty to do beside hunting... Besides the capital, there were few major cities... Besides his interest in anthropology, he had a flair for languages.*

Also used as an adverb: *He was a kind man, but he was many other things besides.*

between

1 If something is **between** two things, these two things are on either side of it, or it joins them or lies on a line joining them.

In an adjunct or after 'be': *He had a pain between his shoulders... At dinner, he was placed between Lords Carrington and Soames... Occasionally, there is a thin layer of sandstone between the two... There must be motels between here and Montauk.*

After a noun: *...the crevices between the stones. ...on the border*

between

between France and Switzerland. ...the dirt road between his house and Grandpa's cabin.

2 If people or things move **between** two places, they move regularly from one place to the other and back again.

In an adjunct: *I have been commuting regularly between the UK and the west coast of America.*

After a noun: *...a civil aviation agreement providing for direct flights between their countries.*

3 If something stands **between** you and a thing or person, it prevents you from having that thing or having a good relationship with that person.

In an adjunct or after 'be': *How to tackle these men who stand between you and the top jobs should be your next preoccupation... A whole series of middle men intervene between the two sides.*

After a noun: *My hostility to culture may have formed part of the barrier between us... It was a veil between herself and Spain which she could not pull aside.*

4 If something happens **between** two times or events, it happens after one and before the other.

In an adjunct: *123 women were reprieved from the death sentence between 1900 and 1949. ...coming in hurriedly between sessions of translating.*

5 The interval of time **between** one event or moment and another is the amount of time that passes after the first event and before the next one.

In an adjunct or after 'be': *There's only twelve days between the two races.*

After a noun: *...the 1000-year period between the end of the Roman occupation and the Renaissance.*

6 You use **between** when indicating a range of ages.

After a noun: *...offering technology-based education to pupils between the ages of 11 and 18.*

In an adjunct: *Between the ages of seven and eleven, girls' preferences changed.*

7 Something **between** one thing and another is a mixture of them both.

After 'something' or the noun 'cross': *He was something between a saint and an artist... He had the same peculiar expression on his face, something between a jeer and a challenge... She's a kind of cross between Lizzie and Janey.*

8 A relationship or interaction **between** two people, groups, or things is one that involves them both.

After a noun: *What is the relationship between language and thought?... Discussion can strengthen bonds between couples... A rally erupted into a brutal battle between police and demonstrators.*

Here are some nouns which are typically followed by **between:**

agreement	contact	merger
alliance	co-ordination	misunderstanding
antagonism	correspondence	partnership
balance	encounter	rapport
battle	feud	relationship
bond	fight	split
breach	friendship	truce
collision	interface	understanding
connection	interplay	
consultation	link	

In an adjunct: *Silence falls between them.*

9 If there is a difference or a similarity **between** people or things, they are different or similar.

After a noun: *The difference between you and me is that you've had a child... There is an interesting similarity between this and the myth of Pandora... So the gap between rich and poor nations widened.*

Here are some nouns which are typically followed by **between:**

contrast	disparity	gulf	similarity
difference	distinction	inequality	
discrepancy	gap	parity	

In an adjunct: *The new tax fails to distinguish between rich and poor.*

10 If you choose **between** two or more things, you choose only one of them.

In an adjunct or after 'be': *When pressed to choose between alternatives, she still explicitly refused... She was torn between what I was trying to make her do and what she thought best... The choice is now between English, French and German at school.*

After a noun: *Clinics in Zimbabwe now give patients a choice between traditional and modern doctors... Either one assertion or the other forms the correct account: and a decision between them is necessary.*

11 When something is shared or divided **between** people, they each have or do part of it, or they both use it.

In an adjunct: *The costs should be divided between all 92 league clubs. ...when child rearing is shared between a couple. ...cases where the kitchen was shared between two households.*

12 If two or more people have something or manage to do something **between** them, they each have or do part of it.

In an adjunct: *I looked in my bag and counted what we'd got between us—fifteen pounds, it was... They managed to win the title nine times between them.*

beyond

1 If something is **beyond** a place or barrier, it is on the other side of it.

In an adjunct or after 'be': *There was a blink of bright light beyond the forest... We were just beyond the range of the big guns... His village lies two miles beyond the border... Beyond the lawn lay Mr Annett's kitchen garden.*

After a noun: *...the long sandy beach beyond the farm... What place was there for a British presence beyond Britain's shores?*

Also used as an adverb: *It stretched for miles, to the river and beyond.*

2 If something happens **beyond** a particular time or date, it continues after that time or date has passed.

In an adjunct: *Few children remain in the school beyond the age of 16. ...the requirements for teachers up to and beyond the year 2000.*

Also used as an adverb: *...a strategy for the 1990s and beyond.*

3 If something extends **beyond** a particular thing, it affects or includes other things.

In an adjunct: *The problems extend beyond Britain's cities... He has expanded his interests beyond painting and sculpture into stage design and film... We're not going to comment beyond that.*

4 You use **beyond** to introduce an exception to what you are talking about.

After an indefinite pronoun or in an adjunct, often followed by an '-ing' clause: *The government could do nothing beyond warning the western governors to be on their guard. ...the only man who knew something about the United States beyond what he had read in magazines... Beyond a cursory acquaintance, he had never been near the Royal circle.*

5 If something goes **beyond** a particular point or stage, it advances or increases so that it passes that point or stage.

In an adjunct: *The nuclear power programme will have proceeded beyond the point where it can easily be stopped... I felt his hands on me, gripping to and beyond the point of real pain.*

6 If something is, for example, **beyond** belief or **beyond** comprehension, it is so extreme in some way that it cannot be believed or understood.

After a link verb or in an adjunct: *The reason was very simple and beyond dispute... The inefficiency of the system was beyond belief... The total number of insects in the world seems beyond any computation... In the course of a year, he had changed almost beyond recognition.*

After an adjective: *Some of the national habits are bad beyond description... I feel humiliated beyond belief.*

After a noun: *There was gold beyond description.*

7 If you say that something is **beyond** someone, you mean that they cannot understand it, do it, or have it.

After 'be': *Her reasoning was quite beyond me... The motives behind artistic impulses were beyond my comprehension... I suspect that an insight on this scale would be beyond the capacity of the human mind... Even the relatively low-cost items may be beyond the resources of many small farmers.*

After a noun: *What happens to us is largely determined by factors beyond our control.*

but

When it is used as a preposition, **but** means the same as **except**.

After an indefinite pronoun: *I could walk across the ice and see nothing but grey skies... I have not encountered anything but extreme courtesy... I could never speak about anything but business to Ivan.*

by

1 If something is done **by** a person or thing, that person or thing does it.

After a past participle: *The meal was served by his armed bodyguards... The chances of being struck by lightning are very small... He was always amazed by her confidence.*

After a noun: *...as a safeguard against attack by one of the shepherds' dogs. ...a deliberate decision by government to resist automation.*

2 If you say that something such as a book, a piece of music, or a painting is **by** a particular person, you mean that this person wrote it or created it.

After 'be': *The paper is by Eulage, of whom you will already have heard.*

After a noun: *I brought him a copy of a book by John Fisher about Emily Hobhouse... Over the bed hung a painting by some Dutch eighteenth-century artist.*

3 If you do something **by** a particular means, you do it using that means.

In an adjunct, followed by a noun with no determiner or an '-ing' clause: *Did you come by car?... Many of the people cooked by Primus stove. ...like a cow being loaded on to a ship by crane... They dined by candlelight... Those who had tried to save themselves by flight were being hunted down and killed... They tried to save themselves by clinging to the wreckage.*

After a noun: *They did not recommend journeys by car.*

4 By is used in phrases which indicate whether or not an event was planned.

In an adjunct: *I gave Castle the wrong notes by accident... Her letter was dropped by mistake into the bay... Whether by design or because he can't help it, he creates a tension which wins over his audience.*

5 By law, **by** a particular rule, or **by** particular standards means according to the law or to the rule or standards.

In an adjunct: *By law, state pensions must be reviewed once a year. ...if pupils refuse to play the game by the rules... The salary was enormous by my standards.*

6 You say that someone is a particular type of person **by** nature, birth, or profession when mentioning their character, nationality, rank, or profession.

In an adjunct, followed by a noun with no determiner: *Sam is English by birth whatever anyone may say... My father, who was a butcher by trade, said, 'The Lord sent the meat for us to eat'.*

7 If you say what someone means **by** a particular word or expression, you are saying what they intend the word or expression to refer to.

In an adjunct: *I now want to explain what I mean by 'expression'... That depends on what you mean by luck, Leonard.*

8 If you hold someone or something **by** a particular part of them, you hold that part.

In an adjunct: *The referee ran up and caught Graham by the shoulder... He sprang over the table and grabbed her by the throat... 'And what might this be?' she enquired, holding up a damp painting by one corner.*

9 Someone or something that is **by** something else is beside it and close to it.

In an adjunct or after 'be': *Barney was standing by my seat when I returned... You're lucky you weren't by the window... He stood by her while she telephoned.*

After a noun: *...the table by the sofa.*

10 When someone or something goes **by** you, they move past without stopping.

In an adjunct: *She also took my hand as we passed by the woods.*

Also used as an adverb: *Another bowler-hatted figure went by.*

11 If you stop **by** a place, you visit it for a short time.

In an adjunct: *They invited us to stop by the house for coffee. ...too many Stotts who had nothing to do but drop by the house and ask after Stanley.*

Also used as an adverb: *I'll drop by later.*

12 If you are **by** yourself, you are alone.

In an adjunct or after 'be': *She sat by herself and waited for service.*

13 If you do something **by** yourself, you do it without anyone helping you.
In an adjunct: *She could perfectly well manage by herself.*
14 If you stand **by** a person or principle, you remain loyal or obedient to them.
In an adjunct: *I would be quite prepared to stand by my observations and comments at any time... It was her duty to stick by James through thick and thin... In most cases, they will abide by the Minister's decision.*
Here are some verbs which are typically followed by **by**:

abide	live	stick
go	stand	swear

15 If something happened or will happen **by** a particular time, it happened or will happen at some time before then.
In an adjunct: *By 11 p.m. all the ships were back... We'll all be dead by then.*
16 If you habitually do something **by** day or **by** night, you do it during the day or during the night.
In an adjunct: *...young men who go about their work by day as peaceable civilians and who by night turn into soldiers.*
17 In arithmetic, you use **by** before the second number in a multiplication or division sum.
In an adjunct: *Multiply the cost per day by the number of days.*
18 You use **by** to talk about measurements of area. For example, if a room is twenty feet **by** fourteen feet, it is twenty feet long and fourteen feet wide.
In an adjunct: *The lake is 450 miles long by 50 miles wide.*
19 If something increases or decreases **by** a particular amount, that amount is gained or lost.
In an adjunct: *Profits have increased by £113 million in eleven years... Department budgets have been cut by 20 per cent.*
20 Things that exist or are produced **by** the dozen, thousand, or million exist or are produced in those quantities.
In an adjunct: *Gillian, who wrote letters by the dozen every week, spent a fortune on stamps. ...a book which sells by the million.*
21 You use **by** between identical nouns to talk about things that happen gradually.
In an adjunct: *Our salaries weren't in fact moving up year by year as projected... He moved his hand bit by bit over the mirror... Carefully pour the oil, drop by drop, into the paste.*

by means of

If you do something **by means of** a particular instrument, method, or process, you use that instrument, method, or process to do it.

close to

In an adjunct: *We climbed down into it by means of a vertical iron ladder... In the end, he hit the mark by means of a simple trick... It would then become possible to protect people by means of vaccination.*

close to

Close has the comparative form **closer** and the superlative form **closest**.

1 If someone or something is **close to** a place or thing, they are near it.
In an adjunct or after 'be': *They live close to Frome... The captain stepped close to Farnbach's side... The river was uncomfortably close to the border.*

2 If you are **close to** a situation or state, you are almost in that situation or state.
In an adjunct or after 'be', often followed by an '-ing' clause: *He came close to dying... I think that I went close to putting them off riding altogether... It was obvious he was close to tears.*

3 If something is similar to something else, you can say it is **close to** it.
In an adjunct or after 'be': *...an exchange of complaints which sometimes came close to bickering... Her status would have been close to that of a slave.*

4 If something is **close to** a particular amount, it is a little less or more than that amount.
After 'be': *The authority's poll tax will be close to £376.*

concerning

You use **concerning** to indicate the subject matter of something that is said, written, or thought.
After a noun: *I want to ask your advice concerning one or two questions... Bettina and I both wrote articles concerning prisons and political prisoners. ...in a bid to allay public fears concerning ownership.*

considering

You use **considering** to show that you are taking a certain fact into account.
In an adjunct: *It wasn't unattractive, considering its function... Considering the circumstances, this was an important win for them.*
Also used as an adverb at the end of a sentence: *She's quite well, considering.*

contrary to

If you say that something is true **contrary to** a belief or statement, you mean that it is true although the opposite is thought or has been said.
In an adjunct: *Contrary to popular belief, the desert can produce crops... Contrary to official predictions of further increases, the prison population has fallen.*

depending on

You use **depending on** to indicate a variable factor that will affect a situation.
In an adjunct: *They will lend up to 90 per cent of the property's value, depending on its age... But the times will vary depending on the classes he has to attend... Different methods are used depending on what results are required.*

despite

1 You use **despite** to introduce something which makes the situation or event you are mentioning seem surprising.
In an adjunct, often followed by an '-ing' clause: *He was very refined despite his occupation... She always had time for a pleasant word, despite having some family problems of her own. ...decisions that were implemented despite much criticism.*
2 If you do something **despite** yourself, you do it although you did not really mean to or expect to.
In an adjunct: *Rudolph laughed and despite herself Gretchen had to laugh too... Jeff grinned reluctantly, pleased despite himself at even this much recognition.*

down

1 If someone or something goes **down** something such as a slope or a pipe, they go towards the ground or to a lower level.
In an adjunct: *They waved as he drove down the hillside... She hurried on down the steps... He emptied the last of the milk down the sink... Tears ran down my cheeks.*
Also used as an adverb: *George waved his shirt up and down.*
2 If you go **down** a road or passageway, you go along it towards one end of it.
In an adjunct: *Karen drove on down the street... He walks back down the corridor... He saw Whitman walking down the pier towards his car.*
3 If you go **down** a river, you go along it in the same direction as the water is flowing.

due to

In an adjunct: *But when you go down the river, don't hit the rocks...
The dead fish drift down the river.*
4 If you go **down** a place, you go to it and into it; a very informal
use.
In an adjunct or after 'be': *Sooner or later all our meetings end up
down the pub... Sometimes I go down the cafe for a sausage-and-
chip lunch.*
5 Something that is situated **down** something such as a road is
situated further along it.
In an adjunct or after 'be': *There's a restaurant down the platform.
...a woman who lives down the road.*
6 If one thing has another thing **down** it, it has it from the top to
the bottom.
In an adjunct: *...a mass of long grey hair that came halfway down
his neck... She emerged with her hair down her back... At the same
time you will feel a strong pull right down the back of your legs.*
Also used as an adverb: *A striped tie hung down to his belt.*

due to

If a situation or event is **due to** something else, it exists or happens
as a result of it. Some people consider that you should only use **due
to** after 'be', and not in an adjunct.
After 'be' or in an adjunct: *Pathologists found that death was due to
police violence... Due to inflation, the general cost of living in
Britain rose by 5% last year.*
After a noun: *Stress due to poor working conditions is one cause of
illness.*

during

1 If something happens **during** a period of time, it happens
continuously, or happens several times between the beginning and
end of that period.
In an adjunct: *He wrote a weekly column for the Guardian during
1963-4... Champagne merchants say that it can be drunk before,
during and after a meal... During all the years of work, he had been
realistic with himself.*
2 If something develops **during** a period of time, it develops
gradually from the beginning to the end of that period.
In an adjunct: *During infancy, the little monkeys form strong
attachments to their owners... Vegetarian societies grew slowly
during the next 150 years... I hope this will become clear to you
during the course of the lectures.*
3 If something happens **during** a period of time, it happens at some
point in that period.
In an adjunct: *The boy disappeared from the hotel during the*

night... She sold the house to the local authority during the crisis months of 1938... He'd given me a strong hint during that phone conversation.

except

The form **excepting** is also used.
You use **except** to introduce the only things or people that your main statement does not apply to.
After an indefinite pronoun or a noun: *There was nothing left except a few bricks... She has no money, no friends except those that live here... The girls all buzzed around, excepting May Noble.*

except for

You use **except for** to introduce the only things or people that your main statement does not apply to or take account of.
After a noun: *I had absolutely no friends except for Tom... He thought he recognized all the faces except for one woman in a shabby fur coat.*
After an adjective: *Now after midnight it is quiet except for an occasional motorcyclist... His mind was empty except for thoughts of her.*
In an adjunct: *There is deep and utter silence here, except for the sound of an Indian tune playing on a record player... Except for such diversions, pond creatures spend their time in an endless search for food.*

excluding

You use **excluding** to introduce someone or something that is not part of a group that you are talking about.
After a noun or in an adjunct: *In 1981 Britain spent nearly 40 billion pounds on inland transport alone (excluding air travel and water freight)... Excluding Greenland and Antarctica, the world has 13.15 billion hectares of land.*

following

Following a particular event means after that event or as a result of that event.
In an adjunct: *The mines had been closed down following a geological survey... Following an emergency meeting, reserve troops were mobilized... The investigation was completely reorganized, following the resignation of the Chairman.*

for

After a noun: *He hasn't been able to sleep well in the days following the fight.*

for

1 If something is intended or done **for** someone, they are intended to have it, use it, or benefit from it.
In an adjunct: *Why are you doing all this for me?... The village had bought it for me.*
After 'be': *Here—this is for you, Ashok. To bring you luck.*
After a noun: *The vicar arrived, bringing with him an unexpected present for me.*
After an adjective: *...cutting down the food supplies available for each person. ...a glossy magazine designed for today's sophisticated woman.*
2 If you work **for** a company or person, they employ you.
In an adjunct: *He worked for a large firm of solicitors.*
3 If someone does something **for** you, they do it so that you do not have to do it yourself. **For** is sometimes stressed in this use.
In an adjunct: *Remove the bones from the trout or ask your fishmonger to do this for you.*
4 If you do something **for** yourself, you do it, rather than someone else.
In an adjunct: *Come up here and see for yourself.*
5 You use **for** when stating the purpose of an object or action, or what someone is trying to get.
After a noun, often followed by an '-ing' clause: *I provided my canary with a bowl for bathing in... He said the best place for the meeting would be Paris... You'll have more than enough money for any equipment you need. ...his campaign for re-election.*
In an adjunct: *Willie went to the desk for the key... Liz had invited the whole group to her house for coffee. ... He crawled about the floor searching for the brush... The policeman was there, waiting for us... For further information see leaflet 49.*
Here are some verbs which are typically followed by **for:**

advertise	bargain	fish	hunt	search
aim	campaign	forage	look	send
apply	fight	grope	scavenge	wait

After 'be': *'You spend all your money.'—'That's what it's for, isn't it?'*
After an adjective, often followed by an '-ing' clause: *...the amount of money available for spending... We also found these diets useful for weight loss.*
6 You use **for** when indicating what someone wants or requests.
In an adjunct: *Perhaps she had longed for a child and never had*

one... He had hoped for some flash of inspiration... We asked for a meeting with the Director.

Here are some verbs which are typically followed by **for:**

appeal	call	hope	lust	press
ask	clamour	hunger	pine	wish
beg	hanker	long	pray	yearn

After a noun: *People have a longing for normality. ...the usual requests for money. ...its demands for greater democracy.*

After an adjective: *They were eager for revenge.*

7 If you leave **for** a place, you intend to go to that place.

In an adjunct: *I'm leaving for Washington on Tuesday morning.*

After a noun: *I boarded the train for New York.*

8 You use **for** when mentioning something that needs explaining or justifying.

After a noun, often followed by an '-ing' clause: *I cannot see any reason for going on... There was no reasonable explanation for her decision.*

In an adjunct after the verb 'account': *There are many elegant theories to account for inflation.*

9 You can sometimes use **for** when giving the reason that something is the case or is done.

After an adjective: *These employers were famous for their meanness.*

After a noun: *...the Cleveland man fighting his conviction for the murder of his wife.*

In an adjunct, often followed by an '-ing' clause: *I hated him for having humiliated me... He apologized for intruding... He was arrested for assault. ...a situation in which infants die for lack of elementary medical care.*

10 If you give someone a present **for** their birthday or **for** some other occasion, you give it to them because of that occasion.

In an adjunct: *She'd received a camera for her fourteenth birthday... What shall I get you for Christmas?*

11 **For** is used after some words to indicate what a quality, thing, or action relates to.

After an adjective: *...to make individuals responsible for their own safety... Be prepared for a little delay.*

After a noun: *Society has not found an acceptable substitute for the family. ...a cure for rheumatism.*

In an adjunct: *Hilary wept for her dead friend. ...having opted for early retirement... I shop now at special boutiques which cater for the fuller figure.*

12 If you feel a particular emotion **for** someone or something, that is how you feel about them.

for

After a noun: *...her hatred for her husband. ...our love for our children.*

Here are some nouns which are typically followed by **for:**

admiration	disdain	enthusiasm	nostalgia
affection	dislike	hatred	partiality
affinity	disregard	love	passion
appreciation	disrespect	lust	predilection
contempt	distaste	mania	weakness

After the adjective 'sorry': *I feel sorry for him.*

13 You can also say that you feel a particular emotion **for** someone when you feel it on their behalf.

After an adjective: *'It's quite a promotion.'—'Of course. I'm delighted for you.'*

14 You use **for** when you mention a person who is involved in an action you are commenting on and whose viewpoint you are giving.

After an adjective or in an adjunct: *She was aware she was making it easy for them to trace the call... That can't have been very pleasant for you... For me, killing you would create more problems than it would solve.*

15 You use **for** when you mention a person or thing in relation to which something has too much, enough, or too little of a quality.

Following 'too' or 'enough': *She wore frocks that were a bit too big for her... He was too heavy for her to carry. ...a room large enough for four to sleep in.*

16 You use **for** when mentioning an aspect of someone or something that is surprising in relation to another aspect of them.

In an adjunct: *She was tall for her age.*

17 You say that something lasts or continues **for** a period of time when indicating how long it lasts or continues.

In an adjunct: *The weather had been bad for several days... We talked for quite a while... For years Mary was unable to find a job.*

18 You say that something goes or extends **for** a particular distance when indicating how far it goes or extends.

In an adjunct: *I walked for miles and miles... The queue stretched for a thousand yards.*

19 If something is planned **for** a particular time, it is planned to happen at that time.

In an adjunct: *The wedding was fixed for 16 June.*

20 You use **for** when indicating how often something has happened before. For example, if something happens **for** the second time, it has happened once before.

In an adjunct: *Before using a pan for the first time, wash it with a sponge.*

21 If you buy, sell, or do something **for** a particular amount of money, you give or receive that amount of money in exchange.

In an adjunct: *...a paperback which he has bought for fifty cents...*
He made an arrangement to rent the property for a very small sum.
22 If you pay or charge a particular amount of money **for** an object
or service, you give or request that amount of money in exchange.
In an adjunct: *He had paid $5,000 for the boat.*
23 You use **for** with 'every' when you give one part of a ratio.
After a number, or a number and a noun: *It worked out at one
teacher for every extra 100 pupils.*
24 If you vote or argue **for** something, you vote or argue in favour
of it, giving it your support.
In an adjunct: *I'll never vote for him again.*
After a noun: *He provided no shred of evidence for these
allegations... The case for more equal relationships between
parents is strong.*
25 If you are **for** something, you support it and approve of it. **For** is
stressed in this use.
After 'be': *Are you for us or against us?*
26 A word **for** another word or **for** a thing means the same as that
word, or refers to that thing.
After a noun: *...'ge', the Greek word for the earth... What's the
proper word for those things?*

forward of

Something that is **forward of** a particular thing is near the front
or is further away from you than that thing; a formal expression.
In an adjunct or after 'be': *The explosion had been in the No.1 cargo
hold just forward of the wing... The line should now be watched
carefully and held lightly between finger and thumb just forward of
the reel.*
After a noun: *The area forward of the valley favoured defence.*

from

1 You use **from** to indicate who or what is the source or provider of
something.
In an adjunct: *Much of their support comes from the political left...
The evidence for this comes from an interesting fossil specimen
found at Koobi Fora... He bought the car from Ford's of
Dagenham... I had inherited it from the late Harold Haze.*
Here are some verbs which are typically followed by **from**:

beg	cadge	extort	inherit	wring
borrow	come	get	obtain	
buy	elicit	glean	receive	

After a noun: *...the ability to evaluate information from a range of* *sources... He unearthed a bottle of eau-de-cologne, a present from a woman admirer.*

2 You use **from** when you say where someone or something started off.

In an adjunct or after 'be': *He came originally from the north-east of England... He's from Philadelphia.*

After a noun: *We were joined by a friend of his, a man from Kansas City. ...vessels made out of semi-precious materials from the East.*

3 You can use **from** to say where someone works.

After 'be': *'He's from the BBC,' Stephen said... He says he's from the New York Times.*

After a noun: *On this principle the man from the ministry continued to visit me.*

4 If someone or something moves or is moved **from** a place, they leave it and go somewhere else.

In an adjunct: *I met Mr Meyers, a kindly man who had come to South Africa from London many years before... Kate retreated from the window and dressed... Blood was streaming from the wound... I produced my own watch from a pocket.*

5 If a person or thing goes **from** place to place, they go to several places. In literary English, this structure is also used to describe leaving one particular place and going to another.

In an adjunct: *...wandering from room to room... Her head bobbed from side to side. ...on the day he'd been transferred from bedroom to verandah. ...so unnerved that he could not pour the liquid from bottle to glass.*

6 If you take one thing or person **from** another, you move that thing or person so that they are no longer with the other or attached to the other.

In an adjunct: *Children were taken forcibly from their mothers... Remove the crusts from the bread... A starling was busy detaching the petals from an anemone.*

Here are some verbs which are typically followed by **from**:

cut	disconnect	separate
detach	remove	take

7 If you return **from** doing something, you return after doing it.

In an adjunct, often followed by an '-ing' clause: *The men as yet had not come back from fighting.*

8 If you are back **from** a place or activity, you have left it and returned to your former place.

After 'be back' or 'be home': *...a phone call telling her boss she'll be late back from lunch... When Harland was home from boarding school, the two of us would go shooting birds. When had all the family last been together with everyone back from university?*

After the adjective 'fresh': *In walked Chris, fresh from a dangerous safari.*

9 If you see something **from** a particular place, you are in that place when you see it.

In an adjunct: *From our cottage, we would see a distant kite swoop down on its prey... From behind his desk, he heard them passing in the corridor... The city, viewed from hundreds of feet in the air, was always full of bustling activity.*

10 If something hangs **from** an object, it is attached to it and hangs underneath it.

In an adjunct: *There, hanging from a peg, was a brand new raincoat... She would toy with the black pearl that dangled from her right ear.*

11 You use **from** when giving the distance between two places. After 'be' or in an adjunct: *The village was barely five miles from the eastern outskirts of Caen... The assault craft were less than a mile from Omaha and Utah beaches... They lived in tents just a few yards from the border.*

12 You can use **from** when you are talking about the beginning of a period of time or the first of a range of things.

In an adjunct or after 'be': *She was to be in New York from June to late September... From now on, you are free to do as you like... Entry fees vary from 50p to £5... We begin counting from zero through to nine and then start all over again.*

13 If something varies **from** thing to thing or **from** one thing to another, it is different in the case of different things.

In an adjunct: *Fees may vary from college to college... The policy on public access varies from place to place... The effect of a given dose of poison will vary from one individual to another... There were radical design alterations from edition to edition.*

14 If someone or something changes **from** one thing to another, they stop being or having the first thing and become or have the second thing.

In an adjunct: *...a year which turned Gillian from a happy, gentle person to an embittered and depressed woman... Language examinations will test the candidate's ability to translate from German into English. ...when interest rates have fallen from 11 to 10 per cent... The water turned from brown to gold. ...by encouraging people to switch from private to public transport.*

Here are some verbs which are typically followed by **from**:

change	fall	switch	translate
convert	graduate	transform	turn

15 If something is made **from** a particular substance, that substance is used to make it.

from

In an adjunct: *Ropes were made from local flax. ...making soap from coconut oil and wood ash.*

16 You use **from** when saying that something is not the same as something else.

After an adjective: *You're quite a bit different from what I expected... Evidently this is an altogether different picture of the world from that which Newton had.*

In an adjunct: *The American political scene differs markedly from that in Western Europe... How can you tell a poisonous mushroom from an edible one? ...his inability to distinguish his friends from his enemies.*

17 You use **from** when mentioning the cause of something or the reason for something.

In an adjunct: *A number of illnesses have resulted from the misuse of these compounds... We all got a tremendous amount of pleasure from your visit... I realized you could die from a cut like that... From my past experience, I think I may safely assume that they will not agree to the plans.*

18 If something is hidden or protected **from** a person or thing, they are not allowed to know, see, have, or harm it.

In an adjunct: *He would never hide this fact from them... You know that withholding information from me is a crime... Measures must therefore be taken to protect pipework from corrosion.*

Here are some verbs which are typically followed by **from**:

conceal	insulate	shelter
guard	keep	shield
hide	protect	withhold

19 If you free someone **from** a state, restriction, or oppressor, you do something so that they are no longer affected by it.

In an adjunct: *Today, with sophisticated machines, we can free man from the harshness of work... Some said that he was eventually released from imprisonment.*

After an adjective: *I am never really free from pain.*

20 You use **from** to indicate that something is being prevented or forbidden.

In an adjunct, followed by an '-ing' clause: *At the same time she'd prevented me from moving around... A security guard in a peaked cap stopped me from leaving the building... Portable yellow metal barriers kept vehicles from circulating in the streets.*

Here are some verbs which are typically followed by **from**:

ban	deter	dissuade	stop
bar	discourage	keep	
deflect	disqualify	prevent	

in

1 Something that is **in** something else is enclosed by it or surrounded by it. If you put something **in** a container, you move it so that it is enclosed by the container.

In an adjunct or after 'be': *In the drawers of a large Italian cupboard I found hundreds of letters... He gathered up the photos and put them back in his briefcase... Most babies have a wonderful time in the bath... He loved to bathe in the river... Billy Stein and Mary Breslow were in the car with him.*

After a noun: *Could he read the labels on packets in the store cupboard?*

Also used as an adverb: *Water poured in over the side of the boat.*

2 If something is **in** a place, it is there.

In an adjunct or after 'be': *There are three bottles in the kitchen... Mrs Brown strolled in the park all afternoon... Do you live in London now? ...multinational corporations based in the United States.*

After a noun: *The table in the kitchen had a tablecloth over it. ...the luckiest man in the world.*

3 A person **in** a piece of clothing is wearing it.

After a noun: *...a small girl in a blue dress. ...an old woman in black.*

In an adjunct or after 'be': *...when I see you walking along in your light-blue suit. ...a tall thin figure dressed in black... Hilary was in her nightdress and dressing-gown.*

4 Something that is covered **in** something else has that thing over its surface.

In an adjunct, usually after a past participle: *The walls of her flat are covered in dirt... Then I noticed that the lectern was draped in white silk bedsheets... Wrap the loaf in some foil and bake for 15 minutes.*

5 If something is **in** a document, book, play, or film, you can read it, see it, or hear it there.

In an adjunct or after 'be': *You didn't mention them in your letter... The change that this entails will be illustrated in the next chapter... Their number is in the phone book.*

After a noun: *Like a man in a comedy film, he pushed out his bare arm and examined the large watch on his wrist.*

6 When you see something **in** a mirror or other shiny surface, you see its reflection.

In an adjunct: *He looked at himself in his shaving mirror.*

After a noun: *She was looking at reflections in the large mirror on her dressing-table. ...the face in the mirror.*

7 Something that is **in** a window is just behind it where you can see it, inside the building.
In an adjunct or after 'be': *There was a sign in the window advertising a laundry marking machine... He stuck a poster in his window.*
After a noun: *...the magazines in the window... She walked along the pavement looking up at the light in his window.*

8 If someone or something is **in** a group, they are part of it.
In an adjunct or after 'be': *Of course, we all enjoy the excitement of being in a crowd... From the first, she was in a special category.*
After a noun: *He seemed set against most of the key people in the company except me.*

9 If you are **in** something such as a play or a race, you are one of the people taking part.
In an adjunct or after 'be': *He may be too small to compete in games... I thought he showed real talent in 'Hamlet'... He was easily the best boxer in the tournament.*

10 If something happens **in** a particular year, month, or other period of time, it happens during that time.
In an adjunct: *I was born in 1910. ...when the grass dies back in autumn... Joe returned to the village in the morning... In the first officer's absence, Demerest would do some of the first officer duties.*

11 If you do something **in** a particular length of time, that is how long you take to do it.
In an adjunct: *I have walked between twenty and thirty miles in a day.*

12 If something will happen **in** a particular length of time, it will happen after that length of time.
In an adjunct or after 'be': *The car should be here in ten minutes.*

13 If someone or something is **in** a particular state or situation, they are experiencing it or being affected by it.
After 'be' or in an adjunct: *...a man who was in an extreme state of distress... Do not run if you are injured and in pain... I have a feeling that she is in grave danger... A chance reunion with Charles Boon would not, in normal circumstances, have gladdened Philip Swallow's heart.*
After a noun: *The thought of a solution to the needs of 3 billion people in crisis seems desperately absurd.*

14 You use **in** to indicate that an emotion causes someone to do something.
In an adjunct: *He started leaping up and down in excitement... I wondered if I could have misunderstood the arrangement in my nervousness.*

15 You use **in** to indicate that when you do something, you do something else as a consequence.

In an adjunct, followed by an '-ing' clause: *He bent down to kiss her forehead. In doing so, he knocked her arm from the armrest.*

16 You use **in** to indicate what something such as an action, belief, or change relates to.

In an adjunct: *Do you believe in ghosts?... She was revelling in her newly acquired freedom. ...a fuller understanding of what is happening in education.*

Here are some verbs which are typically followed by **in:**

assist	embroil	implicate	involve	revel
believe	engage	indulge	join	share
collaborate	fail	interfere	luxuriate	specialize
dabble	gain	intervene	meddle	wallow
deal	glory	invest	mediate	

After a noun: *...developments in the motor vehicle industry during 1966-7. ...just as one acquires skill in golf or skiing or foreign languages... He had sent a note to the court expressing his confidence in me.*

Here are some nouns which are typically followed by **in:**

belief	decline	fall	say
boom	decrease	falling-off	skill
breach	delight	fluctuation	slump
catch	development	improvement	stake
change	diminution	increase	upsurge
confidence	exercise	interest	voice
cut	experiment	part	
cutback	faith	pride	

After an adjective, often followed by an '-ing' clause: *Are you interested in Greek pottery?... I became increasingly involved in politics... I think he was quite justified in refusing to help her.*

17 You use **in** when indicating what aspect of something you are talking about.

In an adjunct: *The electric eel grows to a metre and a half in length... The leaves are rough and grey-green in colour... These aspirations are not now primarily economic in character.*

After a noun: *There really was very little difference in their appearance.*

Here are some nouns which are typically followed by **in:**

difference	equality	similarity
disparity	inequality	variation

18 If someone is **in** things of a particular kind or **in** a particular type of work, that is what their work involves.

After 'be': *He used to be in films... I've been in this business my whole life.*

After a noun: *Maths is no longer a prime requirement for a career in accountancy.*

19 You use **in** to say how someone is expressing something.

in between

In an adjunct or after 'be': *He explained rapidly in French that he had been visiting his girl... 'Eric!' cried Ralph in a shocked voice... We're merely asking you to confirm in writing what you've already told us... A message had been scrawled on the wall in chalk... The letter was in French.*

20 You use **in** to describe how certain people or things are arranged.
In an adjunct: *They stood round me in a circle... There were three men standing in a close group by the lorry.*

21 You use **in** to indicate roughly how many people or things do something.
In an adjunct: *...sensors which would be relatively inexpensive to install in large numbers... In their hundreds the people searched and searched for facts about their ancestors.*

22 You use **in** to indicate roughly how old someone is.
After a noun: *...a stocky man in his thirties.*
After 'be': *She was in her early forties.*

23 You use **in** to introduce the larger number that is part of a ratio.
After a number, or a number and a noun: *Only one in ten of the residents is working-class... One man in five was unemployed.*

in between

1 If something is **in between** things, those things are on either side of it.
In an adjunct or after 'be': *The horizon was like a sandbank, with hollows in between the long blue crests... Scotland were always able to get a man in between the ball and where we wanted it to be.*
Also used as an adverb: *...sets of apartments, with stairs in between.*

2 If you do something **in between** actions of some kind, you do it in the intervals when you are not performing those actions.
In an adjunct: *Elsa had cried all night, in between bouts of telling him that they were disgraced for life. ...tending the gardens, in between visits to various bars.*

including

You use **including** to mention specifically someone or something that belongs to the group of people or things you are referring to.
After a noun or an indefinite pronoun: *Before long everyone, including my mother, had joined in... There were half a dozen plants, including a peach tree growing in a coffee can... His house had a piano in every room including the kitchen and bathroom.*

in favour of

1 If you are **in favour of** something, you support it and believe that it is a good thing to have or do.

After 'be': *The overwhelming majority of the French people were plainly in favour of resistance to the initiative... He was in favour of the retention of capital punishment... I have always been in favour of a voluntary incomes policy.*

In an adjunct: *It has been the players who have spoken out strongly in favour of shorter tours.*

After a noun: *What are the arguments in favour of school uniform?*

2 If you reject one thing **in favour of** another, you choose the second thing.

In an adjunct: *The party had rejected wholesale nationalisation in favour of competitive, selective public enterprise... You will have to temporarily abandon your own needs in favour of theirs.*

3 If a situation or process is biased **in favour of** a group or thing, it helps and supports it.

After an adjective: *Coverage of the election had been biased in favour of the Republicans... The Act is biased in favour of the employers, and is therefore deeply resented by the trade unions.*

In an adjunct: *...discriminating in favour of women.*

in front of

1 If someone or something is **in front of** a particular thing, they are near the front part of it.

In an adjunct or after 'be': *Queues formed in front of the glass doors... Teddy's house was in front of them.*

After a noun: *The man in front of him looked sick.*

2 If you do something **in front of** someone else, you do it when they are present.

In an adjunct: *I don't allow Chris to use that expression in front of me... They are frightened to make mistakes in front of their friends.*

in lieu of

In lieu of something means instead of it, as a substitute or alternative; a formal expression.

In an adjunct: *Most of them were ex-soldiers who had been given a plot of land in lieu of a gratuity.*

inside

The form **inside of** is also used in informal English, especially American English.

1 If someone or something is **inside** a place or a container, they are surrounded by its sides or boundaries.

inside

In an adjunct or after 'be': *Melanie spends more of her life inside prison than out... Put your barley inside a porous sack... At first he thought he was inside a church.*
After a noun: *The hot liquor got to work on the chill inside them.*
Also used as an adverb: *The priest was allowed to go inside.*
2 If you are **inside** an organization, you are part of it and so have knowledge or powers connected with it.
In an adjunct: *Do we want to stay inside Europe? ...whether they should work inside the Labour Party to move it in a leftwards direction.*
After a noun: *Their contact inside the Swiss Intelligence Service office in Berne believes that this was the case.*
3 If you say that somebody has a feeling **inside** them, you mean that they have this feeling but have not expressed it.
In an adjunct or after 'be': *Fury continually rose inside me... Inside him is a vacuum, cold as space.*
After a noun: *I felt the happiness inside me expanding.*
4 If something is **inside** a door, it is in a building, near the door.
In an adjunct or after 'be': *He set the basket just inside the door of his hut.*
5 If you do something **inside** a particular amount of time, you do it before that amount of time has passed.
In an adjunct: *I was back inside twenty seconds... I'll have some men there inside of fifteen minutes.*

in spite of

1 You use **in spite of** to introduce something which makes the situation or event you are mentioning seem surprising.
In an adjunct: *British Rail said the scheme was working well, in spite of early confusion... In spite of the threat of war, he says he remains confident that peace is possible.*
2 If you do something **in spite of** yourself, you do it although you did not really mean to or expect to.
In an adjunct: *Morris was intrigued in spite of himself.*

instead of

If you have or do one thing **instead of** another, you have or do the first thing and not the second, although the second is more usual, or is expected or preferable.
In an adjunct, often followed by an '-ing' clause: *He was wearing a scarf instead of a tie... He accepted the realities instead of resisting them... It pays its staff 60p a mile if they travel by bicycle instead of by car.*

into

1 If someone or something goes **into** a place, thing, or group, they are then in it or part of it.

In an adjunct: *He got into bed... I had to go into town on some business. ...plans to introduce investment and technology into Hong Kong... The river runs into the ocean... The need for low energy consumption should be incorporated into our building regulations.*

After a noun: *Chances of acceptance into the San Diego community are becoming more and more remote.*

2 If someone or something crashes **into** something, they collide with it forcefully.

In an adjunct: *He missed his footing and crashed into the fence... Horch swerved and smashed into a low wall.*

3 You use **into** when saying that someone or something starts being in a particular state or being involved in an activity.

In an adjunct: *He dozed off into a fitful sleep... The project ran into difficulties... I didn't want to go into politics, but I felt I had to. ...going into combat.*

4 You can use **into** with some verbs when you are saying that someone is made or persuaded to do something.

In an adjunct, often followed by an '-ing' clause: *She did not want to stay on, but I talked her into it... I bullied Mother into giving up that awful job in Plymouth... Don't try to con the doctor into prescribing a tranquillizer.*

Here are some verbs which are typically followed by **into:**

brainwash	con	galvanize	push	trick
bully	deceive	lull	seduce	wheedle
coax	delude	mislead	shame	
coerce	frighten	pressurize	talk	

5 If something changes or is made **into** a new form, it then has this form.

In an adjunct: *It takes radiation from the sun and converts it into electricity... It was divided into two sections... He swept a double armful of sand into a pile.*

Here are some verbs which are typically followed by **into:**

blossom	develop	make	turn
change	divide	metamorphose	
convert	evolve	transform	
degenerate	grow	translate	

6 When someone changes **into** clothes of some kind, they put them on.

In an adjunct: *I took off my fancy clothes and changed into slacks... Thomas undressed and got into a clean suit.*

7 You use **into** to indicate what is being investigated.

After a noun: *I embarked on a philosophical enquiry into post-war*

irrespective of

world affairs... ...a number of interesting psychological insights into a child's approach to language.
In an adjunct: *Mr Channon said this was a good, valid point, and he would look into it... It is only now that I have ventured to delve into the deeper meaning of history.*
8 If you lay **into** someone or tear **into** them, you attack them or criticize them.
In an adjunct: *I was going to lay into her but the other two girls grabbed my arms... I tore into them, asking why they were there.*
9 If one thing blends or merges **into** another, there is no clear division between the two things.
In an adjunct: *One day blended into another... Where the land is drier, the vegetation merges into heather moorland.*
10 If something continues **into** a period of time, it continues until after that period of time has begun.
In an adjunct: *...a shift of balance which will continue into the mid 1990s. ...a behaviour pattern lasting into adulthood.*
11 If someone is **into** a particular type of thing, they are very interested in it or like it a great deal; an informal use.
After 'be': *Teenagers are into those romantic novels.*

irrespective of

If something is true or happens **irrespective of** a particular factor, that factor does not affect the situation.
In an adjunct: *Severe steps will be taken against those responsible, irrespective of their rank... There was to be a flat rate charge for each individual, irrespective of where they lived.*

like

1 If someone or something is **like** another person or thing, they have similar characteristics.
After a link verb: *I don't belong here, Mother—I'm not like you... He looked like a sheepdog... I felt like a burglar.*
After a noun: *I'd love to have a room like yours... He even showed something like irritation at times.*
2 If you ask what something or someone is **like,** you are asking for a description or opinion of that thing or person.
After a link verb: *'What is Summerhill like?'—'Well, for one thing, lessons are optional.'... I do believe she forgot what he looked like.*
3 You can use **like** when giving an example of the kind of thing you have just mentioned.
After a noun: *In crowded places like ports and air terminals you must take care of your luggage... Wood chips are used in a range of building products like chipboard and thermal insulation.*

4 You can also use **like** to indicate that someone or something is in the same situation as another person or thing.
In an adjunct: *Like many large women, she felt pressured into hiding her size... He, like everybody else, had worried about it.*
5 If someone behaves or is treated **like** a particular thing, their behaviour or treatment is similar to the behaviour or treatment of that thing.
In an adjunct: *I've watched them like a hawk... The protesters were rounded up like cattle by the police.*

minus

Minus a particular part or thing means with that part or thing missing or removed.
In an adjunct: *Within an hour I was back in Fairacre, minus two back teeth and brimming with thankfulness... One lawyer wants publication of the report, minus any details that could jeopardize national security.*
After a noun: *...a large chair (minus a castor).*

near

The form **near to** is also used, especially for paragraphs 2 and 4.
Near has the comparative form **nearer** and the superlative form **nearest.**
1 If someone or something is **near** a place or thing or **near to** it, they are only a short distance from it.
In an adjunct or after 'be': *He stood near the door... He had been staying with an aunt who lived near Beachy Head... They were near to the French frontier.*
After a noun: *I'm in a telephone box near Victoria Station.*
Also used as an adverb: *The community centre is quite near.*
2 If you are **near to** a situation or state or **near** it, you are almost in that situation or state.
After a link verb or in an adjunct, often followed by an '-ing' clause: *Many millions of people are near to starvation... I came near to killing him... The scheme is near completion... She sounded unlike herself, near tears.*
3 If something happens **near** a particular time or **near to** it, it happens just before or just after it.
In an adjunct: *Sow the seed as near the 1st April as you are able... The President's Reception is always held near the start of the academic year.*
4 If something is similar to something else, you can say it is **near** to it or **near** it.
After 'be' or in an adjunct: *Danny is as near to a brother as I ever*

47

next to

had... Most views were fairly near the truth... There was one incident that came quite near to the science fiction fantasies.
After a noun: *She now feels a more complicated emotion—near to resentment.*
5 If something is **near** a particular amount or **near to** it, it is a little less or more than that amount.
After 'be': *Bank overdraft rates, already down to about 18.5 per cent, should soon be near 18 per cent... The actual number of sufferers may well be nearer half a million.*
After a noun: *...at temperatures nearer 1000 degrees C.*

next to

1 If one thing is **next to** another, it is at the side of it.
In an adjunct or after 'be': *He sat down next to Juris... Her room was next to Marcus's room.*
After a noun: *...the building next to the old chapel.*
2 You can say that **next to** one thing, another thing is the best or most important as a way of indicating what has second place.
In an adjunct: *Next to love Watteau cared most about music... Next to radicalism, religion was the most important factor.*

notwithstanding

Notwithstanding a particular thing means although that thing exists or occurs; a formal word.
In an adjunct: *They mirror each other's experience in certain respects, notwithstanding all the differences in age and personality... She fails to mention that, notwithstanding the legislation, Canada loses far more days through strikes than the UK.*
Also used after what it applies to: *Modern computers, inefficient software notwithstanding, still process data far quicker than brains.*

of

1 You use **of** after nouns referring to amounts or groups to show what substance or thing is involved.
After a noun: *...a bit of paper. ...three pints of boiling water. ...a cup of tea. ...a complicated set of rules.*
2 You use **of** to indicate what group something belongs to or what thing a part or amount belongs to.
After a pronoun, number, or noun: *Several of my fingers were still painful. ...three of his poems. ...the younger of the two women. ...a member of Mr Kuria's family. ...at the top of the hill. ...the family home, where the novelist wrote much of her later work.*

3 You also use **of** when mentioning a date, to indicate what month a day occurs in.

After an ordinal number: *...the 17th of June.*

4 You also use **of** after nouns such as 'kind' or 'sort' to indicate what general type or group you are talking about.

After a noun: *...this new kind of dictionary... Certain types of people come down with certain kinds of ailments.*

5 You also use **of** after nouns such as 'version' and 'form' to indicate what basic thing you are talking about.

After a noun: *...my version of the story... Adair sent me a copy of this letter.*

6 You use **of** to indicate who or what a thing or quality belongs to or is connected with.

After a noun: *...the rights of citizens. ...the smell of the wet garden. ...the importance of the decision. ...the King of Spain.*

7 Of is also used to indicate that someone has a quality or characteristic like the one that a type of person or thing has; a literary use.

After a noun: *Every one of my volunteers is a man filled with the courage of a lion... His eyes were the eyes of a drunkard and a fanatic.*

8 You use **of** to indicate what something relates to or concerns.

After a noun: *...her memories of her childhood there... There was no sign of danger. ...the real cause of the crisis. ...the Department of Employment.*

9 You use **of** with some verbs to indicate something else involved in the action, especially when the action involves knowledge or communication, having a quality or attitude, or removal.

In an adjunct: *Curley had informed them of his intention... He smelled of soap... She did not approve of the decision... Only a disastrous tactical mistake can deprive him of victory.*

Here are some intransitive verbs which are typically followed by **of**:

approve	conceive	dispose	learn	smell
beware	consist	dream	partake	speak
boast	despair	hear	savour	think
complain	disapprove	know	smack	weary

Here are some transitive verbs which are typically followed by **of**:

absolve	avail	convince	divest	warn
accuse	balk	cure	inform	
acquit	cheat	denude	make	
advise	cleanse	deprive	notify	
assure	convict	disabuse	purge	

10 You use **of** with some adjectives to indicate the thing that a feeling or quality relates to.

After an adjective, often followed by an '-ing' clause: *He was not afraid of controversy... I'm very proud of what Bobby has achieved... We like to think that sport is one area free of prejudice... He is capable of doing much better.*

Here are some adjectives which are typically followed by **of**:

afraid	devoid	impatient	scared
appreciative	distrustful	incapable	sceptical
apprehensive	empty	independent	scornful
ashamed	enamoured	indicative	short
aware	envious	insensible	unafraid
bare	expressive	intolerant	unaware
beloved	fearful	jealous	uncertain
bereft	fond	mindful	uncharacteristic
capable	forgetful	neglectful	unconscious
certain	free	nervous	unsure
characteristic	frightened	oblivious	unworthy
conscious	full	possessed	wary
contemptuous	guilty	protective	weary
critical	ignorant	proud	worthy

11 You use **of** with nouns referring to actions to specify the person or thing that is affected by the action or that performs the action. For example, 'the kidnapping of a child' refers to an action affecting a child; 'the arrival of the next train' refers to an action performed by a train.

After a noun: *He called for the removal of the ban. ...guidelines for the control of dogs in public places. ...the emergence of a strong centre party. ...the death of George Gershwin.*

12 You can also use **of** to specify something that occurs and is experienced.

After a noun: *...an attack of food poisoning... Jocasta felt a sudden pang of regret.*

13 You also use **of** to indicate what someone you are referring to creates, affects, or has a particular attitude towards.

After a noun: *...the organizer of the protest. ...supporters of the proposal. ...the owners of the oil tanker.*

14 You can sometimes use **of** to indicate a characteristic or quality that someone or something has.

After a noun: *...a lady of great charm and intelligence. ...material of the finest quality.*

After 'be': *Such international successes are of considerable importance... These lectures are designed to be of general interest to students.*

15 You use **of** when indicating how old someone is or how great an amount is.

After a noun: *...a man of forty... There has been a sales increase of 15 per cent.*

16 You use **of** to indicate the materials or things that form something.
After a noun: *...two rooms divided by a partition of glass and wood... Sprinkle them with a mixture of cinnamon and sugar.*
After the participle 'made': *...a little hat made of wool.*
17 You also use **of** with nouns such as 'gasp' and 'shriek' to indicate the feeling that causes a reaction.
After a noun: *He gave a gasp of amazement. ...a cry of despair.*
18 You also use **of** to say exactly what something is.
After a noun, often followed by an '-ing' clause: *...strong feelings of jealousy... She must address the problem of corruption. ...the joy of seeing her name at the top of the board.*
19 You use **of** in front of dates and periods of time to indicate when the thing you are referring to happened.
After a noun: *He lost his seat in the election of 1974. ...the great conflicts of the past ten years.*
20 You use **of** after nouns referring to the time that an event occurred to indicate what the event was.
After a noun: *The official explanation given at the time of the crash was pilot error. ...on the day of the funeral.*
21 You also use **of** to say what illness or injury caused someone's death.
In an adjunct: *The hospital said Miss Garbo died of heart failure.*
22 You also use **of** before a word referring to the person who performed an action when saying what you think about the action.
After an adjective: *I think it's very nice of him to take it on... I'm sorry about this morning—it was stupid of me.*

off

1 If something moves or is moved **off** something else, it comes away so that it is separate and no longer on the other thing.
In an adjunct: *He had almost fallen off his stool laughing... She walked off the stage... He wiped his fingerprints off the tap... Add mustard powder to the washing-up water to get the smell of fish off silver.*
Also used as an adverb: *Even if I did fall off, I shouldn't hurt myself.*
2 When you get **off** a bus, train, or plane, you leave it.
In an adjunct: *Just get off the train at Byfleet... She is not to be allowed off the aeroplane for any reason.*
After a noun: *The first person off the bus was Miss Maude Bentley.*
Also used as an adverb: *When the train stopped at a small station, he got off.*
3 If you keep **off** a street or a piece of land, you do not go on it.
In an adjunct: *Nothing could keep us off these roads.*

on

Also used as an adverb: *...a notice saying 'Keep off'.*
4 If something is **off** a coast, it is out in the sea, but near land.
In an adjunct or after 'be': *Last night the ship was about 120 miles off the coast of Argentina. ...a ship which sank off the coast of Devon last month... There were masses of fish feeding right off the beaches.*
After a noun: *We stopped at an island just off the Gojjam shore.*
5 If a building is **off** a road or square, it is in a street which joins that road or square.
After a noun: *He had gone to the flat off South Audley Street. ...a complex of nondescript buildings off the Boulevard Mortier.*
After 'be': *My office is just off the Strand.*
6 If you are **off** work, you are not working because you are ill.
After 'be': *Men are frequently off work with nervous headaches.*
Also used as an adverb: *His secretary's off today.*
7 If you keep **off** a subject, you deliberately avoid talking about it.
In an adjunct: *She kept off the subject of Collingdeane.*
8 If you are **off** something, you have stopped liking it; an informal use.
In an adjunct or after 'be': *I'm right off sweet things at the moment.*
9 If an amount of money is taken **off** the price of an item, the price is reduced by that amount.
In an adjunct or after a noun: *Some makers are cutting hundreds of pounds off the big-selling medium-range models... Debenhams offered 20 to 25 per cent off selected purchases.*
Also used as an adverb: *All furniture at 20% off.*
10 If you get something **off** someone or somewhere, you obtain it from that person or place; an informal use.
In an adjunct: *Who did you buy the trumpet off?... ...a picture that we had bought off a stall in the Portobello Road.*
11 If you live **off** a particular kind of food or money, you eat it or use it to live. If a machine runs **off** a particular kind of fuel or power, it uses it in order to function.
In an adjunct: *He had been living off savings accumulated in the previous season. ...machines which run off batteries.*
12 When a radio or television station stops broadcasting, you can say that it goes **off** the air.
In an adjunct or after 'be': *Local radio goes off the air at midnight... They'll be off the air until 7 tomorrow morning.*

on

The form **upon** can sometimes also be used, but is a more formal word.
1 If you are standing or resting **on** or **upon** something, it is underneath you and is supporting your weight.

In an adjunct or after 'be': *He went quietly downstairs and stood on the terrace... On the table were his keys and his pocket-book... There was a photograph of a beautiful girl on Daintry's desk... He sat upon the sweet, cool, grassy verge.*

After a noun: *Suddenly, the telephone on the table behind her rings.*

2 If you put something **on** or **upon** a surface, you move it so that it is then supported by the surface.

In an adjunct: *I put a hand on his shoulder... She flung herself on the floor... He wanted to lay his hand upon her sleeve.*

3 If you are **on** a bus, plane, train, or ship, you are travelling in it.

In an adjunct or after 'be': *He had come out on the bus to visit his friend... As soon as she was on the train, she opened the box.*

After a noun: *'Must be pretty hard to stay detached,' a man on the plane to San Francisco said.*

Also used as an adverb: *A bus came, and several people got on.*

4 If there is something **on** or **upon** a piece of paper, it has been written or printed there.

In an adjunct or after 'be': *He wrote some figures on the chart... He opened up the paper. There was writing on it in pencil.*

After a noun: *We still don't really know what helps children to recognize words on a page.*

5 You use **on** or **upon** when saying what part of your body is supporting your weight.

In an adjunct or after 'be': *Alan lay on his back and stared at the ceiling... He was leaning on his elbow... She was on her hands and knees under a bench.*

6 If you are **on** an area of land, you are there.

In an adjunct or after 'be': *I was born on Honshu, the main island... The hotel was on a hill... They worked on the estate of a rich nobleman.*

After a noun: *...the beaches on the eastern coast. ...a tenant on a farm six miles from town.*

7 If a building is **on** a road, it is next to it.

In an adjunct or after 'be': *Sophie Clark lived on Huntingdon Avenue... The building was on a corner.*

After a noun: *...the house on Sixty-second Street.*

8 If something is **on** or **upon** a vertical surface, a ceiling, or an object, it is attached to it or is sticking to it.

In an adjunct or after 'be': *...the photographs that Mrs Gomez had stuck on the classroom wall... There was sweat upon his forehead... He notices she is wearing a cross on a chain around her neck.*

After a noun: *...looking up at the light fixture on the ceiling.*

'On' can also be used as an adverb: *I can cook and sew buttons on for you.*

9 If you hurt yourself **on** something, you accidentally hit a part of your body against it.

In an adjunct: *He fell over and hit his head on the piano.*

10 You can indicate when something happens by saying that it happens **on** a particular day or part of a day.

In an adjunct or after 'be': *She died on 2 June 1962... We had driven down to Garrod's farm on Sunday morning.*

After a noun: *...after the annual meeting on November 20.*

11 You use **on** or **upon** when mentioning an event that was followed by another one.

In an adjunct, often followed by an '-ing' clause: *On reaching the tent Don and Dougal told me they had reached the top of the ridge that day. ...the money that Ivan had given him on his arrival... They grew up overnight upon starting school.*

12 If something is done **on** an instrument or machine, it is done using that instrument or machine.

In an adjunct: *I was putting away the dishes while she played Chopin on the piano... 'Broadloom' carpets are woven on a loom over six feet wide.*

13 If something is being broadcast, you can say that it is **on** the radio or television.

In an adjunct or after 'be': *It was a song that had been on the radio a lot that winter... It's the sort of thing you hear on the radio.*

After a noun: *Cigarette advertising on television and radio was banned.*

Also used as an adverb: *Is there anything good on tonight?*

14 If something is done **on** or **upon** a particular system, principle, or basis, that is the way it is done.

In an adjunct: *These traps were constructed on the same principle as mouse traps.*

15 Someone who is **on** a drug takes it regularly.

After 'be': *The child should be on continual, regular medication to prevent new infections.*

16 If you live **on** or **upon** a particular kind of food, you eat it. If a machine runs **on** a particular kind of fuel or power, it uses it in order to function.

In an adjunct: *He lived on berries and wild herbs... Not all bats feed on insects. ...dining on smoked mackerel and coleslaw... The refrigerator ran on gas.*

17 If you are **on** a particular kind of income, that is the kind of income you have.

In an adjunct or after 'be': *...the problems of bringing up children on a low wage.*

After a noun: *...workers on low incomes.*

18 If you are **on** a committee or council, you are a member of it.

After 'be' or in an adjunct: *Both of them are on the Executive Committee... There were no women sitting on the Central Committee.*

After a noun: *...the black people on the committee.*

19 If something is **on** a list, it is included in it.

After 'be' or in an adjunct: *The size of telephone directories and the vandalization of telephone kiosks may also be on the agenda... You're not on my list of suspects... Few teachers put examination achievement high on their list of important objectives.*

After a noun: *...the topics on the agenda.*

20 You use **on** to indicate that someone is doing something, especially travelling.

In an adjunct or after 'be': *...when Chris and I were on a trip to Canada... They decided to go on a shopping expedition... A few summers ago Italian friends invited me on a cruise through the Greek Islands... On my other visit I was bolder.*

After a noun: *...if you are a student on a full-time course.*

21 You use **on** or **upon** with some words to indicate what something affects, relates to, or involves, especially when talking about actions involving compulsion, dependence, or emphasis.

In an adjunct: *Financial penalties should not be imposed on parents... Another dinner was forced upon Kitty... Force was used on inmates... It sounded as if his Mum relied on him to do most of the housework... I walked to the station instead of spending money on a taxi... I viewed it with distrust, verging on panic.*

Here are some transitive verbs which are typically followed by **on**:

base	confer	impose	model
bestow	foist	inflict	spend
blame	force	lavish	

Here are some intransitive verbs which are typically followed by **on**:

bet	count	focus	improve	plan
build	depend	frown	infringe	prevail
capitalize	eavesdrop	gamble	insist	rely
check	economize	hinge	intrude	save
choke	embark	impinge	lean	settle
concentrate	encroach	impose	pivot	verge

After a noun: *The effect on Mr Ross was catastrophic... The ban on publicity may now be lifted. ...attacks on the State. ...the emphasis upon the young.*

Here are some nouns which are typically followed by **on**:

assault	burden	emphasis	moratorium
attack	claim	focus	onslaught
attempt	constraint	infringement	restriction
ban	effect	limit	sanctions
boycott	embargo	limitation	

After an adjective, sometimes followed by an '-ing' clause: *The poor are more dependent on the rich than ever before... I was keen on politics. ...those intent on running away.*

Here are some adjectives which are typically followed by **on**:

adamant	contingent	fair	incumbent	unfair
bent	dependent	hard	intent	
conditional	easy	hooked	keen	

22 Books, discussions, or ideas **on** or **upon** a particular subject are concerned with that subject.

After a noun: *...a debate on education. ...information on air pollution. ...advice on marketing and planning.*

Here are some nouns which are typically followed by **on**:

advice	debate	judgement	perspective
agreement	decision	lecture	remark
book	ideas	legislation	report
comment	information	outlook	verdict

In an adjunct: *He just took the text and commented on it. ...meditating upon the bliss of divine union.*

Here are some verbs which are typically followed by **on**:

advise	dwell	meditate	reflect	vote
agree	elaborate	muse	remark	
comment	expand	ponder	report	
decide	lecture	pronounce	speculate	

23 If you spend time **on** something, you spend time doing it, making it, or dealing with it.

In an adjunct: *He was working on a book. ...men engaged on government work.*

After a noun: *...substandard work on dam projects.*

24 If you congratulate or compliment someone **on** something that they have done or that they have, you express your admiration of it.

In an adjunct: *In the locker room later, Thomas congratulated him on his victory... After complimenting me on my work, he informed me of the new arrangements.*

25 If you round or set **on** or **upon** someone, you start criticizing them or attacking them.

In an adjunct: *Arthur rounded on her, eyes gleaming through his glasses... He then turned on Daniel and said he must be mad... I was set upon by older boys and given a beating every morning.*

26 If you stumble or chance **on** or **upon** something, you discover it.

In an adjunct: *He felt certain that he had stumbled on something important... Castle began to regret that he had chanced on that poem... Eventually they came upon a dilapidated shack.*

on account of

If something happens **on account of** something else, that is the reason for it happening.

In an adjunct: *Her parents had been put to death on account of their faith... She was despised on account of her sex... No natural pollen can grow on account of inadequate summer rainfall.*

on board

If you are **on board** a boat, aircraft, or spacecraft, you are on it or in it.

In an adjunct or after 'be': *You knew why I wanted to come on board the Exodus... They informed us that a certain Frank Rogers was on board this aircraft.*

After a noun: *...anxiety over the amount of uranium on board the satellite.*

Also used as an adverb: *I had intended to stay on board.*

onto

1 If someone or something moves **onto** or is put **onto** a horizontal object, the object is then underneath them and supporting them.

In an adjunct: *He fell back onto my bed... She threw her books violently onto the floor... He then poured the beans onto the toast from a saucepan... She put the teapot back onto the warm stove.*

2 If something is fastened or put **onto** an object, it is then attached to it or stays on its surface.

In an adjunct: *She screwed the top back onto her scent bottle. ...a black handbag with sequins sewn onto it. ... He digs his fingers into the black greasepaint and begins smearing it onto his face. ...a concealed bulb which threw theatrical beams of light onto the ceiling.*

3 When you get **onto** a bus, train, or plane, you enter it in order to travel somewhere.

In an adjunct: *She watched the people get onto the train... Slipping past his pursuers, he hurled himself onto the train.*

4 If you hold **onto** something, you hold it firmly.

In an adjunct: *He held onto Lucas's hand... Hang onto that rope whatever happens.*

5 If a speaker gets **onto** or moves **onto** a different subject, they begin talking about it.

In an adjunct: *Then he moves onto the next item... Yeah, I'm coming onto that.*

6 If a door opens or gives **onto** a place, or if a building backs **onto** a place, it is next to that place.

In an adjunct: *French doors opened onto the terrace... The door gave*

on top of

onto a flagged path which skirted the house... The gardens and the houses backing onto them formed the main horizon.
7 If someone is **onto** something, they are about to make a discovery; an informal use.
After 'be', usually followed by 'something': *It seemed that Sabine was onto something, otherwise she would hardly have called Nancy... The police may make mistakes, but when they act this swiftly they're onto a sure thing.*
8 If someone is **onto** you, they have discovered that you are doing something illegal or wrong; an informal use.
After 'be': *Don't forget. I'm onto you, Mrs Bliss.*

on top of

1 If something is situated or put **on top of** something else, it is situated or put over it or on its highest part.
In an adjunct or after 'be': *She took down the box of games which sat on top of the green wooden cupboard... Place the mackerel on top of the cucumber... Newman laid the card on top of the counter.*
After a noun: *...the globe on top of the building.*
2 If something happens or exists **on top of** something else, it happens or exists in addition to it, often causing further problems.
In an adjunct: *On top of that, there had been a newspaper strike in America... She was even doing an Open University course on top of everything else... My father had several hundred pounds a year private income on top of that.*
3 If you are **on top of** a situation, you are dealing with it successfully.
After 'be': *She was composed, eager, and on top of every situation... No batsman this afternoon was ever truly on top of things.*

opposite

The form **opposite to** is also used for paragraph 1, but is less frequent.
1 If one thing is **opposite** another, it is on the other side of a space from it.
In an adjunct or after 'be': *There is a statue opposite the entrance... The road widens, you may note, opposite the Old Bailey... She was thinking more of Mary now than she did when she lived opposite to her.*
After a noun: *...a small house opposite a pub.*
Also used as an adverb: *Opposite is St. Paul's Church.*
2 If one actor stars with another in a film or play, you can say that the first plays **opposite** the second.

In an adjunct: *Two years later, she played opposite Anthony Quinn in the Biblical epic 'Barabbas'.*

other than

1 You use **other than,** usually after a negative, to introduce the only thing or person involved in a particular situation.
After a noun or an indefinite pronoun: *The fact is I don't have a thing with me other than this coat... I was so tired that I could think of nothing other than my cabin and my bunk... No fat other than butter is acceptable in these products.... There was a reluctance to talk about their reports to anyone other than colleagues.*
2 You also use **other than** when you want to specify a group which includes everything of a particular type except the thing mentioned.
After a noun or an indefinite pronoun: *Forensic science is in fact applied most frequently to crimes other than murder. ...recruiting students from groups other than the conventional pool of bright sixth-formers.*

out of

1 If you go **out of** a place, you leave it.
In an adjunct: *Paul got out of the car... He followed Rhoda out of the room... A girl came out of the doorway on the left.*
After 'be': *Once they were out of the air-conditioned restaurant, the smog hurt Stein's eyes.*
2 If you take something **out of** the container or place where it has been, you remove it so that it is no longer there.
In an adjunct: *He took a bag of money out of an inner pocket... She took a rug out of her case.*
3 If you look out or shout **out of** a window, you look or shout away from the room where you are towards the outside.
In an adjunct: *Mark Parker looked out of the window... Yet she would not stop shouting out of the window.*
4 If you are **out of** range of something, you are beyond the limits of that range.
After 'be' or in an adjunct: *...anxiously turning to ensure that Luke was still out of earshot... She watched until they were out of sight.*
5 If you are **out of** the sun or the wind, you are sheltered from it.
In an adjunct or after 'be': *Come in out of the rain... We could go up there a bit. Be out of the wind.*
6 If you get **out of** a situation or activity, you are then no longer in that situation or involved in that activity.
In an adjunct: *There's still a lot to do if we are to get out of trouble. ...unless they elect to opt out of the scheme... I should have talked her out of it.*

outside

After 'be': *I was glad to be out of a bad marriage.*

7 If you get pleasure or profit **out of** doing something, you get it as a result of doing that thing.

In an adjunct, often followed by an '-ing' clause: *He obviously got a sort of joy out of it... She got a lot of fun out of sweeping the front porch of the restaurant... I never made a penny out of it.*

8 If you get something **out of** someone, you persuade them to give it to you.

In an adjunct: *He stands no chance of getting a loan out of them... She flattered Seery and wheedled money out of him.*

9 If you pay for something **out of** a particular sum of money, you use some of that money to pay for it.

In an adjunct: *I was paying for Forio out of eight pounds a week... The relatives do not have to pay these debts out of their own income or savings.*

10 You use **out of** to say why someone does something.

In an adjunct: *I said yes out of politeness... She accepted the job out of curiosity... He used to make large donations out of a sense of duty... Those who remain in primitive housing do so out of poverty alone.*

11 If something is made **out of** a particular substance or thing, that substance or thing is used to make it.

In an adjunct: *They make sandals out of old car tyres. ...a club made out of an old piece of driftwood... Men chisel blocks out of solid rock.*

12 If you are **out of** a type of thing, you no longer have any of it.

In an adjunct or after 'be': *Many of them have simply run out of money... We ought to get some more wood—we're out of green branches.*

13 You use **out of** when indicating what proportion of a group of things you are talking about.

After a number: *Four out of five part-time workers are women... In one group, eight out of ten were unemployed.*

outside

The form **outside of** is also used in informal English, especially American English.

1 If you are **outside** a building or a room, you are not inside it, but you are quite close to it.

In an adjunct or after 'be': *Crowds waited outside the Town Hall for three o'clock... I can't risk the painting going outside the building.*

After a noun: *One of the news-stands outside the station was full of foreign papers and magazines.*

Also used as an adverb: *They stood outside discussing the matter.*

2 If someone or something is **outside** a door, they are not inside a building or room but are near its door.
In an adjunct or after 'be': *There was no-one outside the door.*
3 If people or things are **outside** a place, area, group, or system, they are not in it or are not part of it.
In an adjunct or after 'be': *Not many people have heard of him outside Blackheath... More women than ever are working outside the home... What I've learnt, I've learnt outside of school anyway. ...the schools operating outside the system.*
After a noun: *...influential people both inside and outside government. ...sales to countries outside the EEC.*
4 Something that is **outside** a particular range of things is not included within it.
After 'be': *It was so far outside my range of expectations.*
After a noun: *Art and science are both uniquely human actions, outside the range of anything that an animal can do.*
5 Something that happens **outside** a particular period of time happens before or after that period.
In an adjunct: *You can deposit and withdraw money outside normal banking hours... The fare is cheaper outside of peak hours.*

over

1 If one thing is **over** another or is moving **over** it, the first thing is directly above the second.
In an adjunct or after 'be': *We drew water to heat over an open fire... There is no bridge over the river. ...crouching over a silent keyboard... Over the valley, a full moon was rising... He flew on over the school house.*
Also used as an adverb: *There's an aircraft coming over.*
2 If there is something **over** something else, the first thing is covering the second.
In an adjunct or after 'be': *The blindfold was tied over Ari's eyes... I laid my coat over a nearby barrel. ...as we ate the crumpets, with butter oozing deliciously over our fingers... The ashes were dumped all over the floor.*
3 If you wear one piece of clothing **over** another, the first piece of clothing is closer to the outside than the second.
In an adjunct: *The vicar wore a red and white jacket over his clerical shirt.*
4 If a window has a view **over** a place, you can see the place from that window.
In an adjunct: *High windows looked out over a soft green wooded park... Jim Hess looked out over his country.*
After a noun: *Most rooms have a view over fields.*

5 If someone or something moves **over** an area or place, they move across the surface from one side towards the other.

In an adjunct: *...riding his bicycle over everyone's lawns... They scrambled away over the rocks... We drove back over the hills to the San Fernando Valley.*

6 If you go **over** something such as a river or boundary, you cross it.

In an adjunct: *His Police Jaguar roared over the river in the direction of the village... Then German refugees began pouring over the border into Denmark.*

7 If something is on the opposite side of a road, river, or border, you can say it is **over** the road, river, or border.

After 'be': *The post office is just over the road.*

After a noun: *My son's doing better than I am—in that shop over the road.*

8 If you look **over** something, you look across the top of it.

In an adjunct: *Her husband watched her over the top of his magazine... He smiled over Gant's shoulder at the woman.*

9 If someone or something gets **over** a barrier, they go across the top of it.

In an adjunct: *He was caught before he could jump over the wall... Dan toppled backwards over the sofa.*

10 If someone or something is **over** a particular age or amount, they are more than that age or amount.

After a noun: *Children over the age of one year start their colds with a sudden high temperature... What about those over six foot who have to squeeze themselves into a cinema seat?*

After 'be': *She's well over school leaving age.*

Also used as an adverb: *If you are 70 or over you can get your pension whether you have retired or not.*

11 If you can influence or control people or things, you have influence or control **over** them.

After a noun: *Specialists disagree on the extent of American influence over the British market. ...man's domination over his environment... It provides readers with a feeling of power over their contemporaries.*

Here are some nouns which are typically followed by **over**:

advantage	control	hold	power
ascendancy	dominance	influence	victory
authority	dominion	mastery	

12 You also use **over** to indicate what a disagreement, feeling, thought, or action relates to or is caused by.

In an adjunct: *Starving children were fighting over spilt grain... They were seen gloating over wads of dollar bills. ...Lord*

Boardman, the bank's chairman, who also resigned over the scandal.
Here are some verbs which are typically followed by **over:**

agonize	disagree	fret	haggle	row
argue	drool	fuss	muse	wrangle
brood	enthuse	gloat	quarrel	
clash	fight	grieve	quibble	

After a noun: *In time the misunderstanding over the government's plans would be cleared up.*
Here are some nouns which are typically followed by **over:**

anxiety	debate	outcry
battle	fuss	quarrel
concern	misunderstanding	row

13 If you go **over** something such as a piece of writing, you check it.
In an adjunct: *He comes across in the evening to help me go over my books... She ran her eye over the guest list and sighed.*
14 If something happens **over** a period of time, or **over** a meal or a drink, it happens during that time or meal.
In an adjunct: *It would probably go rotten over the weekend... I did a lot of thinking over Christmas... Over the last twenty years our rural communities have gradually wasted away... Luce once told JFK over lunch, 'I taught Kenneth Galbraith to write'.*

owing to

You use **owing to** when indicating the cause of something.
In an adjunct: *Gary Blackledge missed the last quarter of last season owing to injury... Now, owing to the financial cut-backs, the workshops have been closed.*
After 'be': *It was entirely owing to him that they acquired two bonus points.*

past

1 If you go **past** a person or thing, you pass them as you go somewhere.
In an adjunct: *Then they drove past a grove of chestnuts... A glass flew past his head and smashed against the wall.*
Also used as an adverb: *...as my two colleagues walked past on the way out.*
2 If something is situated **past** a place, you pass that place when getting to it.
In an adjunct: *Just past those houses are the Lispenard Meadows... About a hundred yards past the last houses, take a left on a dirt road.*
After a noun: *...a small castle two miles past the village.*

3 You use **past** when you are stating a time which is thirty minutes or less after a particular hour.
After a number, 'half', or 'a quarter': *By ten past nine the final version was finished... They came for Superintendent Thomas at a quarter past ten... It was half past twelve.*
Also used as an adverb: *We'll try to finish early—about twenty five past.*

4 If someone or something is **past** a state or stage, they are no longer in that state or at that stage.
After 'be', sometimes followed by an '-ing' clause: *It is past its peak... Once they were past infancy, they were absorbed into the adult household... I'm past caring now about people's feelings.*
After a noun: *It has the decadence of an empire past its peak.*

5 If something is **past** belief or description, for example, it cannot be believed or described.
After 'be': *...exaggerations that are past belief... My complexion is past redemption.*
After a noun: *It was exhilaration past description.*

pending

If something is done **pending** a future event, it is done as a temporary measure because that event may make other action necessary; a formal word.
In an adjunct: *The hospital said the unit had been closed pending an investigation... Many charge payers have withheld payment pending the outcome of a legal test case.*

per

You use **per** to express rates and ratios. **Per** is put in front of the single unit involved in the rate or ratio.
After a noun or number: *...a new record of 318 miles per hour... Petrol costs around 30p per gallon here... They spent $73 per head on defence last year.*

plus

You can use **plus** when mentioning an additional thing or amount.
In an adjunct: *It has 16 class teachers, plus a teacher who works with children with special needs... Cleaners working for the agency get £2.45 an hour plus an agency fee of £4 per session.*

preparatory to

If you do something **preparatory to** doing something else, you do the first thing before doing the second thing, as preparation for it.
In an adjunct, usually followed by an '-ing' clause: *He was aligning*

the cuffs of his trousers, preparatory to draping them over a hanger... She had just drawn a deep breath, preparatory to embarking on a tedious summary of the lecture.

prior to

If something happens **prior to** a particular event or time, it happens before that event or time; a formal expression.

In an adjunct: *...the professor who corrected the manuscript prior to publication... Prior to that he was in the film industry. ...those widowed prior to 1973.*

After a noun: *In the four years prior to the Act, the rate of decline increased.*

regarding

You can use **regarding** to indicate the subject matter of something that is said, written, or thought.

After a noun: *This did give valuable information regarding Lloyd George's character... A big difficulty is the confusion regarding qualifications.*

In an adjunct: *Regarding this last item, let me discuss an example of what I mean.*

regardless of

If something happens **regardless of** a particular thing, it happens, and the existence or nature of that thing does not affect it.

In an adjunct: *They are taught to respect everyone, regardless of race... Regardless of the result, the present conflict threatens serious damage to the Church.*

round

The form **around** is also used.

1 If there is something **round** or **around** something else, the first thing surrounds the second thing or exists on every side of it.

In an adjunct: *I put my arms round her... He hung a garland of flowers round Tusker's neck... Little crowds would gather around them to listen.*

After a noun: *...the barbed wire round the big estates. ...the squalor and degradation around them.*

Also used as an adverb: *We crowded round.*

2 If something moves **round** or **around** something else, it moves in a circle with that thing at the centre of the circle.

In an adjunct: *He would dance round them excitedly.*

Also used as an adverb: *They just seemed to be riding round and round.*

3 If something such as a discussion centres **round** or **around** a particular thing, that thing is the main thing in it.

In an adjunct: *Next day the talk centred around the events in London... My life revolved around Margaret's daily visits.*

4 If you go **round** or **around** a place, you go to several different parts of it.

In an adjunct: *I wandered round the orchard... I trotted round town getting advice from various experts.*

After a noun: *...a walk round the estate.*

Also used as an adverb: *They won't want anyone else trampling around.*

5 If you go **round** or **around** a corner or obstacle, you move past it in a curve, so that you finish on the other side of it.

In an adjunct: *As I came round the corner, he caught my arm... The blonde secretary put her head round the door of Bruno Lazlo's office... Mr Willet stepped round a tombstone.*

6 If there is a way **round** or **around** a problem or difficulty, there is a solution to it.

After the noun 'way': *If you are a woman, it will be assumed that he is the guest, not you; the only way round this is to become a Dame... As usual, Jefferson had a way around the difficulty.*

In an adjunct after 'get': *These provisions were intended to get round the perennial problem of non-application of the law at local level.*

7 If you hang **round** or **around** a place, you stay there for a while, not doing much.

In an adjunct: *I enjoyed hanging around Parliament listening to debates.*

save

You use **save** to introduce an exception to what you have just said; a formal use.

After a pronoun or noun: *...nations with little in common save a history of Commonwealth links... The next election will be fought with every party save the Greens pledged to membership of the EC.*

save for

You use **save for** to introduce an exception to what you have just said; a formal expression.

In an adjunct: *Tomorrow the report will be completed save for the controversial clause 31... At length, save for an occasional rustle, the shelter was silent.*

since

1 If something has happened **since** a time or event, it has happened at some time or continuously in the period after that time or event. In an adjunct, with a verb in a perfect tense, sometimes followed by an '-ing' clause: *This has been going on since July... This has been the experience of all Governments since 1945... I had dreamed of China since childhood... Since leaving Styal, I have reverted to my former slapdash methods of cooking.*
Also used as an adverb: *He threw his stuff in a bag and left. I haven't seen him since.*
2 If you say that something is the biggest, best, or first thing of a particular kind **since** another thing of the same kind, you mean that it is the biggest, best, or first thing of that kind that has occurred from that time until now.
After a noun: *...the first significant change in pictorial space since Cubism... It's the best thing since sliced bread.*

than

1 **Than** is used to link two parts of a comparison.
After a comparative adjective or adverb: *For some time, Wendy had been more radical than me... The Japanese scripts were more difficult than the Chinese... Two people could survive more easily than one... A stronger man than himself would not have hesitated.*
2 **Than** is also used to link two parts of a contrast.
In an adjunct, usually after 'rather': *It had been a scuffle rather than a fight... An age of leisure, rather than unemployment, was in prospect... It was more a lodge than a banqueting house.*

thanks to

You use **thanks to** when mentioning the person or thing that caused something to happen.
In an adjunct: *The town centre had a narrow escape from destruction, thanks to 100 firemen, who contained the blaze.... Thanks to the new network, clerks will be able to deal with all the payments at one time.*

through

1 If someone or something moves **through** something such as a hole or pipe, they go directly from one side or end of it to another.
In an adjunct: *The rain poured through a hole in the roof... They attempted to gain access through a side entrance... It proceeds through the tunnel and emerges coated with chocolate.*
Also used as an adverb: *The Ante-Room leads through into the Breakfast Room.*

through

2 If you cut **through** something, you cut it in two pieces or make a hole in it.

In an adjunct: *...cutting through a crust... The fish must have chewed right through it... He put a bullet through his girlfriend's eye.*

3 If you move **through** a group of things or a mass of something, it is on either side of you.

In an adjunct: *She zigzagged her way through the other guests... He trotted through the sand.*

4 If you go or move **through** a place, you go across it from one side to the other.

In an adjunct: *I was travelling through Athens on my way home from the Lebanon.*

After a noun: *I had been planning this trip through Mexico for over a year.*

Also used as an adverb: *I was just passing through.*

5 If you get **through** a barrier or obstruction, you get from one side of it to the other.

In an adjunct: *Nobody gets through the barriers except officials... We can go through the checkpoints together... Morris paid his pound and pushed through a baize curtain and a swing door.*

Also used as an adverb: *Only 200 demonstrators got through.*

6 If you see, hear, or feel something **through** an object, the object is between you and the thing you can see, hear, or feel.

In an adjunct: *We had spoken to each other in the booth, through glass, on telephones. ...looking through the lens of a camera... She kissed his skin through his shirt.*

7 If something happens or exists **through** a period of time, it happens or exists from the beginning of that period to the end.

In an adjunct: *Through the years there was, of course, a great deal of rebuilding... We would leave Nairobi at midday and drive through the night to Ferguson's Gulf.*

8 If something happens from a particular period of time **through** another, it starts at the first period and continues until the end of the second period; used in American English.

In an adjunct, usually after a prepositional phrase with 'from': *They lived there from early February through Thanksgiving 1967... I was in college from 1927 through 1932.*

9 If you go or live **through** an experience, especially a difficult or exciting one, it happens to you.

In an adjunct: *We've been through a big transition... She proceeded through her pregnancy with a great deal of apprehension. ...the boys who had gone through High School with her... He was a great friend of mine and saw me through all the hard times.*

10 If you are some of the way **through** a task, you have completed that much of it.

After 'be' or in an adjunct: *He was not yet halfway through 'Sense and Sensibility'... Two-thirds of the way through the race the wind suddenly blew up to gale-force.*

Also used as an adverb: *Halfway through, Hawk had started grinning.*

11 If you look or go **through** a lot of things, you look at them or deal with them one after the other.

In an adjunct: *I looked through a small booklet... He thumbed through the reports once more... To wade through all the papers is an impossibility.*

Here are some verbs which are typically followed by **through**:

browse	glance	look	sift	wade
flick	go	rifle	skim	work
flip	leaf	run	thumb	

12 If an idea or proposal goes **through** a committee or other official body, it is accepted and put into practice.

In an adjunct: *We could not be sure that we could carry sanctions through Parliament.*

After a noun: *Its passage through Parliament will be further troubled by a campaign against it.*

13 If one thing happens **through** another, the second thing is the cause of the first.

In an adjunct: *He always managed to find me, usually through a series of unbelievable chances... Many of the audience walked out through sheer boredom.*

14 If you achieve something **through** particular methods, you use those methods to achieve it.

In an adjunct: *We persuade through fear... Forecasting has already been substantially improved through computer analysis.*

throughout

1 If something happens **throughout** a period of time or an event, it happens during the whole of it.

In an adjunct: *This feeling of uncertainty exists for most people throughout life... Throughout the day, Mrs Pringle maintained a sullen silence... Throughout his career his main concerns have been with politics.*

Also used as an adverb: *Colonel Williams remained seated throughout.*

2 If something happens or exists **throughout** a place, it happens or exists in all parts of it.

In an adjunct: *He is famous—not only in England but throughout*

till

the world... I've included throughout this book quite a lot of simple, cheap ideas... They have branches throughout London.
Also used as an adverb: We were given £15,000 initially to equip the centre throughout.

till

1 If something happens **till** a particular time or event, it happens and then stops at the time mentioned.
In an adjunct, often after a prepositional phrase with 'from': You can stay till three if you like. ...the huge Franciscan church that was there till the Reformation... I worked from seven till seven each day. ...from breakfast till lunch.
2 If something does not happen **till** a particular time, it does not happen before that time but happens or starts at that time.
In an adjunct, with a negative clause: She didn't come downstairs till about a quarter to eight... He did not finish till the small hours of the morning.

to

1 If someone or something goes **to** a place, they move towards it until they arrive there.
In an adjunct: Adam went to the station to meet Sheila... The doctor walked over to the door and opened it... I took the book and threw it to the other end of the room.
After a noun: ...on the long journey to Calcutta. ...a visit to the theatre.
2 If you go **to** a concert, party, or other event, you go where it is taking place.
In an adjunct: ...accompanying their grandfather to a football match... You must come to dinner... A night or two later we were all invited to a party at a film studio.
After a noun: Three months ago, he had received an invitation to Julie's wedding.
3 If something is attached **to** something larger or fixed, the two things are joined together.
In an adjunct: We tied him to a kitchen chair... He untwisted the wire fixed to the cork of the second bottle... His tongue stuck to the roof of his mouth.
4 You use **to** when indicating the position of something. For example, if something is **to** your left, it is nearer your left side than your right side.
In an adjunct or after 'be': Ahead and to the left loomed the long dark line of the Ridge... The Killer Whale broke the surface no more than twenty yards to the north of me.

After a noun: *...the black shapeless masses to the left and right of the road.*

5 You use **to** when indicating who or what receives something or has an action or feeling directed towards them.

In an adjunct: *He gave the money to the cook... He showed the letter to Barbara... Mother waved to us through the window.*

Here are some verbs which are typically followed by **to**:

beckon	give	point	signal
demonstrate	offer	show	wave

After an adjective: *Molly was devoted to her sister... Helen seemed utterly indifferent to his words... She was always wonderfully kind to me.*

Here are some adjectives which are typically followed by **to**:

courteous	fair	kind	sympathetic
cruel	faithful	loyal	unfair
devoted	friendly	nice	unfaithful
disloyal	indifferent	partial	unkind

After a noun: *It is a gift to the people of Hartford. ...cruelty to animals... The threat to democracy was real... She was appointed as assistant to the General Secretary.*

6 If you say something **to** someone, you want that person to listen and understand what you are saying.

In an adjunct: *A number of people had complained to the church officials about it... My father and my uncle haven't spoken to each other for fifteen years... They started to explain their plan to Bradlee.*

Here are some verbs which are typically followed by **to**:

announce	chat	mention	preach	talk
apologize	complain	mumble	report	write
boast	confide	murmur	say	
brag	explain	mutter	speak	

7 A memorial **to** someone is intended to remind people of that person.

After a noun: *...the monument to the father of English poetry, Geoffrey Chaucer.*

8 You use **to** when indicating the form or state that someone or something starts to have.

In an adjunct: *His relief changed to anger. ...a desire to return to full-time education... They envisaged inflation falling to about 10 per cent a year.*

Here are some verbs which are typically followed by **to**:

change	degenerate	promote	turn
convert	fall	return	

to

After a noun: *...his rise to power. ...the transition from daylight to darkness. ...a return to old-style stability.*

9 You use **to** with some words to indicate what something is connected with or compared with.

In an adjunct: *The same law applies to everyone... As we waited, Jenny succumbed to a last-minute panic... Bothwell is said to have confessed to his part in the conspiracy... A former girl-friend compared his smile to a snake's.*

After a noun: *At first it seemed like the answer to all my problems. ...his abrupt and violent reaction to my casual announcement. ...the introduction to the first volume of his diaries.*

After an adjective: *The nutritional needs of a cat are broadly similar to a dog's... That would make us more vulnerable to attack. ...the belief that material goods are essential to a happy life.*

Here are some adjectives which are typically followed by **to**:

accustomed	fundamental	parallel	unaccustomed
adjacent	identical	preferable	used
allergic	immune	proportional	useful
central	impervious	sensitive	vital
comparable	indebted	similar	vulnerable
equal	inferior	subordinate	
equivalent	irrelevant	superior	
essential	married	susceptible	

10 You use **to** when indicating the person whose opinion or viewpoint you are giving.

In an adjunct, with a link verb: *It looks fine to me... She seems in rather a hurry to me... It is the spontaneity and flexibility of American schools which is most impressive to an outside observer.*

After an adjective: *...safety standards which are acceptable to the workers themselves.... Any attitude she adopted would have been distasteful to him.*

11 You use **to** when indicating someone's feelings about an event or situation.

In an adjunct: *To his amazement, she was delighted... To my relief, next morning the fever had vanished.*

12 You use **to** when indicating a sound that occurs at the same time as an action.

In an adjunct: *...carrying the cup high around the arena to the applause of their fans... I woke early to the sound of rain pattering on the tent.*

13 You use **to** when indicating the time or part of something at which something ends.

In an adjunct, after a prepositional phrase with 'from': *He worked from dawn to dusk... He was covered from head to foot with a fine white dust... The entire theatre, from top to bottom, should be transformed.*

14 You use **to** when indicating the last thing in a range of things.
After 'everything from' or 'anything from': *...offices handling everything from espionage to assassination... Colleges of education may have anything from a few hundred to nearly 2,000 students.*
After a number, before another number: *...a number of five to eight digits.*

15 You use **to** when you are stating a time which is less than thirty minutes before an hour.
After a number or 'a quarter': *At ten to nine she was ready to leave... It was a quarter to eleven.*
Also used as an adverb: *I'm afraid it's only ten to.*

16 You use **to** in ratios and rates.
After an amount: *His car did fifty miles to the gallon... Use four parts of sand to one of cement.*

together with

You use **together with** to emphasize that another person or thing is involved in something.
In an adjunct: *His son Lee and daughter Stacey were saved, together with a friend, Mr Peter John Griffiths... Drain the beans and add them to the soup, together with the stock or water.*

towards

The form **toward** is also used.
1 If you move, look, or point **towards** or **toward** someone or something, you move, look, or point in their direction.
In an adjunct: *'I'm going towards Chelsea,' she said, opening the door... As she nodded in agreement, he edged toward the door... He looks back towards me... She gestured towards the bartender.*
2 If there is a shift **towards** or **toward** a particular situation or thing, that situation or thing is becoming closer or more popular.
After a noun: *There has been a shift in values towards children and conventional family life. ...a steady advance towards equality. ...the trend towards large farms.*
In an adjunct or after 'be': *...plans to assist the liberal governments in Poland and Hungary to move towards a market economy... At the moment the trend is definitely towards arts-based students.*
3 If you do something **towards** or **toward** the achievement of a particular result, you do something that might help to achieve it.
In an adjunct: *Very little is being done towards the promotion of contemporary art... We shall have to work towards a solution.*
4 If you give money **towards** or **toward** something, you give it to help pay for that thing.
In an adjunct: *BR contributed £154,000 towards safety*

improvements... Only 54 million pounds went towards capital investment.

5 If there is a bias **towards** or **toward** a group or thing, that group or thing is favoured or supported more than other ones.

After a noun: *It's modern, progressive, with a bias towards the arts... There will be a bias towards those two sectors.*

After an adjective: *...when the selection is clearly biased towards wealth or lineage.*

6 If you have a particular attitude or duty **towards** or **toward** someone or something, that is your attitude or duty in relation to them.

After a noun: *He was full of ill-will towards mankind in general... The Committee criticized the IBA for its permissive attitude towards investment in local radio... As captain of this vessel, I have responsibilities towards both passengers and crew.*

In an adjunct: *I think this was the first time she realized how warmly we felt towards her.*

7 If something happens **towards** or **toward** a particular time, it happens just before that time.

In an adjunct: *Tension heightened towards the end of July... Towards the end of the century men began to wear more comfortable clothing... Towards Christmas, Howard got a large royalty cheque.*

8 If something is **towards** or **toward** part of a place or thing, it is near that part.

After 'be' or in an adjunct: *Most of it is toward the rear where it is out of his sight... This information is usually towards the back of the document... Towards the top, the heat haze shimmered through wisps of smoke.*

under

1 If a person or thing is **under** something, they are directly below or beneath it.

In an adjunct or after 'be': *Try to avoid having a fitted carpet under the dining table... He slept under hedges... There was a cask of beer under the bench.*

After a noun: *Stuart tossed the paper towel into the bin under the sink.*

2 If something is **under** the earth or **under** water, it is some way below the surface of the earth or the water.

In an adjunct or after 'be': *She has her home deep under the earth. ...the mechanism which enables diving birds to spend long periods of time under water.*

Also used as an adverb: *Animals that strayed into the bog were trapped and sucked under.*

3 If you go **under** something, you move from one side of it to the other by passing below it.

In an adjunct: *A wicked draught blew under the door... The water passes under the wall.*

4 Something that is **under** a layer of something, especially clothing, is covered by that layer.

In an adjunct or after 'be': *It is worth investing in a long-sleeved top to wear under your tracksuit... Under the long overcoat, the director was in evening clothes... Under their film of fat, the cold sausages were pink.*

5 You can use **under** to say that a person or thing is being affected by something.

After 'be' or in an adjunct: *Everything is under control... The case was still under consideration... We were under arrest... Casey's business dealings had come under Congressional scrutiny... The monuments were made in 1682 under Wren's supervision.*

After a noun: *He listed some of the people under investigation.*

6 If something happens **under** particular circumstances or conditions, it happens when those circumstances or conditions exist.

In an adjunct: *This must under no circumstances be allowed to happen... Most panels will provide adequate heat under conditions of good sunlight.*

7 If something happens **under** a law, agreement, or system, it happens because that law, agreement, or system says that it should happen.

In an adjunct: *Under existing legislation, the planning authority has a lot of power... Very few people have to my knowledge been released under this law... Marshall was obliged to observe that under the Constitution no crime had been committed.*

After a noun: *No beneficiary under a will may receive a single penny until then. ...its obligations under the Atlantic Treaty.*

8 If something happens **under** a particular person or government, it happens when they are in power.

In an adjunct: *The banquet was an institution which flourished greatly under Queen Elizabeth.*

9 If you work **under** someone, they are your teacher or boss.

In an adjunct: *The explorer Pinzon had served under Columbus... He showed himself naive for anyone who had worked under Harold Macmillan... His father had been a captain under Morris Eller.*

10 If you do something **under** a particular name, you use that name instead of your real name.

In an adjunct: *He made an arrangement to write for the Evening Post under a pseudonym... He was travelling under an assumed name.*

underneath

11 You use **under** to say which section of a list, book, or system
something is classified in.
In an adjunct or after 'be': *The library actually classified these
books under Light Romance... This information is sorted and filed
under different headings... Under Liszt she found two biographical
volumes.*
12 If someone or something is **under** a particular age or amount,
they are less than that age or amount.
After 'be': *Less than ten per cent of members are under forty.*
After a noun: *Whooping cough can be a serious disease, especially
in a baby under 2. ...promising delivery within 24 hours for parcels
under 25kg.*
Also used as an adverb: *Treatment will be free for everyone aged 17
and under.*

underneath

1 If a person or thing is **underneath** something, they are directly
below or beneath it.
In an adjunct or after 'be': *His dog slept underneath his desk... We
also printed a comment underneath it... Lampone reached
underneath the seat and found the key.*
After a noun: *Plate after plate smashed on the tiles underneath the
sink.*
Also used as an adverb: *He drew back the white cotton bedspread
and the blanket underneath.*
2 Something that is **underneath** a layer of something, especially
clothing, is covered by that layer.
In an adjunct or after 'be': *Perhaps there were more bulky garments
underneath the red and white striped jerseys then... Now the
spider's underneath your dress.*
Also used as an adverb: *He picked at the new wallpaper to see
whether his painting still existed underneath.*
3 You use **underneath** when you are talking about feelings and
emotions that people try to keep hidden.
In an adjunct: *Underneath it all, he hates his mother... Underneath
that tough exterior there is a core of old-fashioned religious values.*
Also used as an adverb: *They keep getting angrier underneath
without knowing what to do about it.*

unlike

1 You can use **unlike** to contrast the nature, situation, or
behaviour of one person or thing with that of another person or
thing.
In an adjunct: *Mrs Hochstadt, unlike Etta, was a careful shopper...
Dogs, unlike other animals, have to be licensed.*

2 If one thing or person is **unlike** another, the two things or people are different.

After 'be': *It was quite unlike any flu I'd experienced before. ...as though teachers were somehow unlike other folk.*

After a noun: *It was a book quite unlike any other book I've read recently.*

3 If you describe someone's behaviour as being **unlike** them, you mean it is surprising because it is different from their typical behaviour.

After 'be': *It's so unlike him to be late.*

until

1 If something happens **until** a particular time or event, it happens and then stops at the time mentioned.

In an adjunct: *I work until three... They talked until dawn.*

2 If something does not happen **until** a particular time, it does not happen before that time but happens or starts at that time.

In an adjunct, with a negative clause: *The rush-hour wouldn't start until eight o'clock... You don't need to pay contributions until after your sixteenth birthday... Until recently children were not allowed to play near these sacred rocks.*

up

1 If you go **up** something such as stairs, a ladder, or a slope, you move higher.

In an adjunct: *Len carried Allie up the stairs... My father appears, wheeling his bicycle up the hill.*

Also used as an adverb: *They climbed up inside the tower.*

2 If you go **up** a road, you go along it towards one end of it.

In an adjunct: *She watched a young woman walk up the street with a baby in a pushchair... He turned left up the Rue de Rennes.*

3 Something that is situated **up** the road is situated further along the road.

After 'be' or in an adjunct: *The hotel is just a couple of blocks up the road... What about a drink or two up the road, eh?*

Also used as an adverb: *There's a police station further up.*

4 If you go **up** a river, you go along it towards its source.

In an adjunct: *The barge was towed up the river to the edge of town.*

After a noun: *...a voyage up the Nile.*

up against

If you are **up against** something or someone that is hard to deal with, they are obstructing or opposing you.

After 'be' or in an adjunct: *The authorities know they are up*

upon

against a powerful commercial force... The first time I did this I came up against an unforeseen problem.

upon

1 **Upon** is used in several of the same ways as **on,** but is more formal. See **on.**

2 You use **upon** between two identical nouns or numbers to emphasize that there are large numbers of the thing referred to; a literary use.

After a noun: *...shrouded in layer upon layer of material... I just lay there for hour upon hour, trying to work out what he meant... Beyond, we could see thousand upon thousand, packed together.*
In an adjunct: *Crisis followed upon crisis.*

3 If an event or time is **upon** you, it has just started affecting you; a literary use.

After 'be': *I am convinced the invasion will be upon us by dawn... Now that autumn was upon us, we needed wood for heat.*

up to

1 If you are **up to** a part of your body in an amount of a substance, it reaches that part of your body.

After 'be' or in an adjunct: *She was up to her knees in mud... She walked into the water, sinking up to her ankles in the mud on the pond bottom.*

2 If something is **up to** a particular standard or amount, it has reached that standard or amount.

After 'be': *His clothes and shoes were not up to his usual standard... I was up to 195 mph as I moved out to the left for the overtaking manoeuvre.*

3 You say that something happens **up to** a particular date or event to emphasize that it happens until that date or event.

In an adjunct: *The use of perspective remained part of an artist's training right up to 1945... Schoenberg continued to explore new ways of making music right up to his death.*

4 If you say that it is **up to** someone to do something, you mean that it is their responsibility to do it.

After 'be': *It is up to the individual to find out what suits him best... It's up to you what you tell him... Now the next move was up to the Allies.*

5 If you are **up to** doing something, you are well enough or capable enough to do it.

After a link verb, often followed by an '-ing' clause: *If you don't feel up to writing it alone, we can do it together... The heat made him feel he wasn't up to more... As ever, Haringey were up to the challenge.*

6 If you say that someone is **up to** something, you mean that they are secretly doing something, probably something bad; an informal use.

After 'be': *I had no idea what Karin was up to, but I feared the worst.*

up until

You say that something happens **up until** a particular time or event to emphasize that it happens until that time or event.

In an adjunct: *This practice was continued up until the Second World War... Up until last night, I'd never even raised a finger to her.*

via

1 If someone or something goes **via** a particular place, they go through there on the way to another place.

In an adjunct: *We had to fly to Hamilton via Wellington. ...a transit visa to return to London via Moscow... The Baltic republics are most readily approached from Britain via Scandinavia.*

After a noun: *A flight to London via Karachi was arranged for him.*

2 If you do something **via** a particular means or person, you do it by making use of that means or person.

In an adjunct: *The owners could be traced via a central registry... Its flight plan can be modified during flight via a communications link with ground controllers... I got the three pictures you sent via Mum.*

with

1 If one person or thing is **with** another, they are together in one place.

After 'be': *'Where's Caroline?'—'She's with Margaret.'*

In an adjunct: *Life would be easier if I could live with my husband... They spotted me and came up to sit with me on the sandhill. ...a leg of lamb, served with new potatoes.*

After a noun: *Veteran soldiers told the new men with them what to expect.*

2 If you do something **with** someone else, you both do it together or are both involved in it.

In an adjunct: *I enjoyed working with Hitchcock... I've discussed*

*the matter with my colleagues... This engineering firm has
collaborated with the University over a number of years.*
Here are some verbs which are typically followed by **with**:

ally	collaborate	discuss	socialize
amalgamate	collide	fraternize	speak
associate	confer	interact	trade
chat	conspire	merge	work
coexist	dance	negotiate	
cohabit	debate	share	

After a noun: *My next private discussion with him took place a year
later. ...his nation's alliance with the Soviet Union... I wanted to
maintain my friendship with her.*
3 If you fight, argue, or compete **with** someone, you oppose them.
In an adjunct: *You heard how the boy was arguing with him...
Dreyfus wrote a lengthy paper heaping scorn on those who
disagreed with him.*
Here are some verbs which are typically followed by **with**:

argue	compete	fight	row	vie
bargain	disagree	haggle	spar	wrangle
clash	feud	quarrel	struggle	

After a noun: *...in the event of an American war with a foreign
power... He began to tell me about a quarrel with his landlord.*
4 If you do something **with** a tool, object, or substance, you do it
using that tool, object, or substance.
In an adjunct: *Jim broke up the frozen mass with a hammer... He
moistened his lips with his tongue... Mend torn sheets with press-
on tape.*
5 If someone stands or goes somewhere **with** something, they are
carrying it.
In an adjunct: *Eva woke an hour later to find Sally standing by the
bed with a cup of coffee... Then she said: 'Wait', and went off for a
minute; she came back with some dresses.*
After a noun: *...hundreds of men with binoculars and rifles.*
6 Someone or something **with** a particular feature or possession
has that feature or possession.
After a noun: *...a very old woman with a wrinkled face. ...taxpayers
with incomes under $50,000 a year. ...a blue dress with a full skirt.
...pieces of paper with marks on them.*
7 Someone **with** an illness has that illness.
After a noun: *...a child with a temperature.*
In an adjunct: *Mike was in bed with 'flu.*
8 If something is filled or covered **with** a substance or **with** things,
it has that substance or those things in it or on it.
After an adjective: *The walls were covered with bookshelves. ...a
dark veil, embroidered with red and blue flowers... Nobody's going*

to go to the beach if it's crawling with cops... The windows were thick with grime.

Here are some adjectives which are typically followed by **with**:

adorned	emblazoned	inundated	piled
awash	embroidered	laden	rich
bursting	encrusted	littered	riddled
caked	engraved	loaded	studded
clogged	festooned	ornamented	stuffed
cluttered	filled	overgrown	suffused
covered	flecked	overloaded	swamped
crawling	furnished	packed	teeming
crowded	heaped	padded	thick
draped	heavy	painted	tinged
edged	infested	patterned	wreathed
embellished	inlaid	peopled	

In an adjunct: *Cover the fish with the mushrooms... The pottery section fairly bristled with exciting things.*

9 If you are, for example, pleased or cross **with** someone or something, you have that feeling towards them.

After an adjective: *She got rather angry with me when I tried to intervene... No-one was satisfied with what they had got.*

Here are some adjectives which are typically followed by **with**:

angry	disappointed	furious	pleased
annoyed	displeased	happy	satisfied
besotted	dissatisfied	impressed	unhappy
bored	fascinated	infatuated	unimpressed
content	fed up	obsessed	unsatisfied

After a noun: *...their dissatisfaction with society.*

10 You use **with** to indicate what a state, quality, or action relates to, involves, or affects.

After an adjective: *I was as familiar with the case as anyone... No-one connected with drugs will be tolerated in any way... Perhaps competition was simply not compatible with harmony... I have been careless with money ever since. ...a doctor who is good with children.*

Here are some adjectives which are typically followed by **with**:

acquainted	consistent	identical	mixed up
afflicted	conversant	impatient	occupied
commensurate	engaged	incompatible	parallel
comparable	faced	inconsistent	patient
compatible	familiar	infected	popular
concomitant	frank	intoxicated	unacquainted
confronted	free	involved	unconnected
connected	friendly	level	unfamiliar

After a noun: *The problem with institutions is that they are run by people... He began having trouble with his digestion... His skill with explosives had already been remarked on.*

In an adjunct: *Nona would help with the laundry and housework... I only made two mistakes with the pay envelopes... The task of the court is to decide on how to proceed with the case... We must combine theory with practice... I asked them to provide me with an assistant.*

11 If you part **with,** dispense **with,** or finish **with** something, you no longer have it or use it.

In an adjunct: *The snag is, of course, that you have parted with the money once and for all... I think we will soon see juries dispensed with in criminal trials.*

12 If you side **with,** hold **with,** or agree **with** someone or something, you support them.

In an adjunct: *When the matter went to the full Cabinet, Ministers sided with Mr Brooke... I didn't hold with capital punishment.*

13 You use **with** when indicating the manner of an action or the feeling that someone has when they do something.

In an adjunct: *The campaign was conducted with remarkable skill and tenacity... With some reluctance, the church authorities agreed.*

14 You use **with** when indicating a sound or gesture that is made at the same time as an action.

In an adjunct: *With a sigh, he rose and walked slowly away... He fell back with a great scream and a look of surprise—dead... He landed with a crash in one of the trees.*

15 You use **with** when indicating the feeling that makes someone have a particular appearance or type of behaviour.

In an adjunct: *My sister went white with rage... I was shaking with fatigue.*

16 You use **with** when mentioning the position or appearance of someone or something at the time that they do something, or what someone else is doing at that time.

In an adjunct: *She lay with her head against the back of the seat... He advanced into the room with both hands extended... The keeper came loping up the lane with the dog padding at his heels.*

17 You use **with** when mentioning a current situation that is a factor affecting another situation.

In an adjunct: *Even now, with all the pressures off her, she was unable to rest... With inflation in West Germany rising, this caution is understandable.*

18 You use **with** when making a comparison or contrast between the situations of different people or things.

In an adjunct: *You and I can go on borrowing but we have to go on paying the interest. It is the same with a company... It's different with each individual.*

19 If something increases or decreases **with** a factor, it changes as that factor changes.

In an adjunct: *The chance of getting a free meal from your employer increases with status.*

20 If something moves **with** a wind or current, it moves in the same direction as the wind or current.

In an adjunct: *...letting both boat and net drift with the tide.*

21 If someone says that they are **with** you, they mean that they understand what you are saying; an informal use.

After 'be': *Sorry, I'm not quite with you.*

within

1 If something is **within** something else, it is contained inside that thing; a formal use.

In an adjunct or after 'be': *The casket is kept within an iron chest wrapped in asbestos... They generate electricity within their bodies... The well was drilled within the power station grounds.*

After a noun: *The books and periodicals within the library are arranged by subject.*

Also used as an adverb: *...a box with dials on the outside and a complex assembly of gear wheels mounted within.*

2 You use **within** when you are describing something that exists or happens among members of a group or as part of the workings of an organization.

After a noun: *It ensured a balance of forces within society. ...discontent within the local community... A good accountant can easily camouflage troubles within his company.*

In an adjunct: *Working within an existing organization has a lot of advantages.*

3 You can say that someone has a feeling **within** them when they have this feeling but have not expressed it; a literary use.

In an adjunct: *...the high spirits that bubbled within her... Deep within him lived a secret dread.*

After a noun: *A man looks at the love or anger within himself and says 'So, this is me.'*

Also used as an adverb: *Neither was that outward self apparently affected by the turmoil within.*

4 If something happens **within** a particular period of time, it happens before the end of that period.

In an adjunct: *Within a matter of weeks she was crossing the Atlantic... The balance may well tip within our lifetimes... Use wild mushrooms within 24 hours of picking.*

5 If you are **within** a particular distance of a place, you are less than that distance from it.

In an adjunct or after 'be': *D.P. Moon was now within twelve miles of Utah Beach... The strategic missile has a good chance of landing within half a mile radius of its target. ...mothers who live within walking distance of free clinics.*

6 If something is **within** sight, **within** earshot, or **within** reach, you can see, hear, or reach it.

In an adjunct or after 'be': *Ash did not know that he had been born within sight of those snows... Bond stood within earshot of the desk... They were almost within reach of their goal.*

7 If something is **within** a particular limit or set of rules, it does not go beyond it or is not more than what is allowed.

In an adjunct or after 'be': *...a Party which works within the British system of Parliamentary democracy. ...keeping within budgets... It is well within the 25 per cent limit for foreign holdings of US airlines.*

without

1 If someone or something is **without** something, they do not have it.

In an adjunct or after 'be': *He sits there on a hot evening without a care in the world. ...a bottle whose label I couldn't read without my spectacles... There I was in Paris alone without the slightest idea of how to find Harriet... They are going to find themselves without jobs in a year or so.*

After a noun: *...inadequate houses without gardens... We had cakes without sugar.*

2 If one thing happens **without** another thing, or if you do something **without** doing something else, the second thing does not happen or occur.

In an adjunct, often followed by an '-ing' clause: *We were refused permission to see him without explanation... We shall inform you without delay... Without warning, Boylan punched him... He cast votes on their behalf without consulting them... In most workplaces a whole range of chemicals are used without people even knowing what they are.*

3 If you do something **without** a particular feeling, you do not have that feeling when you do it.

In an adjunct: *'Yes,' I said, without much conviction... Kunta ate without pleasure... He described this incident without emotion.*

4 If you do something **without** someone else, they are not in the same place as you or are not involved in the same action as you.

In an adjunct: *I'm not going anywhere without you today... We could have a good evening without him... The funeral can go on without me. ...when Romeo himself dies rather than live without Juliet.*

worth

1 If something is **worth** a particular amount of money, it can be sold for that amount or brings someone that amount.

After 'be': *A good farm in Lincolnshire is likely to be worth around three million pounds... The tournament was worth £75,000 to the winner... Who decides how much they are worth?*

After a noun: *She has given away jewellery worth millions of pounds... He will graduate shortly and is already negotiating for a job worth $35,000.*

2 If something is **worth** a particular activity or effort, it is likely to be useful or interesting.

After 'be', often followed by an '-ing' clause: *These shops are well worth a visit... You may be wasting your time, but it's worth a try... Having a career and being a mother is worth the effort... The cathedral's well worth seeing, you know.*

Part Two

The Combinations

A

abandon to abandon yourself **to** an emotion. *I wanted to abandon myself to primitive sensations.*

abhorrent be abhorrent **to** someone. *The constant struggle for advantage was abhorrent to him.*

abide to abide **by** a law or agreement. *The press should abide by a charter of good practice.*

ablaze be ablaze **with** lights or colourful things. *The Hall was ablaze with massed flowers and exotic fruits.*

abound to abound **with** things or **in** things. *The larger artificial lakes abound with birds and wildlife... The place abounds in rumours.*

absent be absent **from** a place or thing. *The police discovered I was absent from my house... References to the 'armed struggle' were conspicuously absent from the President's speech.*

absolve to absolve someone **from** or **of** blame, responsibility, or guilt. *You'll notice he's careful to absolve the young officer of any blame... It had the effect of absolving him from responsibility.*

absorbed be absorbed **in** something. *Anne had been too absorbed in her own hopes.*

abstain to abstain **from** something enjoyable. *I have kept myself fit all my life, abstaining from drink and tobacco.*

abundance in abundance. *The essential aggressiveness and skills were there in abundance.*

accede to accede **to** a request or demand. *...his reluctant refusal to accede to their request.*

acceptable be acceptable **to** someone. *What we've got to do is find a government which is acceptable to the people.*

access access **to** a place, person, or thing. *...an organization for those interested in maintaining free access to the countryside.*

accessible be accessible **to** someone. *...an institution which is reasonably accessible to the public.*

accident 1 by accident: not deliberately. *I gave Castle the wrong notes by accident.* 2 in an **accident:** in a violent crash or collision. *Thirty-six people were killed yesterday in Australia's worst ever road accident.*

acclimatize to acclimatize **to** a new situation or environment. *People acclimatize to altitude at different rates.*

accompaniment 1 to the accompaniment of a sound. *The procession continued on its way to the accompaniment of frenzied cheers.* 2 an accompaniment **of** something; an accompaniment **to** a particular thing. *Authoritarian regimes seem to be an almost inevitable accompaniment of national poverty. ...a sauce served as an accompaniment to veal or fish.*

accord of your **own accord:** willingly. *He had been hoping that*

I would crack and leave of my own accord.

accordance in accordance with a rule or system. *The Secretary of State will distribute national resources in accordance with this formulation.*

account 1 an account **of** an event. *He gave an account of his wartime exploits.* 2 **on no account:** used as a strong negative. *On no account give her my home address.* 3 be **of no account:** be unimportant. *Everything they say is of no account.* 4 to account **for** something. *He was always prepared to account for his actions... Children's needs account for a good part of the family budget.*

accountable be accountable **to** someone **for** your actions. *This would be a public agency, accountable to Parliament... All these institutions are accountable for what they do.*

accusation an accusation **of** something **against** someone. *Their careers are threatened by accusations of incompetence... The accusation against us was that we were giving the country a bad name overseas.*

accuse to accuse someone **of** doing something wrong. *He was accused of inciting violence.*

accustomed be accustomed **to** something. *They are getting accustomed to the idea.*

ache 1 to ache **for** something. *She had been aching for recognition for a long while.* 2 to ache **with** a feeling. *I lay aching with misery.*

acknowledge to acknowledge someone or something **as** a particular thing. *Zuse acknowledged it as one of the best films ever made.*

acquaint to acquaint someone **with** a fact or subject. *...to organise groups for self-defence and acquaint them with the use of arms.*

acquainted be acquainted **with** someone or something. *I wish to know how you came to be acquainted with those people. ...the new Renaissance men and women, acquainted with great literature.*

acquiesce to acquiesce **in** something or **to** something. *Ordinary conscripts, too, were ultimately to participate or acquiesce in such horrors... Rather than embarrass his hosts, Sihanouk acquiesced to their demands.*

acquit to acquit someone **of** a charge or **on** a charge. *On the day they were acquitted of murder charges, we held a celebration... He was acquitted on all charges.*

act 1 to act **on** advice, orders, or information. *Acting on my instructions, my lawyer paid a week in advance for his private care.* 2 to act **as** something or **like** something. *...spreading the rope on the floor of the ledge to act as a rough cushion... They obviously believe that union executives must act like managing directors.* 3 to act **for** someone. *Lawyers acting for the government have argued that such changes would be against the public interest.*

action 1 **in action:** fighting or doing something. *George Farr had been wounded in action in the Sahara... Study them in action as often as possible and get to know their movements.* 2 **out of action:** not functioning. *All three tanks were very quickly put out of action.*

adamant be adamant **about** something or **on** something; be adamant **in** opposing or refusing something. *These women are adamant about denying any ties or similarities to their mother... I'm sorry, son, but Murray is adamant on this... The leaders of the teaching profession have been* *adamant in opposing the notion of unqualified assistants.*

adapt to adapt **to** something new or different. *They will then be able to adapt to a variety of jobs.*

add 1 to add one thing **to** another. *Sugar should not be added to any of these milks.* 2 to add **to** something. *She knew that she ought not to add to her companion's misery.* 3 to add up **to** something. *All these factors combined add up to a strong incentive to buy more machines and employ fewer men.*

addicted be addicted **to** a drug or an enjoyable activity. *He was addicted to wine and French brandy... It was a magazine of popular science, the kind of reading I had become addicted to.*

addition in addition; in addition **to** something. *In addition, he proposed three other changes... A baby would sometimes drink as much as a quart of milk in addition to a full meal.*

address to address someone **as** something. *She always addressed me as 'my daughter'.*

addressed be addressed **to** someone. *The letter was addressed to 'Mr and Miss Paget'.*

adept be adept **at** doing something. *I had never been adept at controlling people.*

adhere to adhere **to** a thing, rule, or view. *...a substance which prevents the fibres from adhering to each other. ...ensuring that professional standards are adhered to.*

adjacent be adjacent **to** something. *...in the shower adjacent to the cell.*

adjudicate to adjudicate **in** a dispute, **on** the point at issue, or **between** the people involved. *...powers to adjudicate in inter-union disputes. ...committees to consider and adjudicate on supplier and customer claims... We cannot sensibly adjudicate between these rival explanations.*

adjunct an adjunct **to** something or **of** something. *Years ago, puddings used to be eaten as an adjunct to meat... Even leisure had been reduced to an adjunct of capitalism.*

adjust to adjust **to** a new situation. *We waited for our eyes to adjust to the darkness.*

administer to administer a drug **to** someone. *Prison officers had helped to administer a sedative to him.*

admiration 1 admiration **for** someone or something. *...modern admiration for Greek art.* 2 **in admiration of** something. *Many of us are lost in admiration of his ability to concentrate on his own thoughts.*

admire to admire someone **for** a quality they have. *He admired the British troops for their courage and endurance.*

admission an admission **of** guilt or failure. *The admission of guilt is hard. ...after this rare and revealing admission of doubts.*

admit 1 to admit **to** a crime or fault. *He couldn't admit to any weakness in front of others.* 2 to admit **to** someone that you have done something. *Earlier Irene had admitted to Mr Stewart that she had wondered whether there was any connection between the two events.* 3 to admit someone **to** a club or institution. *Constable was not admitted to full membership of the Academy until eight years before his death... When admitted to the clinic in January 1976, she weighed just 5.4 kilos.*

admonish to admonish someone **for** doing something. *He admonished us for not arranging enough cocktail parties.*

adopt to adopt someone or something **as** something. *The local constituency party had adopted him as its candidate.*

adorn to adorn something **with** things. *She wanted to make the room her own, to adorn it with treasures.*

adorned be adorned **with** things or **by** things. *...a series of steps and banks adorned with fountains... Its facade is adorned by an impressive sculpture.*

advance in advance **of** an event or thing. *They wanted their musicians to rehearse in advance of the company's arrival.*

advantage 1 an advantage **over** someone. *The smoker has an enormous advantage over the non-smoker during moments of stress.* 2 be **to** your **advantage**. *It is to your advantage to keep him as happy and relaxed as possible.*

advertise 1 to advertise **for** someone to do a job. *Jimmie advertised for a researcher about a month ago.* 2 to advertise something **as** a particular thing. *Compact cars were again advertised as 'the biggest and most luxurious of them all'.*

advertisement an advertisement **for** a product. *...advertisements for cosmetics.*

advice advice **on** something or **about** something. *They began giving him advice on how to run the business. ...if you need advice about your education.*

advise 1 to advise **against** doing something; to advise someone **on** a particular matter. *The doctor advised against tiring him... Your local health office will advise you on the necessary requirements.* 2 to advise someone **of** a fact. *...failure to advise them of the accident within the specified time limit.*

affection affection **for** someone or something. *...his respect and affection for Guy.*

affiliated be affiliated **to** a group or **with** a group. *He was not affiliated to any human rights group. ...an experimental group affiliated with the Royal Shakespeare Company.*

affinity an affinity **with** something or someone or **for** something or someone. *Anne felt an affinity with the Day Nurse... I have had a growing affinity for lost causes.*

afflicted be afflicted **by** something or **with** something. *In spite of precautions, you may be afflicted by mice... Only other sufferers know what it is like to be afflicted with this disease.*

affront an affront **to** someone or something. *Such a move would be a grave affront to the Trade Union Movement.*

afraid 1 be afraid **of** someone or something: be frightened by them. *I'm afraid of spiders.* 2 be afraid **for** someone: be worried that they are in danger. *She was afraid for her children.*

aftermath the aftermath **of** a serious event. *...in the aftermath of the war.*

aggression aggression **towards** someone or **against** someone. *...aggression towards the outsider. ...the aggression against their group.*

aghast be aghast **at** something. *I'm aghast at how Billy is being educated.*

agitate to agitate **for** something you want or **against** something you dislike. *...squatters whose leaders had been agitating for political reforms... There is now a vigorous body of opinion agitating against the use of chemical fertilizers.*

aglow be aglow **with** something. *Daniel, his eyes aglow with inspiration, took his leave.*

agonize to agonize **over** something. *He didn't agonize over which tie to wear.*

agree 1 to agree **with** someone **on** or **about** a matter; to agree **with** what someone says. *I agree with Dr Marlowe that you're not the* *right person. ...if two people cannot agree on the meaning of a word... No two teachers will agree about everything... I agree with everything you've said.* **2** to agree **on** an action that is jointly worked out. *We agreed on this arrangement towards the end of 1951.* **3** to agree **to** an action proposed by someone else. *Castle agreed to a picnic.* **4** to agree **with** something: to approve of it. *Note that I do not agree with this habit—I simply record it.*

agreeable be agreeable **to** someone or something. *...a subject which was agreeable to both my parents.*

agreement **1** agreement **between** people or **among** people **on, about,** or **as to** a particular matter. *This statement underlines the agreement between the two sides on many issues... There is widespread agreement among people as to which changes in their lives require major adaptations... There is very little agreement about objective standards.* **2** be **in agreement.** *We were always in agreement on this matter.*

aid **1 in aid of** something: intended to help something. *...social functions in aid of worthy charities.* **2 with the aid of** something or someone: using something or helped by someone. *The grey dye was washed out with the aid of a solvent.*

aim **1** to aim something **at** a target. *He aimed at the far wall and squeezed the trigger.* **2** to aim **at** or **for** something desirable. *All Fair Rent Associations aim at helping people with real housing needs... We should aim for more nursery schools.* **3** the aim **of** achieving something; the aim **of** an action or activity. *...the party's aim of attracting 500,000 votes at the next election... The aim of the terrorists is to halt our peaceful progress towards the elections.*

air by air. *Some freight movement was possible by air.*

akin be akin **to** something. *They could not help feeling something akin to relief.*

alarmed be alarmed **by** something or **at** something. *...the owner came running into the street alarmed by the clatter of broken glass... Doctors are alarmed at the progressive deterioration of the population's diet.*

alert **1** be alert **to** something or **for** something. *In assessing progress, we have to be alert to the landmarks... He kept his senses alert for a sign.* **2** to alert someone **to** something. *The press had been alerted to my presence.* **3** be **on the alert.** *The very formality of his question put Helen on the alert.*

alibi an alibi **for** a time. *Her aunt's supposed to be her alibi for the night.*

alien be alien **to** someone or something. *They are habits strange and alien to the British people.*

alienate to alienate someone **from** someone or something. *Such attitudes have a tendency to alienate a boy from his father.*

align to align yourself **with** someone **against** someone else. *He found himself in the pre-war years aligned with Churchill and Eden against Chamberlain.*

alive **1** be alive **with** things. *The main street was alive with pushcarts and bicycles.* **2** be alive **to** a problem or situation. *I am fully alive to the problems facing the industry.*

allegiance someone's allegiance **to** a person, group, or country. *...the workers' allegiance to the Labour Party.*

allergic be allergic **to** a substance. *...people who are allergic to cow's milk.*

alliance an alliance **with** another group or person or **between** two groups or people; an alliance

against someone or something. *...a group which formed an alliance with the Liberal Party... An alliance between her party and the Bolsheviks had collapsed... They created a formidable alliance against syllabus reform.*

allied be allied **to** something or **with** something. *Allied to the concern for efficiency is a concern for training people to do certain jobs... Many nations are not specifically allied with either capitalism or communism.*

allocate to allocate something **to** someone or something. *...the money which is allocated to education or other purposes.*

allot to allot something **to** someone. *A substantial sum had been allotted to her in Harold's will.*

allow to allow **for** something. *He failed to allow for the unexpected.*

allude to allude **to** something. *I have already alluded to the energy problem in some of the earlier chapters.*

ally 1 /əˈlaɪ/ to ally yourself **with** someone you support **against** someone else. *The mother should not be seen to ally herself with the children against the father.* 2 /ˈælaɪ/ an ally **against** someone else. *The only role in which Jane would accept Marsha was as an ally against Lynn.*

alternate /ˈɒltəncɪt/ to alternate **between** two things or states; to alternate **with** something else. *He alternates between moderation and militance... The white sand alternates with rocks.*

alternative an alternative **to** something else. *...improving the public transport system to make it an attractive alternative to the private car.*

amalgamate to amalgamate **with** something else. *Their inclination was to conquer nature, not amalgamate with it.*

amazed be amazed **at** something or **by** something. *Both were amazed at their good fortune... You will probably be amazed by the warmth of your welcome.*

amenable be amenable **to** something. *She was amenable to whatever I suggested.*

amount to amount **to** something. *The statements amounted to blackmail.*

amused be amused **by** something or **at** something. *He was not amused by the stories I related... Marcks was slightly amused at the role he was supposed to play.*

amusement amusement **at** something. *She smiled in amusement at my Western logic.*

analogous be analogous **to** something else. *Is Bud Scully's case analogous to that of John Brown?*

anathema be anathema **to** someone. *Taxes were always anathema to the Americans.*

anger anger **at** something or **against** someone. *Alexandra was filled with anger at Ned's betrayal of their secret sign. ...a consuming and useless anger against his mother.*

angle 1 to angle **for** something. *People began angling for the best offices and furniture.* **2 at an angle.** *He wore a tall, white chef's cap at a rakish angle.*

angry be angry **about** something or **at** something; be angry **with** someone or **at** someone. *He had been angry about the article... I wasn't hurt—just angry at having made a mistake... Are you angry with me?... He'd sounded so angry at me when I'd told him.*

announce to announce something **to** someone. *She announced firmly to the assembled relatives that she herself intended to take sole charge of the boy.*

annoyed be annoyed **with** someone **for** doing something; be annoyed **at, by,** or **about**

something. *I was annoyed with myself for wasting a day... Mr Neumann seemed annoyed at this suggestion... She had been annoyed by her friend's reaction to her news... I used to get annoyed about it all.*

answer 1 an answer **to** a question, problem, or letter. *The answer to both questions is yes... At first it seemed like the answer to all my problems.* 2 **in** answer; **in** answer **to** a question. *...concepts which had been formulated in answer to these questions.* 3 to answer **to** a particular description. *No one answering to their description used any form of public or private transport out of town.*

answerable be answerable **to** someone **for** something. *The Secretary of State is answerable to Parliament... Mr Fromstein is now answerable for that money.*

antagonism antagonism **to** or **towards** someone or something; antagonism **between** people. *...a general antagonism to technologically based society. ...antagonism towards authority. ...a basic antagonism between workers and management.*

antagonistic be antagonistic **to** or **towards** someone or something. *Ian is openly antagonistic to the media... A daughter may be surprisingly antagonistic towards her father at times.*

antidote an antidote **to** or **for** a poison or unpleasant situation. *The antidote to unhappiness is community feeling. ...an antidote for their melancholy.*

antipathy an antipathy **to** or **towards** someone or something. *...the antipathy of many outside the country to the policies pursued there... This perhaps explained her antipathy towards Koda Dad and his son.*

antithesis the antithesis **of** something. *Most television is the antithesis of art.*

anxiety anxiety **about, over,** or **for** something or someone. *...anxiety about money. ...anxiety over nuclear weapons. ...our anxiety for their welfare.*

anxious 1 be anxious **about** someone or something. *We are all rather anxious about Maurice.* 2 be anxious **for** something that you want. *He was anxious for good marks.*

apologist an apologist **for** something or **of** something. *...an outspoken apologist for psychiatric practices in his country. ...apologists of the capitalist system.*

apologize to apologize **to** someone **for** something. *I even felt like apologizing to them... I do apologize for causing all this disturbance.*

appalled be appalled **at** something or **by** something. *I was appalled at the prospect... He was appalled by what was happening.*

apparent be apparent **to** someone. *My mistake in choosing Rick became apparent to me.*

appeal 1 to appeal **for** something that you need. *He appealed for local volunteers to work long hours for six weeks.* 2 to appeal **to** someone **against** a decision. *He appealed to a higher level... We appealed against this conviction and won.* 3 to appeal **to** someone: to seem attractive to them. *The novelty of this appeals to him.* 4 the appeal **of** someone: their attractive qualities. *It is impossible to understand the appeal of this charmer.*

appetite an appetite **for** something. *...an insatiable appetite for power.*

applicant an applicant **for** a job; an applicant **to** a college. *Seven other applicants for the post turned up for the interview. ...successful applicants to Oxford University.*

apply 1 to apply **to** an organization **for** something such as a job. *He had only applied to one college... I applied for a job on the railway.* 2 to apply **to** something or someone. *The same rule applies to parents.* 3 to apply something **to** something else. *...the force applied to the bar.* 4 to apply yourself **to** something. *Mrs Oliver applied herself to an examination of the address book.*

appointment an appointment **with** someone. *I've got an appointment with Mr Orpen.*

appreciation 1 appreciation **of** or **for** something that someone has done for you. *...by showing their real appreciation of his efforts. ...her lack of appreciation for all he had done for her.* 2 appreciation **of** the significance or quality of something. *He had a keen appreciation of the power and dangers of the media.*

appreciative be appreciative **of** something. *I had always been appreciative of his writing.*

apprehensive be apprehensive **about** something or **of** something. *I felt a little apprehensive about the choice... I was apprehensive of strangers.*

approach 1 an approach **to** a place. *...Aldersgate Street, for many centuries the main approach to London from the North.* 2 an approach **from** someone. *Mrs Thatcher said she welcomed the approach from Mr Gorbachov.* 3 an approach **to** something. *...his rational approach to life.*

appropriate /əˈprəʊprɪət/ be appropriate **to** or **for** something or someone; an appropriate thing **for** something or someone. *...an education system appropriate to local needs. ...clothing appropriate for hot climates... It was an appropriate start for a party of this kind.*

approval 1 approval **for** or **of** a proposal **by** someone; the approval **of** someone. *I was given McPherson's approval for the plan. ...justice department approval of any proposed changes in local election laws... We've got to decide which ones to put forward for approval by the Faculty Committee... The authorities' arrangements should be subject to the approval of the Secretary of State.* 2 the approval **of** someone: the fact that they like something. *...her dependence on the approval of others.*

approve to approve **of** something or someone. *I don't usually approve of new methods.*

approximate /əˈprɒksəmeɪt/ to approximate **to** something. *...stories which vaguely approximated to the truth.*

aptitude an aptitude **for** doing something. *In engineering management, an aptitude for languages may be important.*

arbiter an arbiter **of** something; an arbiter **between** two people or groups. *...the final arbiter of human destiny. ...Germany's renewed status as arbiter between East and West.*

argue 1 to argue **with** someone **about** or **over** something. *There was no point in arguing with him... They were arguing about politics as they played... We would then argue over the merits of the individuals concerned.* 2 to argue **for** something or **against** something. *Benn argued for a massive extension of public ownership... Bratkowski also argued against active resistance.* 3 to argue someone **out of** a plan. *His wife and friends argued him out of this ambition.*

arise to arise **from** or **out of** something. *...any consequences arising from our decision... I am sure their policy arose out of concepts of elitism.*

armed be armed **with** something.
...*army officers armed with machine guns.*

arrange to arrange something **with** someone. *She arranged with the principal of her school to take the necessary time off.*

arrest to arrest someone **for** a crime or **on** a particular charge. *He was arrested for drunken driving... The police arrested her on a charge of conspiracy to murder.*

arrive 1 to arrive **at** or **in** the place you were going to. **from** the place you were in before. ...*by the time we arrived at Victoria Station... We arrived in Queenstown at about 4 a.m. ...having just arrived from the Caribbean.* 2 to arrive **at** a conclusion or decision. *I had arrived at a conclusion on the basis of the only facts then available to me.*

ascendancy ascendancy **over** someone else. *Liverpool confirmed their ascendancy over Everton with a 2-1 win.*

ascribed be ascribed **to** a cause or person. *Illnesses of every kind were ascribed to witches.*

ashamed be ashamed **of** something or **about** something. *He felt ashamed of his selfishness... Inside, she felt ashamed about being a failure.*

ask 1 to ask someone questions **about** something. *He asked me about my work.* 2 to ask **for** something or someone you want. *We asked for sandwiches and tea.* 3 to ask **after** someone: to ask how they are. *Mrs Boismortier has been by the house several times, asking after you.* 4 to ask something **of** someone. *All that is asked of the reader is that they approach it step by step with an open mind.*

aspire to aspire **to** something. *You were not expected to aspire to excellence.*

assault an assault **on** or **upon** someone or something. ...*armed assaults on homes, stores and warehouses.*

assent 1 to assent **to** a proposal. *58% of ConsGold shareholders have assented to the takeover offer.* 2 the assent **of** someone in authority. *The student had to gain the assent of two tutors to his statement.*

asset 1 an asset **to** a person or organization. *He was a great asset to the Committee.* 2 the assets **of** a company or person. *70% of the assets of manufacturing companies were foreign-owned.*

assign to assign something **to** someone. ...*if there are two or more staff people assigned to one group of children.*

assimilate to assimilate people **into** a group. *These individuals may not be fully assimilated into the ruling class.*

assist to assist someone **in** a task or **with** a task. *The navy will assist in the trials... His pupils will assist the local schools with English studies.*

associate /əsəʊsɪeɪt/ 1 to associate something **with** something else. ...*the firm confidence that we normally associate with the Victorian age.* 2 to associate **with** someone. *Vaughan has been associating with a known criminal.*

association in association **with** someone else. ...*working in association with the Peruvian National Institute of Culture.*

assure to assure someone **of** something. *I believed that being an intellectual assured me of a higher life.*

astonished be astonished **at** something or **by** something. *I was astonished at the speed of the reaction... I am always astonished by their kindness.*

astonishment astonishment **at** something. ...*her astonishment at her sister's departure.*

atone to atone **for** something wrong. *Francis atoned for his lapse with inspiring play in the second half.*

attach 1 to attach something **to** something else. *This string is attached to the outside of the peg.* 2 to attach **to** something. *A certain romance attaches to opera singers.*

attached be attached **to** someone or something. *I really was very attached to him.*

attack 1 an attack **on** a person or place. *...attacks on defenceless civilians.* 2 an attack **of** an illness. *...an attack of gastro-enteritis.*

attempt 1 an attempt **at** doing something. *He made an attempt at appearing to be in control.* 2 an attempt **on** someone's life. *Fears that an attempt on Mr. Mandela's life might be made were being taken seriously.*

attend to attend **to** something or someone. *I shall attend to that matter shortly.*

attendance 1 attendance **at** an event or institution. *Saturday's attendance at the Wimbledon tennis championships was 28,077.* 2 in attendance; in attendance **on** someone. *There was no longer any reason to keep Ashok in attendance on him.*

attest to attest **to** something. *This letter clearly attests to her sanity.*

attired be attired **in** clothes of some kind. *He was at least six feet tall, elegantly attired in a fur-collared cashmere coat.*

attitude someone's attitude **to** something. *...his own personal attitude to life.*

attract to attract someone **to** someone or something. *...that quality which had first attracted him to her.*

attraction 1 someone's attraction **to** something. *I was unable to account for this strange attraction to a country I had never seen.* 2 the attraction **of** something

interesting or appealing. *Half the attraction of climbing is playing with danger.*

attribute /ətrɪbjuːt/ to attribute something **to** a person or cause. *The death of Mrs Thurston was attributed to the horrors she had witnessed. ...a remark attributed to Lord Northcliffe.*

attuned be attuned **to** something. *...being attuned to other people's moods.*

audition to audition **for** acting or singing work, or **for** someone such as a director. *...when Elizabeth Taylor auditioned for the lead in National Velvet.*

augur to augur well or ill **for** something. *This augurs well for your career.*

auspices under the auspices of someone. *The committee was assembled under the auspices of the Sunday Times.*

authority 1 authority **over** someone. *...men with complete authority over their children.* 2 an authority **on** a particular subject. *...Edith Standen, a distinguished authority on tapestry.*

avail 1 to avail yourself **of** something. *Some people might wish to avail themselves of the ministry's services.* 2 to no avail; be **of** no avail. *The young lieutenant continued to plead with the captain, but to no avail... It seemed as if all the pleading and threats were of no avail.*

available be available **for** someone, **as** something, or **for** a purpose. *...cutting down the food supplies available for each person... Geography is also available as a B.Sc. course in the college. ...the police manpower available for this task.*

average on average. *People move house on average once every eight years.*

aversion an aversion **to** something. *...the average citizen's*

profound aversion to doing what
he or she is told.

avid be avid **for** something. *More
and more correspondents arrived—
all avid for good, sensational
stories.*

awaken to awaken **to** a fact. *In
middle age, they awaken to the
realization that they don't know
anyone.*

award to award something **to**
someone. *...medals awarded to
those who fought in the Free
French Forces during the Second
World War.*

aware be aware **of** something.
*...waiting for some sign that he
was aware of her presence.*

awash be awash **with** something.
The plain was awash with water.

B

back to back **onto** a place. *...in our
little garden, which backs onto the
other gardens of the square.*

background the background **to**
an event; a background **of** a
particular kind of thing. *The
background to the case had been
the subject of great controversy.
...against this background of
continuing unrest.*

backlog a backlog **of** things to be
dealt with. *...the backlog of
unprocessed applications.*

bad 1 be bad **at** doing something.
The Romans were bad at science.
2 be bad **for** someone or
something. *Nobody wants to talk
about it because it's bad for
business.*

badge a badge **of** a quality or
status. *A mastery of reading and
writing was a badge of class.*

bail to bail someone **out of** a
difficult situation. *...even if he
bailed me out of financial trouble
now.*

balance 1 to balance **on**
something. *Soon the bird learned
to balance on the edge of my hand.*
2 to balance one thing or idea
against another. *He had to
balance what they wanted against
what their rivals wanted.* 3 a
balance **between** things or **of**
things. *...the balance between
teaching and research. ...a balance
of forces within society.* 4 be **off
balance:** be unsteady or confused.
He was almost thrown off balance.
5 be **in the balance:** be uncertain.
*Everything was still in the
balance.* 6 **on balance:** after
considering all the facts. *On
balance, there seems little doubt
that they are following the wiser
path.*

balk 1 to balk **at** something
unpleasant. *However, Mr Sorrell is
likely to balk at such a price.* 2 to
balk someone **of** something they
wanted. *...in order to balk the
court of any opportunity of making
a decision.*

ban 1 to ban someone **from** an
activity or place. *They had banned
me from all contact with them...
They were banned from state
schools.* 2 a ban **on** something.
*The ban on publicity may now be
lifted.*

banish to banish someone or
something **from** a place or thing or
to another place. *...to banish
hunger and poverty from the
earth... Even the Foreign
Secretaries are banished to
another room.*

bank 1 to bank **with** a particular
bank. *The case involved a
company which banked with
Barclays.* 2 to bank **on** something
happening. *It is possible that he
may relent, but don't bank on it.*

bar to bar someone **from** a place or
from doing something. *Foreign
relief agencies were barred from
the disaster area... The defendant
is almost invariably barred from
participating in his trial.*

bare be bare **of** something. *The rooms were largely bare of furniture.*

bargain 1 to bargain **with** someone **for** something. *He's now in a better position to bargain with Russia... Japanese steel producers usually join forces to bargain for coal supplies.* 2 to have not bargained **for** something unexpected. *This was one complication he had not bargained for.*

bark to bark **at** someone or something. *Their dog came in and started barking at me... 'Just do me a favour!' he barked at the crowd.*

barrier a barrier **to** something that is prevented. *...the single greatest barrier to reform.*

base 1 to base something **on** or **upon** something else. *...a class system based on land ownership.* 2 a base **for** a system, method, or particular task. *It forms a base for later discussion.*

basic be basic **to** something. *...the fear of the unknown which is basic to the behaviour of all animals.*

basis 1 the basis **for** or **of** an idea, system or method. *Past experience is the best basis for a sound judgement... Curiosity is the basis of learning.* 2 **on the basis of** something. *No fair-minded juror would convict me on the basis of such evidence.*

bask to bask **in** the sun or **in** approval or attention. *They basked in the warmth of public approval.*

bastion a bastion **of** something which is preserved; a bastion **against** something which is resisted. *...the bastions of privilege at the apex of the class structure. ...the principal bastion against this aggression.*

bathe 1 to bathe **in** water. *Bathing in the sea is no longer possible there.* 2 to be bathed **in** light or sweat. *The stage was bathed in blue light... Gant realized that his body was bathed in a sweat of relief.*

battle 1 a battle **between** two groups; a battle **with** or **against** another group. *...the battle between the gods and the giants. ...the God who helped us in our battle with the British. ...its battles against the government.* 2 a battle **for** something that you want, **against** something that you want to stop, or **over** something that is in dispute. *...the battle for safer and healthier working environments... He did fight in the battle for New York Island. ...the battle against cancer. ...the battle over next year's budget.*

beam to beam **at** someone. *They beamed at each other.*

bear to bear down **on** or **upon** someone or something. *...swerving to avoid a huge lorry that bore down on them.*

beckon to beckon **to** someone. *He beckoned to me: 'Come here, Hugh.'*

beg to beg **for** something; to beg money or food **from** someone. *Peter begged for more stories. ...kids begging cigarettes from passers-by.*

begin 1 to begin **with** something or **by** doing something. *The pamphlet begins with the heading 'A party of Nationalism and Patriotism'... He began by apologizing profusely about what had happened.* 2 to begin **as** something of a particular kind. *This book began as a survey of higher education.* 3 to begin **with** a particular letter. *All government agencies have a code name beginning with OD.*

belief a belief **in** something. *...affirming their belief in his innocence.*

believe 1 to believe **in** the existence of something. *I don't believe in God.* 2 to believe **in** something you are in favour of. *They believe in equality.*

belong

belong to belong **to** a person, thing, or group. ...*a toy telescope belonging to one of my children... He also belonged to an organization called the Young Front.*

beloved be beloved **of** a type of person. ...*the big windows beloved of modern architects.*

belt 1 be **below the belt**: be unfair. *I felt Weatherby's next question was a little below the belt.* 2 **under your belt**: achieved. *He starts today's race with two victories under his belt.*

beneficial be beneficial **to** someone or something. ...*reforms beneficial to the mass of people.*

beneficiary a beneficiary **of** something. *They are perceived as beneficiaries of the industrial system.*

benefit 1 to benefit **from** something or **by** something. *The children benefit from knowing their fathers better... One-parent families will benefit by this reform.* 2 **for the benefit of** someone: in order to help them. ...*to use this new tool for the benefit of all mankind.* 3 be **of benefit to** someone; **to the benefit of** someone: helping them. *Algeria was not willing to risk a single citizen in a cause that could be of no direct benefit to herself. ...to forge stronger links between voters and politicians, to the lasting benefit of both.*

bent be bent **on** or **upon** doing something. *They seemed bent on avenging his death.*

bequeath to bequeath something **to** someone. *General Compson had bequeathed the gun to him.*

bereft be bereft **of** something. ...*crumbling slums bereft of the most basic amenities.*

beset be beset **by** or **with** difficulties, danger, or problems. *Daniel found himself beset by technical difficulties. ...a society that is beset with profound contradictions.*

besotted be besotted **with** something. *He was besotted with the country and its people.*

bestow to bestow something **on** or **upon** someone. *I want to thank them for the honour they want to bestow on me.*

bet to bet **on** the outcome of something. *Zvereva was asked if people should bet on her to win the Championship.*

betray to betray someone or a secret **to** an enemy. *I know he would never betray me to anybody... These phrases betray their real intentions to the opposition.*

beware to beware **of** something. *Beware of becoming too complacent.*

bewildered be bewildered **by** something or **at** something. *The policemen, bewildered by the racket, had stopped too... 'Just a minute,' Uri said, somewhat bewildered at the rapid turn of events.*

biased be biased **against** someone or something; be biased **in favour of** or **towards** someone or something. ...*this tendency of judges to be biased against workers in such cases... Educational opportunity is heavily biased in favour of middle-class, urban people... Home-ownership policies are biased towards the preferences of the rich.*

bid 1 to bid **for** something at an auction. ...*if you are planning to bid for the property that you want at an auction.* 2 a bid **for** something you want. *Mobil has also made a bid for the company.*

bill the bill **for** something that you are buying; a bill **for** a particular amount. *The bill for my uniform came to ten pounds... He remembered the bill for more than twelve dollars that Boylan had paid.*

bind to bind someone **to** a person, group, or thing. *...the ties which bind him to his colleagues.*

bit to bits. *If it turns out you're not who you say you are, I'll blow you to bits.*

blame 1 to blame someone or something **for** a bad situation or event. *Each man has blamed the other for starting the fight.* 2 to blame a bad situation or event **on** someone or something. *Police blamed the violence on excessive drinking.*

blasphemy blasphemy **against** something that is sacred. *...alleged blasphemy against Islam.*

blaze 1 to blaze **with** light, colour, or a strong feeling. *The cottage gardens blaze with irises and lilies... Her face blazed with joy.* 2 a blaze **of** light or colour. *When night falls, the village is a blaze of lights.*

blend 1 to blend one thing **with** another; to blend two or more things **into** something new. *...a dessertspoon of cornflour blended with a little milk... Bach and Brahms blended into this weird sound.* 2 a blend **of** two or more things. *These are a blend of a variety of oils. ...a strange and wistful blend of voices.* 3 to blend in **with** or blend **into** the background. *Don't be conspicuous, blend in with your surroundings... Tree snakes are green, but they blend so well into foliage.*

blind 1 be blind **to** something that you are unaware of. *A bribe makes people blind to what is right... Most customers are completely blind to what a waitress is doing.* 2 be blind **with** a feeling. *A moment before, I'd been blind with anger.*

blossom to blossom **into** a new, form or state. *Karen began to blossom into womanhood.*

blow 1 a blow **on** or **to** a part of someone's body, **from** a weapon. *He had received a blow on the cheek bone... He had been killed by a blow to the brain... A single slashing blow from a sword had broken Tuku's back.* 2 a blow **to** someone or **to** their hopes or pride. *...yet another blow to hopes of the early capture of the killer.* 3 a blow **for** something you support or **against** something you do not support. *I did my best to strike a blow for modern science... President Garcia described the arrest as a blow against subversion.* 4 to blow money **on** something expensive or trivial. *'I'm going to keep the money.'—'To blow it on drinks?'*

blueprint a blueprint **for** or **of** something in the future. *...a blueprint for survival... Every cell in our bodies contains this essential blueprint of life.*

boast to boast **to** someone **about** something or **of** something. *She boasted about her acquaintance with him to her friends... They boasted of their prowess.*

boat by **boat.** *People could get to France and then come over by boat.*

bode to bode well or ill **for** someone or something. *It bodes well for his future.*

boil to boil down **to** something. *It boils down to mutual agreement.*

bolt to bolt something **to** or **onto** another thing. *...simple pulleys with flat plates bolted to the rim... A two-way radio was bolted onto the roof.*

bombard to bombard someone **with** questions or ideas; to bombard something **with** things. *...bombarding them with a bewildering series of suggestions... He bombards male insects with radioactive particles to sterilise them.*

bond a bond **of** a particular kind **between** two or more people. *...strengthening the bond between members of the group. ...a bond of mutual dependence and love.*

bone

bone to bone up **on** a subject. *It is difficult for mature students to bone up on the sciences.*

book 1 a book **by** someone **about** something or **on** a particular subject; a book **of** different pieces of writing. *...the subject of a book by Morton M Hunt... She had written a book about her childhood. ...a book on communism. ...a book of poems.* **2** to book someone **for** committing an offence. *This was the twenty-third time he had been booked for poaching deer.* **3** to book **into** a hotel. *He's booked into the hotel for two nights.*

boom a boom **in** a particular activity or type of event. *High profitability is helping to fund the boom in investment.*

boon a boon **to** someone. *Baby-sitters are a boon to parents.*

border 1 the border **between** or **of** two countries; the border **of** one country **with** another. *...the border between the two American nations. ...near the border of Spain... The border with Hungary was closed.* **2** to border **on** another country. *...other small countries that border on the Soviet empire.* **3** to border **on** another state, feeling, or way of behaving. *I cultivated an air of politeness bordering on subservience.*

borderline the borderline **between** two things; the borderline **of** something. *The novel examines the borderline between fact and fiction... I have not been able to discover where the borderline of fantasy begins and ends.*

bored be bored **with** something or **by** something. *By then he was bored with the project... He seemed bored by the proceedings.*

born 1 to be born **to** parents: used to refer to the time when a baby is born. *The twins were born to a surrogate mother.* **2** be born **of** particular parents: be the child of those parents. *...a thirty-nine-year-old lawyer, born of Quaker parents in California.* **3** be born **of** a particular feeling or activity. *...fear born of hate or distrust.*

borrow 1 to borrow money or a possession **from** someone or **off** someone. *Jeremy had to borrow a cloth from the barman... He was persuaded to authorize the police to borrow his house key off the next-door neighbour.* **2** to borrow an idea or word **from** a person, piece of writing, or language. *Its title is borrowed from Wilde's decorative phrase in De Profundis.*

bother 1 not to bother **with** or **about** something that you could do, use, or deal with. *We won't bother with the candles. ...a mystery that he felt too contented to bother about solving.* **2** not to bother **about** something that might worry you. *Don't bother about me. I'm fine.*

bothered be bothered **about** something worrying. *You're getting all bothered about nothing.*

bound 1 be bound **by** a rule, law, or restriction of some kind. *They are bound by the rules of the game.* **2** be bound **to** something or someone else. *I find myself more firmly bound to my people than ever before.* **3** be bound **for** a destination. *...a plane bound for Jersey.* **4** be bound up **with** a particular problem, situation, or activity. *The problem of poverty is bound up inextricably with the problem of riches.*

boundary 1 the boundary **of** a country or region; the boundary **between** two countries or regions. *...the boundaries of the new states. ...the boundary between the Free State and the Eastern Province.* **2** the boundary **between** two types of thing. *...the child who seems automatically to know the boundary between freedom and licence.*

bow /baʊ/ **1** to bow **to** someone, as a mark of respect. *Agassi bowed to all four sides of the court before hugging his coach.* **2** to bow **to** pressure, or someone's wishes, demands, opinions, and so on. *The Chancellor bowed to City advice.* **3** to bow **out of** an activity. *David Lean bowed out of appearing.*

boycott a boycott **of** something, **on** something, or **against** a thing or country. *...the boycott of examinations by academics. ...the international boycott on sporting links with South Africa... Hardliners called for a boycott against British goods and companies.*

brace to brace yourself **for** something bad. *Police are bracing themselves for a spate of shootings.*

brag to brag **to** someone **about** something. *She had overheard him bragging to his comrades about how he had been followed.*

brainwash to brainwash someone **into** thinking or doing something. *...consumers brainwashed into believing that factory products are superior.*

brake a brake **on** or **upon** development or activity. *...seeing age as a brake on progress.*

brand to brand someone **as** a particular kind of person. *They are branded as failures.*

breach **1** a breach **of** an agreement or rule. *...a serious breach of prison regulations.* **2** be **in breach of** an agreement or rule. *He was technically in breach of contract.* **3** a breach **in** a wall or barrier. *...the only breach in the wall's defences.* **4** a breach **between** two friends or relatives. *There had been a total breach between them some years after her second marriage.*

break **1** to break **with** a group, colleague, or tradition. *In 1960 he finally broke with the party.* **2** a break **with** a group, colleague, or tradition. *...the catalyst in bringing about its break with Labour... The break with the past has been dramatic.* **3** to break someone **of** a habit. *Cecil used to chew his nails before I broke him of it.* **4** to break some bad or surprising news **to** someone. *On our return, I broke the bad news to Jimmy.* **5** to break **for** a meal or drink. *By mid-morning he was finished with this task, and broke for a cup of coffee.* **6** a break **in** an activity or state. *The fights were seen as a break in the monotony.* **7** a break **from** something that is boring or unpleasant. *It heralded a complete break from the apathy of their normal lives.* **8** to break **into** a building. *...the man who had broken into his home and murdered his wife.* **9** to break **into** laughter, song, a run, and so on. *When Rudolph saw her, he broke into a run.* **10** to break **out of** an undesirable way of life. *He feared to break out of the conventional life which had slowly suffocated him.* **11** to break **through** a barrier. *When they broke through the door, they discovered gold.* **12** to break away **from** a person or group. *A group broke away from the parent body.* **13** to break in **on** someone or a conversation or activity. *It seemed a pity to break in on his enjoyment.* **14** to break out **in** spots or a sweat. *When I saw their faces, I broke out in a sweat.*

bridge **1** a bridge **over** or **across** something such as a river. *...the bridge over the Charles River. ...joined onto the castle by a covered bridge across the moat.* **2** a bridge **between** different people, groups, or things. *Industrial designers frequently act as a communication bridge between other team members.*

brief in brief: used when giving a summary. *The facts, in brief, are as follows.*

brim

brim to brim **with** a particular emotion. *The New Zealanders, who have trained this week, are brimming with confidence.*

bring 1 to bring a person or thing **with** you **to** a place; to bring something **to** a person. *...a book which she had brought back with her to France... Occasionally she brought Caro to London... She brought the drink to me and set it on the table.* 2 to bring a quality or thing **to** or **for** a person, thing, or place. *A new pair of shoes brings more happiness to a child than a new car brings to a grown man... Small improvements in the population situation can bring massive benefits for the poorest countries.* 3 to bring something **to** an end or stop. *It took several letters to bring the relationship to an end.* 4 to bring shame **on** a group; to bring trouble **on** yourself. *This would have brought great shame on all concerned.* 5 to bring a response **from** someone. *This last remark brought sniggers from the choir.* 6 to bring someone or something **into** a particular state or situation. *...sentiments which would later bring him into conflict with Party leadership.* 7 to bring a charge **against** someone. *No charge of murder was brought against them.* 8 to bring someone out **in** spots. *Sometimes people think some food or other brings them out in a rash.*

brink on the brink **of** an event or experience. *Cunard was on the brink of bankruptcy.*

bristle to bristle **with** a large quantity of things. *...five ships bristling with radar and radio antennae... This topic bristles with unanswerable questions.*

brood to brood **over** something, **on** something, or **about** something. *I sat back and brooded over what I'd done... I brooded on the problem of the best use I could make of my freedom... Oldham found himself brooding about the police and the woman.*

browse to browse **through** a magazine or book. *Browse through the following pages and choose a holiday just right for you.*

brush 1 a brush **with** someone. *We were still agitated by the brush with the police.* 2 to brush up **on** a subject. *He definitely needed to brush up on his knowledge of rural American customs.*

bubble to bubble **with** a lively quality. *His wife, Marie, bubbled with vitality.*

buckle to buckle down **to** a task. *Crick could now buckle down to his thesis.*

budge not to budge **on** a matter or not to budge **from** your idea or decision. *He refuses to budge on design principles he knows to be sound... But do what they might, the British would not budge from their immigration policy.*

budget to budget **for** something that you will have to spend money on. *Electricity, gas, and telephone bills can all be budgeted for.*

build 1 to build something **into** a system or thing. *...as you build greater challenges into your personal fitness programme.* 2 to build something **on** or **upon** a principle or basis. *This morality was built on two foundations.* 3 to build **on** something that has been achieved. *The fourth job is to build on this progress.*

bulge to bulge **with** a mass of something. *I suppose you've come back with your pockets bulging with money.*

bulk in bulk. *When you deal in fine porcelain, you can't order in bulk.*

bully to bully someone **into** doing something. *They try to bully us into buying their products.*

bulwark a bulwark **against** something undesirable or **of** something that is preserved. *...bulwarks against chaos. ...its* *past role as a bulwark of the regime.*

bump 1 to bump **into** a person or object. *As she backed away, she bumped into someone behind her.* 2 to bump **into** someone you happen to meet. *A week ago the two men had bumped into each other in Goodge Street.*

burden 1 a burden **on** someone or something; be a burden **to** someone. *This system would place intolerable burdens on teachers... I tried not to be a burden to my father.* 2 to burden someone **with** a problem. *However, I mustn't burden you with my problems.*

burdened be burdened **with** or **by** something troublesome or heavy. *Many were burdened with the special equipment that their particular jobs demanded... He was burdened by a huge civilian population that had to be fed.*

burning be burning **with** anger or humiliation. *The jailers were silently burning with rage.*

burst 1 to burst **into** tears, laughter, song, or flames. *She burst into tears and fled.* 2 to burst **in on** someone. *He suddenly burst in on me during a meeting.*

bursting be bursting **with** energy, happiness, or excitement. *The children were there, bursting with life as usual.*

bury 1 to bury a dead person **in** a place. *He wished to be buried in the churchyard.* 2 to bury your face or head **in** something. *She buried her face in her hands and sobbed.*

bus by bus. *He had returned home by bus.*

busy 1 be busy **with** something you are dealing with. *...if you are busy with your hobbies.* 2 to busy yourself **with** something. *He busied himself with plates and cups and saucers.*

butt the butt **of** jokes or **for** teasing. *The butt of the satire is a pompous, ageing scientist... His*

brash matiness made Simon an obvious butt for humour.

buy to buy something **from** someone. *He had bought the equipment from a salesman.*

buzz to buzz **with** conversation. *The room buzzed with excited questions.*

by-product a by-product **of** a process or thing. *Oxygen is released into the atmosphere as a by-product of photosynthesis.*

C

cab by cab. *Mr and Mrs Simpson came by cab.*

cadge to cadge something **off** someone or **from** someone. *The troops cadged a few cigarettes off us. ...the drinks they could cadge from others.*

caked be caked **with** a substance. *His fingers were caked with grime.*

call 1 to call someone **by** a particular type of name. *He never called her by her first name.* 2 to call **on** someone who is at home. *Peter and I called on her in her cottage.* 3 to call **for** someone in order to take them somewhere. *What time shall I call for you?* 4 to call **on** someone to do something. *The keeper called on Father to help him.* 5 to call **for** something to be done. *He called for massive increases in defence spending... Something more radical was called for.*

campaign to campaign **for** something or **against** something. *...campaigning for legal and political equality. ...environmentalists campaigning against nuclear weapons.*

capable be capable **of** doing something. *The workers were no longer capable of bringing about revolution... The car is capable of a top speed of 170 mph.*

capitalize

capitalize to capitalize **on** or **upon** something. ...*people who have capitalized on violence.*

car by car. *We had to travel seventy miles by car.*

care 1 to care for someone: to look after them. *She has cared for other people's babies.* 2 to care **for** or **about** someone: to feel affection for them. *Does he care for her?... They care about each other.* 3 not to care **for** someone or something: to dislike them. *General Ravenscroft didn't care for him much... I didn't care for the way he called me 'mister'.*

case 1 the case **for** doing or having something. *This is clearly a case for breaking with tradition. ...the case for more individual freedom.* 2 the case **for** or **against** someone who is on trial. *...the case for the defence. ...the case against David Poindexter.*

cash to cash in **on** a situation. *I don't blame businessmen for cashing in on their success.*

cast 1 to cast an actor **as** a character in a play. *I remember being cast as Julius Caesar.* 2 to cast doubt **on** something. *The opposition were casting doubt on the official conclusion.*

catch 1 to be caught **in** an unpleasant situation. *She was caught in a cruel dilemma.* 2 to catch up **with** someone who is in front of you. *Kevin raced to catch up with him.* 3 to catch up **on** something you have not had time to do. *This will help you catch up on the housework.* 4 to be caught up **in** a situation. *You are bound to be caught up in events.* 5 to catch up **with** a criminal. *The police caught up with them in the end.*

categorize to categorize someone or something **as** a particular thing. *Many of them had been categorized as insane... The group would have been categorized as belonging to the extreme end of the political spectrum.*

cater to cater **to** or **for** people or their needs. *...a college catering to the rich... Newspapers cater for a variety of tastes.*

cause cause **for** a feeling or type of behaviour. *There was some cause for concern... They were unable to see any cause for rejoicing.*

cede to cede territory or power **to** another country or person. *Part of the mainland was ceded to Great Britain... His government had to cede power to the black majority.*

ceiling a ceiling **on** something such as prices or wages. *...the 6 per cent ceiling on sales growth.*

central be central **to** something. *Information technology is central to improving productivity.*

centre to centre or be centred **round, around,** or **on** something. *College life is centred round hall, chapel and lodgings. ...a training programme which is centred around the study seminar... Interest has centred on the use of solar energy.*

certain be certain **of** something or **about** something. *It was so dark that no-one could be certain of what was happening... People are not certain about the consequences.*

certainty with certainty. *We couldn't say with certainty that the child would be abnormal.*

certify to certify someone or something **as** being a particular thing. *Exported beef must be certified as coming from approved farms... Nevertheless, we cannot certify the moon as completely uninhabited.*

chafe to chafe **at** or **under** an undesirable situation. *The neighbouring farmers chafed at the delay... They had been chafing under the stern rule exercised by the village headman.*

champion a champion **of** a cause, principle, or group of people. *...a champion of the First Amendment. ...the champion of the proletariat.*

chance 1 the chance or chances **of** something happening. *They had a good chance of winning the 1953 election... His chances of success are pretty good.* **2 by chance:** used to talk about events that are not planned. *...a man whom he might have met by chance.*

change 1 a change **of** something. *The world went through a great change of climate.* **2** a change **in** a particular thing or person. *There would be a major change in Egyptian foreign policy.* **3** be a change **from** something. *The decision was a sharp change from past procedure.* **4** to change **from** one thing **to** or **into** another. *The country gradually changed from forest to muddy plain... Britain changed her foreign policy from one of force to one of appeasement... His laughter changed abruptly to a cry of pain... His face seemed to have changed into a mask of hatred.* **5** to change **into** a different set of clothes. *She changed into her street clothes.* **6** to have change **for** a banknote. *Have you got change for a fiver?*

characteristic be characteristic **of** someone or something. *...that reliance on themselves which had been characteristic of the British. ...those large, curved tiles so characteristic of East Anglia.*

characterize 1 to characterize someone or something **as** a particular thing. *His published diary will cover more than 2000 pages, and he characterizes it as an autobiography.* **2** to be characterized **by** a particular feature. *...public awareness that is characterized by strong feelings of distrust... The future is more likely to be characterized by inflation than unemployment.*

charge 1 to charge a sum of money **for** goods or a service. *They charge ten pence for them... The museum will still charge for admission.* **2** to charge someone **with** an offence. *A grand jury charged Williams with murdering Cater... Evangelina was charged with sedition.* **3** the charge **against** an accused person. *The judge announced that he was dropping all charges against Franklin.* **4 in charge; in charge of** someone or something: responsible for them. *I'm in charge now... I was in charge of Sarah and Pam. ...the man in charge of the building.*

charged be charged **with** a quality or feeling. *...an atmosphere that was highly charged with emotion.*

chat 1 to chat **to** or **with** someone **about** something. *Jane chatted to Nell about all the people she'd heard from... He strolled down the road and chatted with the passers-by.* **2** a chat **with** someone **about** something. *I had a chat with Joy Lemoine about old times.*

chatter to chatter **about** something. *We caught twenty or thirty fish and chattered about it for weeks.*

cheat 1 to cheat **at** a game. *I never cheat at cards!* **2** to cheat someone **of** or **out of** something. *She is likely to be robbed or cheated of her land... I bet he cheated you out of that trust money.*

check 1 to check **on** or check up **on** someone or something. *Poirot checked on a point here and there... The Council had checked up on her and decided that she was too old.* **2** to check **with** someone that something is correct or possible. *You won't do anything without checking with the Organization?* **3** to check **into** or **out of** a hotel. *He checked into a small boarding house... The following morning he checked out of the hotel.* **4** to check in **at** a hotel or airport. *He checks in at the hotel at four o'clock.*

cheque 1 by cheque. *The groundsmen are also paid by cheque.* **2** a cheque **for** a particular amount. *He will receive*

choke

a cheque for £300 and a glass tankard.

choke to choke **on** something you are eating or drinking. *Miller seemed about to choke on his drink.*

choked be choked **with** a substance. *...a little fountain choked with mud.*

choose 1 To choose someone or something **as** a particular thing. *A few weeks ago you were chosen as the new Bishop of Jarrow.* **2** To choose someone or something **for** a particular purpose or occasion. *Mr Stokes had been chosen for the job... I chose a yellow dress for that night.*

chum to chum up **with** someone. *You could have chummed up with Maclean.*

cipher in cipher: written in a secret code. *Most of us wrote in cipher.*

circumference in circumference. *Its artificial lakes are ten or twenty kilometres in circumference.*

circumstance in the circumstances; under the circumstances. *In the circumstances his sense of humour was amazing... Under the circumstances this was hardly surprising.*

cite to cite something **as** an example, a reason, or evidence. *She cited differences of opinion as the reason for her departure... Low wages were cited as the main cause for dissatisfaction.*

clad be clad **in** particular clothes. *She was clad in 17th-century costume.*

claim 1 a claim **for** something you think you are entitled to. *...a claim for compensation.* **2** your claim **to** a particular status. *The Labour Party could reassert its claim to popular leadership.* **3** a claim **on** or **upon** someone or their time.

They have a claim upon our loyalty.

clamour to clamour **for** something you want. *I was always clamouring for work.*

clamp 1 to clamp one thing **to** another. *...a steel trap clamped to the cygnet's leg.* **2** to clamp down **on** people or their activities. *The authorities were seeking to clamp down on trade union activity.*

clash 1 to clash **with** someone **over** something. *Its chairman was already clashing with Benn over this proposal... Catholic youths clashed with police in Belfast.* **2** to clash **with** another thing. *The use of reason would have clashed with the strong mystical element.*

class to class someone or something **as** a particular thing. *Such men should not be classed as common labourers.*

classify to classify someone or something **as** a particular thing. *Literacy education is classified as 'education for the disadvantaged'.*

claw to claw **at** someone or something. *Connie clawed at his face.*

cleanse to cleanse someone or something **of** something undesirable. *His body should be cleansed of all sin.*

cling 1 to cling **to** someone or something. *She clung to Mrs Hochstadt's arm.* **2** to cling **to** an idea or way of behaving. *Both parties clung to the principles of social democracy.*

clogged be clogged **with** things. *Herald Square was clogged with people... Our minds are clogged with false opinions.*

close /kləʊs/**1** be close **to** a place, thing, or state. *The restaurant was quite close to the airport... This is close to the truth... I had been close to being killed.* **2** be close **to** someone you like. *I had grown so* *close to Hattie that it hurt to see her leave.* 3/kləʊz/ to close in **on** someone you are attacking. *The Mandinkas closed in on Soumaoro's forces.*

closeted be closeted **with** someone. *Worried airline officials have been closeted with their bankers all this week.*

close-up in close-up. *...pictures of terrible casualties, shown in close-up.*

clothed be clothed **in** particular clothes. *She was clothed in a crumpled school uniform.*

clue the clue **to** something that you are trying to solve or understand. *I had the clue to something that had long baffled me.*

clutch to clutch **at** something. *She clutched at my hand.*

cluttered be cluttered **with** objects. *...a kind of platform, cluttered with crates and churns.*

coach by coach. *We usually go by coach.*

coast 1 **on the coast:** on land next to the sea. *The family was at one of their other houses on the coast.* 2 **off the coast:** in the sea near to the coast. *...a ridge 250 miles off the coast of Mexico.*

coat to coat a surface or object **in** something or **with** something. *Shake the pan to coat the mushrooms in fat. ...glass coated with aluminium.*

coax 1 to coax someone **into** doing something. *He may be able to coax her into going along with him.* 2 to coax someone **out of** a place or state. *He wouldn't let anyone coax him out of his house again... She would tenderly coax the poor girl out of her depression.*

code in code. *...information typed in code.*

coerce to coerce someone **into** doing something. *The employers*

tried to coerce them into signing an illegal agreement.

coexist to coexist **with** another thing, person, or group. *...a fish species which can coexist with other marine life.*

cohabit to cohabit **with** someone. *She has no intention of cohabiting with the father of her baby.*

coil to coil **round** or **around** something. *...a tree with a snake coiled round it.*

coincide to coincide **with** another event. *Dottie's departure coincided with Toby's marriage.*

collaborate to collaborate **with** someone **in** something or **on** something. *We should collaborate with other colleges in putting forward proposals. ...a system in which a university and an industrial firm collaborate on major programmes of research.*

collide to collide **with** someone or something. *He collided with one of the men from the ship... The car stalled as it collided with the bank.*

collision a collision **with** something or **between** two things. *...the danger of collision with another ship. ...a collision between two cars.*

colour in colour: used of films, television programmes, or photographs. *They had photos of themselves printed in colour.*

comb to comb a place **for** something. *The district had been combed for recruits.*

combination in combination **with** something or someone. *They were tested in combination with other chemicals... The head teacher, in combination with his colleagues, arranges the teaching of the groups of pupils.*

combine to combine one thing **with** another. *Her writing combines objectivity with a deft management of style. ...a perfect*

come

example of professional expertise combined with personal charm.

come 1 to come **to** a place. *At last he came to Philadelphia.* **2** to come **from** or **out of** a place. *Whole families came from neighbouring villages to look at her... Roger and Maurice came out of the forest.* **3** to come **from** a place: to have been born there. *She comes from New Zealand... Where do you come from?* **4** to come **from** something: to be the result of it. *The wealth of industrial society could only come from the toil of the masses.* **5** to come **to** a person or **to** their mind. *Vague thoughts and memories came to her... A scene came to his mind.* **6** to come **to** or **into** a particular state. *The argument came to an end... They hid when I came into sight... He first came into prominence when he finished fifth in the Tokyo Olympics.* **7** to come **to** or **onto** a particular topic. *I'm going to come to that in a minute... You then come onto the whole question of Northern Ireland.* **8** to come **to** a particular amount. *My income now comes to £65 a week.* **9** to come **on, upon,** or **across** something or someone: to find or meet them by chance. *A few hours later they came upon a beautiful plain... Sometimes he came across snapshots of himself and Hilary.* **10** to come **as** a surprise, shock, or relief. *The news came as a relief.* **11** to come **in** a particular form or colour. *This device comes in two parts... Few people realise that ladybirds come in different colours.* **12** to come **by** a possession: to obtain it. *Everyone knows how Barbara came by her fur coat.* **13** to come **between** two people: to spoil their friendship. *I believe he wanted to come between you and Celia.* **14** to come **under** criticism or attack. *It would soon come under very heavy pressure.* **15** to come **under** someone's authority or control. *Day*

Nurseries come under the Department of Health and Social Security. **16** to come down **to** a particular consideration: used when mentioning the most important consideration. *When it comes down to it, they're all on the side of the employers.* **17** to come in **for** blame or criticism. *His Department has come in for special criticism.* **18** to come out **with** a remark. *He actually came out with a word of praise... He came out with 'Of course you have met my niece before.'* **19** to come round **to** something. *We shall have to come round to their way of thinking... He had come round to loving her.* **20** to come up **against** a problem or difficulty. *Everyone comes up against that hurdle sooner or later.* **21** to come up **for** discussion or election. *Financial obligations and partnerships now come up for review.* **22** to come up **to** a particular standard. *It never really came up to expectations.* **23** to come up **with** a proposal or suggestion. *The people of a neighbouring kingdom came up with a tempting proposition.*

command 1 be **in command**; be **in command of** a situation or group of people. *Colonel Wentworth was in command... Jones was in command of the attack.* **2 under** someone's **command:** commanded by them. *...troops under French command.* **3 at** someone's **command:** possessed and able to be used by them. *...a writer who has both elegance and passion at his command.*

commend to commend something **to** someone. *I commend this book to anyone interested in family morals... This tidy division of functions may commend itself to theoreticians.*

commensurate be commensurate **with** something. *Their position in* the social hierarchy is not commensurate with their income.

comment to comment **on** or **upon** something. *The presenter commented on the huge capacity of computers.*

commentary a commentary **on** or **upon** something. *...a series of commentaries on Jane Austen... It was a terrible commentary on her frustration and loneliness.*

commiserate to commiserate **with** someone **on** or **over** something unfortunate. *I commiserated with him on his ill luck.*

commit 1 to commit yourself **to** something. *At the age of 40, he has committed himself more and more to motor racing... I couldn't commit myself to having her indefinitely.* 2 to commit money or resources **to** something. *The company must commit its entire resources to the project.*

committed be committed **to** something. *He is committed to his own career.*

common 1 be common **to** several people or things. *...the fear of dogs common to all tramps. ...the ugly style common to engineering and technical writing.* 2 **in common with** someone or something; have something **in common.** *Young, in common with his contemporaries, has realised that the old combinations work best... The two nations had little in common.*

communicate 1 to communicate **with** someone. *We're trying to communicate with all different kinds of people... You've got to be able to communicate with each other.* 2 to communicate an idea or feeling **to** someone. *The function of reading aloud is to communicate the writer's meaning to one or more listeners.*

company 1 **in** someone's **company:** with them. *...spending the whole day in the company of young children.* 2 **in company**

with someone: accompanied by them. *He returned to the office in company with his colleagues.*

comparable be comparable **to** something or **with** something; a comparable thing **to** something else. *The length of a sound wave is comparable to the size of a human skull... The efficiency of electric cars is comparable with that of petrol cars. ...government support on a comparable scale to that given to owner-occupiers.*

compare to compare one thing or person **to** or **with** another. *He can be compared to a patient undergoing psychoanalysis... As an example, I'll compare freedom with marriage.*

comparison in comparison **to**, in comparison **with**, or **by** comparison **with** someone or something. *In comparison to her, Valechka was a model of discretion... Man is immeasurably privileged in comparison with most of his fellow creatures... They are well off by comparison with almost anybody else.*

compatible be compatible **with** something or someone. *Private ownership is compatible with a high degree of equality... I wanted lawyers who would be compatible with each other.*

compensate 1 to compensate **for** something that is bad, lost, or damaged. *Artificial snow cannot compensate for the general lack of real snow... The sense of relief more than compensates for any losses you may incur.* 2 to compensate someone **for** something unpleasant that has happened to them. *...plans to compensate patients for damage caused by medical negligence.*

compete to compete **against** someone or **with** someone. *He has competed against the finest athletes in Britain... US companies are having to compete with giants from Europe and Japan.*

competent

competent be competent **at** or **in** a particular skill, job, or subject. *...an educated man, who was also competent at his job... People can be helped to be competent in personal affairs.*

competition in competition **with** someone or something. *We are not in competition with people who sell equipment at the lowest prices.*

complacent be complacent **about** a situation. *The Department are giving a warning not to be complacent about the success in cutting accident statistics.*

complain to complain **to** someone **about** something, or to complain **of** something. *Thomas knew that people had complained to Uncle Harold about his fights... She never complained about the noise or the traffic... The officers complained of a shortage of staff at Risley.*

complement 1 a complement **to** a particular activity or thing. *The quiet good humour of his wife made a perfect complement to his more ebullient nature.* 2 a specified complement **of** people or things. *By the time the crew reached the west coast, 44 of the original complement of 150 were dead... He lacks a full complement of teeth.*

complementary be complementary **to** something. *The roles of the sexes are complementary to one another.*

complete complete **with** something: used to mention something extra which is included with a larger thing. *He bought a lovely Beverly Hills mansion, complete with swimming pool.*

complex a complex **about** a problem or bad experience. *...a boy who had an inferiority complex about his size.*

complexities the complexities **of** something. *He worked hard to master the complexities of tax law.*

compliance compliance **with** an order, law, or set of rules. *The Department of the Environment expects compliance with EC standards to be achieved by the end of this year.*

compliment 1 to compliment someone **on** something or **for** doing something. *Thomas tried to smile, to compliment Mrs Jardino on her sense of humour... She is to be complimented for handling the situation so well.* 2 **with** someone's **compliments.** *Send him a copy of the dictionary with our compliments.*

comply to comply **with** an order, request, or set of rules. *New vehicles must comply with certain standards.*

composed be composed **of** particular things or people. *The book is composed of essays written over the last ten years.*

composite a composite **of** several different things. *This scene is a composite of features from villages in North Wiltshire where Tanner lived.*

composition in composition: used to say what something consists of. *The organization is mainly working class in composition.*

compounded be compounded **of** different things or **from** different things. *The old soldier cast me a glance, compounded of despair and amusement... His acting is compounded from theories of different kinds.*

comprised be comprised **of** particular things or people. *The medical profession is largely comprised of responsible, caring, and competent practitioners.*

compromise a compromise **between** two things. *Co-operative tenure is a compromise between owning and renting.*

con to con someone **into** doing something. *Barry may con*

unsuspecting people into paying
him for golf lessons.

conceal to conceal something
from someone. *We had to worry
about concealing our intentions
from the Mexicans.*

concede to concede something **to**
someone. *The government has
conceded the political initiative to
fundamentalist opponents. ...the
title she conceded to Steffi Graf
last year.*

conceive 1 to conceive **of**
something. *I can conceive of no
circumstances in which we would
give in.* 2 to conceive one thing **as**
another thing; to conceive **of** it **as**
another thing. *A politician
conceives the world as being a
variety of conflicting values... The
need to conceive of the house as a
place of recreation and work.*

concentrate to concentrate **on** or
upon something. *Once you've got
all these distractions, you can't
really concentrate on the play...
Mr Hattersley concentrated
particularly on the provisions
made for women in the social
charter.*

concentration 1 concentration
on something. *His concentration
on civil rights has improved his
popularity.* 2 a concentration **of** a
thing or substance. *A low
concentration of fertilizer may be
used in the solution... Large
concentrations of capital were in
the hands of merchants.*

concern 1 concern **about, over,** or
at something. *I would share your
concern about prison conditions.
...the growing public concern over
the treatment of circus animals...
The teachers expressed their
concern at the increasing levels of
classroom violence.* 2 to concern
yourself **with** or **about** something.
*I'd dearly love to see more women
concerning themselves with such
vital issues... It's interesting you
should concern yourself so much
about Dave.* 3 be **of** concern.

*Increasing zinc pollution is also of
concern.*

concerned be concerned **with**
something or **about** something.
*I'm more concerned with efficiency
than expansion... We are very
concerned about the breakdown in
family life.*

conclude 1 to conclude **from**
evidence or facts that something is
true. *It would be easy to conclude
from this that the whole idea was a
failure.* 2 to conclude **with**
something. *The article concluded
with a demand for more American
aid.*

conclusion in conclusion. *In
conclusion, let me suggest a
number of practical applications.*

concomitant 1 be concomitant
with something. *I was aware of
the high moral standards
concomitant with the name I bore.*
2 a concomitant **of** something.
*Decreased mobility is often a
concomitant of old age.*

concur to concur **with** someone or
something that they say. *When we
are satisfied, we will concur with
those calling for sanctions... We've
concurred with everything
MacGregor has ordered, and it's
been to no avail.*

condemn 1 to condemn something
as bad or unacceptable. *The
remark has been widely
condemned as racist.* 2 to condemn
someone **for** something they have
done. *The Council condemned the
Government for allowing the sale
of fireworks to children.* 3 to
condemn someone **to** a particular
punishment or unpleasant
situation. *...a murder for which her
mother had been condemned to
death... Lack of education
condemns them to extreme
poverty.*

condense to condense a speech or
piece of writing **into** a shorter form
or **into** a shorter time. *Act One
was condensed into about seven
minutes.*

condition

condition 1 a condition **of** something or **for** something to happen or exist. *We insist on the granting of human rights as a condition of financial aid... The right of our nation to independence is a condition for world peace.*
2 **out of condition:** unfit. *The men are exhausted and badly out of condition.*

conditional be conditional **on** or **upon** something. *The issue of a licence was conditional on the production of certain documents... Their support was conditional upon further reductions in public expenditure.*

conducive be conducive **to** something. *The absence of natural light and sunshine is not conducive to mental and physical well-being.*

confer 1 to confer **with** someone. *In 1943 Churchill went in the Queen Mary to confer with Roosevelt.* 2 to confer a title or award **on** or **upon** someone. *Baron de Reuter's title was conferred upon him in 1871.*

conference in **conference:** in a meeting. *The party remained in conference until 1 o'clock.*

confess to confess **to** something that is bad, unacceptable, or illegal, or to confess **to** someone. *Fourteen per cent confessed to travelling on public transport without paying... The man's companion claimed that Mr X had confessed to him.*

confide 1 to confide a secret **to** someone. *Last month he confided to me his latest scheme... A 15-year old pupil confided to her parents that she was pregnant.* 2 to confide **in** someone. *Lonnie doesn't believe in confiding in doctors.*

confidence confidence **in** a person or thing. *She has an unshaken confidence in her own abilities.*

confine to confine yourself **to** a particular thing or place, or to be confined **to** it. *Unionist MPs have confined themselves to matters relating specifically to Northern Ireland... The conflict was confined to the Peking area... A number of those previously confined to bed have become mobile.*

confirm to confirm someone **in** a belief, opinion, or intention. *It confirmed him in his belief that England was no longer the sort of place in which he wished to live.*

conflict 1/kɒnflɪkt/ to conflict **with** something. *My wife thought that my plans might conflict with a book that she and her first daughter were having published.* 2/kɒnflɪkt/ **in conflict; in conflict with** someone. *Full employment and economic viability are in conflict... Many parents were alarmed to find themselves in conflict with the church.*

conform to conform **to** or **with** a law, demand, or wish. *Imported drugs must have packaging that conforms to UK standards... It was held that all intellectual activity must conform with an accepted, approved ideology.*

conformity in **conformity with** something. *This new Act is not in conformity with international law.*

confronted be confronted **by** or **with** something unpleasant or difficult. *Bill stared, as if confronted by a policeman about to make an arrest... The controllers were confronted with a sudden build up of traffic.*

confuse to confuse someone or something **with** another person or thing. *You must be confusing me with my sister... I had noticed that several times she confused left with right.*

congratulate to congratulate someone **on** or **upon** something; to congratulate someone **for** doing something. *Let me be the first to congratulate you on a wise decision... Councils were being congratulated for economising.*

connect 1 to connect one person or thing **to** or **with** another. *There was a lack of qualified staff to connect lamps to the cable network... A causeway connects the island to Guernsey... The Communist Party is more interested in connecting itself with the mainstream of the Labour movement.* 2 to connect **with** a train, bus, plane, or coach. *This train connects with a bus service to Worcester.*

connected be connected **with** something. *You need two references, preferably from people connected with the racing industry.*

connection 1 a connection **to** or **with** something, or a connection **between** two things. *...the rail connection to the tunnel... Mr Ikeda has denied any connection with the case... Musicologists are investigating the connection between Schumann's mental illness and his music.* 2 **in connection with** something. *Harry Hearns had been arrested in connection with a fatal shooting.*

conscience on your **conscience**. *I can't accept it, I'd have all those poor people on my conscience.*

conscious be conscious **of** something. *Recalling it now, she was conscious of a sharp pang of guilt. ...squirming a little, conscious of his filthy appearance.*

consent to consent **to** something. *The Vice-President announced that he would consent to several television appearances.*

consequence 1 the consequence **of** a situation or event. *Higher mortgage rates are a consequence of higher interest rates.* 2 **in consequence** of something: as a result of it. *Five workers were laid off in consequence of a dispute in which they were playing no direct part.* 3 **of consequence:** important. *These are fringe parties, of no real consequence.*

consider to consider a person or thing **as** something. *I consider twenty-nine minutes as the absolute limit... They do not consider a child as important.*

consideration under **consideration.** *Further debt reduction moves have been under consideration.*

consign to consign someone or something **to** a particular place, position, or person. *Her daughter had been consigned to Lizzie's care... This dreadful Government deserves to be consigned to the dustbin of politics.*

consist 1 to consist **of** particular things or people. *The trap consists of a hollowed-out coconut chained to a stake... The sample consisted of 10,000 adult males.* 2 to consist **in** a particular activity or thing. *Progress in future may consist in finding ways of reducing the Gross National Product.*

consistent be consistent **with** something. *These proposals are quite consistent with the modified plan.*

console /kənsəʊl/ to console someone **with** something or **by** doing something. *I lay in the bath and consoled myself with Bob Dylan's latest album... She tried to console me by saying that I'd probably be happier in a new job.*

consort /kənsɔːt/ to consort **with** a particular person or group. *More important, you should not have consorted with the enemy.*

conspire to conspire **with** someone **against** another person. *He feels that you conspired with the students to weaken the authority of the senior staff... The restrictions are there to prevent people conspiring against the state.*

constrained be constrained **by** someone or something. *A lot of men feel constrained by society's image of masculinity.*

constraint a constraint **on** someone, or the constraints **of** something. *The constraint on most doctors is lack of time. ... the constraints of the market economy.*

construe to construe a situation, event, or statement **as** something. *The judge could have construed my attendance at the trial as a violation of the bail order.*

consult to consult **with** someone **about** something. *He became suspicious on receiving another request to consult with the chairman of the town council... She made no secret of her annoyance that she was not consulted about the legal implications of the agreement.*

consultation 1 consultation **with** someone **about** something, or **between** two or more people. *Budgets will be fixed after consultation with heads and governors... It's a question of winning consultation about management plans... There would still be a long process of consultation between the Foreign Office, Buckingham Palace, and the Kremlin.* **2 in consultation with** someone. *They have promised to implement reforms in consultation with black leaders.*

consumption for someone's **consumption.** *Some of this meat would be unfit for human consumption. ...what politicians say for public consumption.*

contact 1 contact **with** someone or **between** two or more people. *We are the only people who have any real contact with the general public... There was very little contact between the people in the University.* **2 in contact with** someone or something. *We were very closely in contact with our writers.*

contempt 1 contempt **for** someone or something. *Rani made no secret of the contempt she felt for the older woman. ...a cynical contempt for truth, justice, or decency.* **2 beneath contempt;** be **beneath** someone's **contempt.** *...a despicable act, beneath contempt... The poor were beneath her contempt.* **3 in contempt; in contempt of court:** a legal term. *The court order ruled that they are theoretically in contempt... His words were held to be in contempt of court.*

contemptuous be contemptuous **of** someone or something. *The Prime Minister was contemptuous of Press criticisms.*

contend to contend **with** a problem or difficulty. *They had to contend daily with appalling conditions.*

content /kɔntɛnt/**1** be content **with** something. *A lot of unattached ladies in mid-life seem to be content with their lot.* **2** to content yourself **with** something. *She hadn't said much but had contented herself with smoking cigarettes and smiling.*

contention be in contention; be **in contention for** something: be competing or be likely to win something. *Three players are in contention to win the title... Warwickshire are still very much in contention for the championship.*

context 1 in context. *I think one has to see the oil issue in context.* **2 out of context.** *This remark was taken completely out of context.*

contingent be contingent **on** something. *Grants are to be contingent on continuing academic progress.*

continue to continue **with** something. *He was prepared to let them continue with the task... The series continued with a performance of The Threepenny Opera.*

contract 1/kɔntrækt/ to contract **with** someone to do something. *A* general practitioner contracts with the state to provide a medical service. 2/kɒntrækt/ be **under contract to** someone. *I was then under contract to a finance company.*

contrary /kɒntrəri/1 **on the contrary:** used to say that the opposite is true. *There was nothing dowdy or ugly about her dress; on the contrary, she had a certain private elegance.* 2 **to the contrary:** used when indicating that one thing contradicts another. *This method, despite thousands of published statements to the contrary, has no damaging effects whatsoever.* 3 be contrary **to** something. *She claimed that this was contrary to the sex discrimination act of 1975.*

contrast 1/kɒntrɑːst/ a contrast **with** or **to** another thing, or a contrast **between** two things. *His work would give the dancers a good contrast with their usual style... The ship was spartan, a poor contrast to her sumptuous successors... There could hardly be a greater contrast between the two painters.* 2 **in contrast with** something; **in contrast to** something. *It has been a decade of outstanding creative achievement, in contrast with the depressing Seventies... Gordon's friends were uncertain, in contrast to their usual boldness of manner.* 3 /kɒntrɑːst/ to contrast one thing **with** or **to** another thing. *I cannot help contrasting her attitude with that of her friends... His accent contrasted curiously with the earthiness of his language... Phaedrus is a bizarre person when contrasted to the people that surround him.*

contribute to contribute **to** something or **towards** something. *The worry and strain contributed to a long and painful illness... They had contributed towards the cost of the scheme.*

control 1 control **over** something or **of** something. *Workers should have more influence and control over production... Steve Cowper called on the group to take control of the clean-up operation.* 2 be **under control.** *The Asian republic of Uzbekistan has been brought under control.* 3 **beyond** someone's **control; outside** someone's **control.** *The delays were caused by events beyond the company's control. ...motives so deep that they are outside our conscious control.* 4 **in control of** someone or something. *She was in control of herself completely... I was beginning to feel that I was in control of events.*

convenience at someone's **convenience.** *I left the blankets outside my room for my landlady to remove at her convenience.*

converge to converge **on** or **upon** a particular place or person. *Seventy trucks and thirty personnel carriers converged on the square... Two men converged on the card players and told them gambling was illegal.*

convergence a convergence **of** or **between** two or more things. *...the predicted convergence of the industrialized societies... The President's formula has ended a movement towards convergence between the states.*

conversant be conversant **with** a particular task or topic. *You will need to be fully conversant with the running of the household.*

converse 1/kɒnvɜːs/ to converse **with** someone. *None of them had ever been left alone to converse with Captain Paget.* 2/kɒnvɜːs/ the converse **of** something. *Another cliche, the converse of the first, is that people who live in the same place all their lives are insular and bigoted.*

conversion conversion **from** one belief, system, or method **to** another. *...the conversion from*

convert

guerrilla fighting to organized warfare.

convert /kənvɜːt/ to convert something **from** a particular state **to** a different state, or **into** something else. *They slept on pallets in a dormitory converted from a storehouse... He knew the formula for converting kilometres to miles... Trying to run with an injured ankle may convert a mild injury into a severe one.*

convey to convey something **to** a particular place or person. *Thousands of Angolans had been conveyed to the square in military trucks... She feels no hesitation conveying such feelings to her daughter.*

convict /kənvɪkt/ to convict someone **of** or **for** a crime. *...a judge who convicted five men of a single murder... Only two were subsequently convicted for motoring offences.*

conviction the conviction **of** someone **for** a crime. *...the trial and conviction of Oliver North. ...a criminal conviction for fraud.*

convince to convince someone **of** something or **about** something. *The talks did convince her of how urgently they wanted progress... A senior consultant is far from convinced about the worth of Blythe's work.*

convoy be in convoy. *...one of eight trucks moving in convoy.*

co-operate to co-operate **with** a person, rule, or order. *100 prison officers have been suspended for refusing to co-operate with new shift arrangements.*

co-ordination co-ordination **between** people or things. *...the problem of poor co-ordination between different parts of the Health Service.*

cope to cope **with** a difficult task, problem, or situation. *...schools that specialize in coping with handicapped children... People who have just arrived are going to*

have problems coping with our demands.

corrective a corrective **to** a particular attitude, account, or quality. *This analysis provides an important corrective to the traditional view.*

correlate to correlate **with** something. *Age often correlates with conservatism.*

correspond 1 to correspond **with** something or **to** something. *This view corresponds less and less with reality... He finds it difficult to make his words correspond to the music.* 2 to correspond **with** someone. *He began to correspond with other shell collectors.*

correspondence correspondence **with** someone or **between** people. *He is engaged in correspondence with nearly one hundred writers... I have seen some of the correspondence between the War Office and the Colonel.*

couched be couched **in** a particular style of language. *Here was a resolution couched in forthright terms.*

counsel to counsel someone **about** or **against** something. *He counselled each of us about our present and future goals... I would strongly counsel the new administration against complacency.*

count 1 to count **against** someone. *It would count heavily against me if I got the Director into trouble.* 2 to count **as** something. *Horses are usually free, but a horse-box counts as a trailer and you will be charged accordingly.* 3 to count **for** something. *So all his feeling, thinking, and writing counted for nothing.* 4 to count **on** or **upon** someone or something. *Give my apologies—I'm afraid they were counting on me.* 5 to count **to** or count up **to** a particular number. *I counted up to one thousand seven hundred.* 6 to count **towards**

something. *I think his exams will count towards his apprenticeship.*

counter to counter something that is bad or harmful **with** a particular action or **by** saying or doing something. *Labour should counter this propaganda with a series of press statements... Disease problems are countered by rotating crops.*

coupled be coupled **with** something. *He had similar linguistic abilities, coupled with a love of exotic places and cultures.*

course be on **course**; be **off course**. *He was at the wheel again, with the Morning Rose back on course... Northerly winds swept Phillips and his crew off course.*

court 1 **at court:** at the court of a king or queen. *The king had commanded his presence at court.* 2 **in court:** in a court of law. *The latter made a statement that was used against the judge in court.* 3 **out of court:** without going to a court of law. *Be careful about settling out of court without first consulting the union.* 4 **on court:** on a court where you play a game such as tennis, netball, or squash. *On court, Billie Jean has taken risks.*

courteous be courteous **to** someone. *He was quiet, and courteous to the staff.*

cover 1 to cover one thing **with** another. *Pour this mixture into a pie dish and cover it with mashed potatoes.* 2 to cover up **for** someone. *Once I'd covered up for you, it was my word against theirs.*

covered be covered **in** something or **with** something. *Her mouth was bruised and covered in blood... Malpas in Cheshire, like most of the country, is covered with a blanket of snow.*

crack 1 a crack **between** two things. *He made a crack between two of his fingers and peeped through.* 2 a crack **in** something. *Water appeared to be seeping*

though a crack in the wall. 3 to crack down **on** someone or something. *...the Special Investigation Unit assigned to crack down on the drug trade.*

craving a craving **for** something. *The craving for imported goods continues.*

crawling be crawling **with** something. *...cheeses covered in mould and crawling with maggots.*

craze a craze **for** something. *...the craze for inflatable bananas.*

crazy be crazy **about** something. *Julie was crazy about music and liked to sing.*

credit 1 to credit someone **with** something, or credit something **to** them. *I used to credit you with a bit of common sense... The original songs were not credited to a composer or lyricist in the programme.* 2 credit **for** doing something. *He's never had enough credit for the job he did.*

crick a crick **in** your neck. *I got a crick in my neck lying on this bed.*

crime a crime **against** a moral code, rule, or standard. *The Labour leader condemned the killings as a crime against humanity.*

criterion a criterion **for** something or **of** something. *Competition should be the only criterion for assessing mergers... Economic relationships should be dominated by the criterion of ownership.*

critical be critical **of** someone or something. *The family has always been critical of their achievements.*

criticize to criticize someone **for** or **over** something that is wrong or foolish. *Francis criticized the players for being greedy and lacking pride in their performance... He was increasingly criticised for obstinacy... Some of her colleagues have criticized her over the introduction of the new tax.*

cross 1 a cross **between** one thing and another. *The black gown made him look like a cross between a*

crowd

preacher and an avenging angel.
2 to cross one animal or plant **with**
another. *The main hybrid used in
pig farming was crossed with the
British Saddleback variety.* **3** to
cross a word or words **off** a list. *We
crossed the days off our home-
made calendars.*

crowd 1 to crowd **around** or
round someone or something.
*Children were always crowding
around the ticket booth.* **2** to crowd
into a place. *Outside, shiny cars
crowd into the square.*

crowded be crowded **with**
something. *The pier was crowded
with anxious parents waiting for
their children.*

cruel be cruel **to** someone. *How
could you be so cruel to poor
Rhoda?*

cry 1 to cry out **against** something.
*People are crying out against the
new laws.* **2** to cry out **for**
something. *The VAT office is
crying out for new staff.*

cull to cull information or ideas
from a particular source. *The
story is culled from legend.*

culminate to culminate **in** or **with**
a particular result or outcome.
*Their last tour culminated in four
nights at Wembley Stadium... The
whole event will culminate with
the traditional fireworks on Friday
night.*

cure 1 a cure **for** an illness or
disease. *Eating is the best cure for
jet-lag.* **2** to cure someone **of** a
habit or attitude. *He must try and
cure himself of this tendency to
daydream.*

curse a curse **on** or **upon** someone.
There is a curse on this family.

cursed be cursed **with** something.
*It is the elephant's misfortune that
it has been cursed with a pair of
tusks.*

cut 1 to cut **across** a place. *We cut
across the grass to a relatively
secluded spot.* **2** to cut **through**
something. *Their voices cut
through the murmured prayers.*

3 a cut **in** something such as
expenditure, quality, or an
amount. *President Bush
announced a ten per cent cut in US
forces.* **4** to cut back **on** something
such as expenditure or quality.
*Many manufacturers cut back on
the quality of the keyboard.* **5** to
cut down **on** something. *You
should cut down on dairy produce.
...companies who need to cut down
on administrative waste.* **6** to cut
someone off **from** something.
*Success threatened to cut her off
from him... Liverpool prides itself
on its uniqueness, the way it is cut
off from the rest of the country.*
7 to cut someone **out of** an
activity. *I don't think I should be
cut out of the trip.* **8** be cut out **for**
a particular job or activity. *I'm not
really cut out for this kind of work.*
9 be cut up **about** something.
*They sent her home; she seems
awfully cut up about it.*

cutback a cutback **in** something
such as expenditure, quality, or
amount. *...the cutback in public
services.*

D

dab to dab **at** something. *He dabbed
at her cheek with a handkerchief.*

dabble to dabble **in** an activity. *I
sometimes dabbled in commercial
art.*

dally to dally **with** an idea or plan.
*He began to dally with the idea
that she might be looking for him.*

damage damage **to** something. *It
can cause damage to the liver,
heart, and kidneys... My only
concern is the damage to your
reputation.*

dance 1 to dance **with** someone.
*Alverio says he was dancing with
friends at a nightclub.* **2** to dance
to a particular kind of music. *They
do not dance to classical music.*

danger 1 be **in danger**; be **in danger of** something: be likely to be harmed. *Do you realize that you may be in danger?... It is in danger of collapsing.* 2 be **out of danger**: be no longer likely to be harmed. *Once he was out of danger, the doctors were able to investigate the causes which led to his collapse.*

date 1 a date **with** someone. *He was late for his date with Julie.* 2 to date **from** or date back **to** a particular time. *...a rococo shop front that dates from about 1760... The use of money dates back to the time when human societies first became large and efficient.*

dawn to dawn **on** or **upon** someone. *It never dawned on her that her life was in danger.*

day by day. *The birds feed mainly by day.*

deal 1 to deal **with** something that needs attention. *When they had dealt with the fire, another crisis arose... They have to deal with children who've been drinking in the lunch-hour.* 2 to deal **with** a particular subject. *The book deals with the pursuit of Rommel's army after El Alamein.* 3 to deal **in** a particular type of goods. *He dealt in all domestic commodities.*

dealings your dealings **with** someone. *I kept him informed of my dealings with cabinet ministers... I've never had any dealings with Gertrude.*

dear be dear **to** someone. *...long stretches of sand with rocks and pools so dear to children.*

debate 1 a debate **on, over,** or **about** something. *...this debate on the future guidelines for social spending. ...the debate over the extent and scope of public ownership. ...the unending debate about tobacco.* 2 to debate **with** someone. *He debated with his foreman on the state of the crops... Bernstein debated with himself for a while.*

debt in debt. *Her husband drank and was deep in debt.*

deceive to deceive someone **into** doing something. *One can easily be deceived into feeling everything was justified... Readers were deceived into the mistaken belief that the advertisements were genuine.*

decide to decide **on** or **upon** something. *Have you decided on how we should act?... Already their first production had been decided upon.*

decision a decision **on** or **about** something. *A decision on the issue might not be necessary... He never made a swift decision about anything.*

decked be decked **with, in,** or out **in** something. *...raised mounds decked with garlands and flowers. ...twin beds decked in rich cream-coloured brocade... They were decked out in embroidered coats.*

decline a decline **in** something or **of** something. *...a decline in standards. ...the decline of the Liberal Party.*

decrease a decrease **in** something. *The tax on fuel will encourage a decrease in petrol consumption.*

dedicate 1 to dedicate yourself **to** something. *He dedicated himself to the solution of routine problems.* 2 to dedicate a book or piece of music **to** someone. *She dedicated her first book 'Under the Net' to Raymond Queneau.*

dedicated be dedicated **to** something. *...a man dedicated to his craft.*

default 1 **by default**: because something has not happened. *Much of what I was doing had fallen to me by default.* 2 **in default of** doing something: because of not doing it. *You can even be sent to prison in default of payment.* 3 to default **on** an amount of money that you owe. *The film company has already defaulted on one payment.*

defect

defect 1/diːfɛkt/ a defect **in** or **of** something. *There are a number of defects in this view. ...the defects of Western society.* 2/difɛkt/ to defect **from** one place or organization **to** another. *The composer's son defected from Russia earlier this year... Taylor defected to the Liberals in 1906.*

defence defence **against** something. *...a baby's defence against infection.*

defer to defer **to** someone. *Children were expected to defer to their parents in everything.*

deference **in** deference **to** someone or **to** their wishes. *He changed his name to Weinreb in deference to his grandfather.*

defiance **in** defiance **of** a rule or order. *His son had come in defiance of his father's strict orders.*

deficient be deficient **in** something. *Cow's milk is deficient in vitamins C and D.*

deficit **in** deficit. *...a country whose balance of payments was permanently in deficit.*

definition **by** definition. *A democracy has by definition to be independent.*

deflect to deflect someone **from** something. *She had no reason to be deflected from her usual mode of life.*

degenerate /didʒɛnərɪt/ to degenerate **into** or **to** something. *Her work has degenerated into a series of sexual puns and metaphors... Their acting often degenerated to an infantile level.*

degree **by** degrees. *Her hatred of Philip had grown by degrees to be the dominant passion of her life.*

delight 1 the delights **of** an activity or experience. *The Victorians developed a great passion for the delights of cruising.* 2 to delight **in** an activity or experience. *He delights in controversy.*

delude to delude someone **into** believing something. *We must not delude ourselves into imagining that we are being educated.*

deluge to deluge an organization or place **with** something. *They deluged the Ministry with letters... Five minutes later the hotel was deluged with uniformed police.*

delusion **under** a delusion. *She continued to drink, under the delusion that she was immune to it.*

delve to delve **into** something. *They delved into their desks for their pens. ...delving into the secrets of nature.*

demand 1 a demand **for** something. *There was a heavy demand for goods and services.* 2 the demands **of** a type of activity. *...the demands of factory work.*

demonstrate to demonstrate something **to** someone. *They need to demonstrate to children just what cheating means... The appropriate action is then demonstrated to them.*

denounce 1 to denounce someone or something **as** a particular kind of thing. *They were being denounced as traitors.* 2 to denounce someone **for** something they have done. *But many in the crowd denounced him for not going far enough.*

denude to denude something **of** a quality or feature. *Winds swept the plain, denuding it of all vegetation.*

depart 1 to depart **from** a way of doing things. *He departed from custom on this occasion by taking a bath... The party departed from the principle that all members were equal.* 2 to depart **from** a place. *They finally departed from the stage.* 3 to depart **for** a place. *The man was already late in departing for Bilyarsk.*

depend to depend **on** or **upon** something or someone. *France* depended equally on Algerians and Moroccans... He argued that security depended upon disarmament.

dependent be dependent **on** or **upon** someone or something. *They are still dependent on their parents... Now, as never before, one's future is almost wholly dependent upon education.*

depict to depict someone or something **as** a particular kind of thing. *In the picture, judges are depicted as sheep... The human hunter is often depicted as a savage killer.*

deprive to deprive someone **of** something they have or want. *The players were deprived of their instruments... She was deprived of sleep for fourteen days.*

derive 1 to derive pleasure or an advantage **from** something. *They derive enormous pleasure from their grandchildren... How was I to derive any sort of living from that one acre?* **2** to derive or be derived **from** a particular source. *Soil derives from many kinds of rock. ...principles derived from religious doctrine.*

descend 1 to descend **on** or **upon** a place or person. *Silence would descend on the meadow. ...schoolgirls descending upon him with teasing cries.* **2** to descend **to** a type of behaviour. *All too soon they will descend to spreading scandal and gossip.*

descended be descended **from** someone. *He was descended from the founder of the Settlement.*

describe to describe someone or something **as** a particular thing. *One Labour M.P. described him as 'the most hated man in Parliament'... She described Mr Black's allegations as being completely untrue.*

design by design. *...events which did not occur by design.*

designate /dɛzɪɡnɪt/ to designate someone or something **as** a

particular thing. *The Prime Minister designated Mahathir as his successor. ...areas designated as 'wilderness'.*

desire desire **for** something. *The desire for home ownership is still strong... You cannot suppress the desire for liberty.*

desist to desist **from** doing something. *...forlorn hopes that they would desist from snowballing each other... The publishers persuaded the author to desist from such references.*

despair to despair **of** doing something; to despair **of** something existing or being successful. *He despaired of ever having the courage to ask her... We would be very unwise to despair of democracy.*

desperate be desperate **for** something. *I was desperate for money at the time... He was my idol—I was desperate for him to win.*

destined 1 be destined **for** a particular experience or thing. *...horses destined for slaughter... He seemed destined for a conventional career in the City.* **2** be destined **for** a particular place. *...a flight destined for Italy.*

detach 1 to detach yourself **from** a situation or a group of people. *Arab Africa had begun to detach itself from external control... She detached herself from the group and wandered over towards me.* **2** to detach one thing **from** another. *...a scheme to detach the western states from the rest of the United States.*

detail details **of** or **about** something. *The bank gave no details of the agreement... Give me a few details about your wife's route to Swaziland.*

detention in detention. *He was in detention awaiting trial.*

deter to deter someone **from** doing something. *That will not deter him from breaking the law again.*

detract

detract to detract **from** something good. *This should not be allowed to detract from their achievement.*

detrimental be detrimental **to** something. *Plantation forestry is also detrimental to wildlife.*

develop to develop **from** one thing **to** or **into** another thing. *She has developed from a youthful, smiling enthusiast to a hardened professional... Some of them developed into very strange creatures indeed.*

development a development **in** a field of activity or a type of thing. *...some exciting new developments in cancer science.*

deviate to deviate **from** a particular method, standard, or idea. *...people who deviate from society's ideas of what is normal... We have never deviated from our belief that abortion is a moral evil.*

devoid be devoid **of** a quality or thing. *His work is totally devoid of merit.*

devolve to devolve or be devolved **to, on,** or **upon** someone. *Considerable powers would be devolved to the regional administrations... The labour of finding food should devolve on the men.*

devote to devote yourself, your time, or your energy **to** something. *They devote themselves to working for social justice. ...those who devote their energies to party politics.*

devoted 1 be devoted **to** someone or something. *Nicola remained devoted to her sister... For the last two years of his life he was devoted to weight-training.* 2 be devoted **to** a particular subject or activity: be used entirely for it. *Reykjavik has a surprising number of museums devoted to a single artist... Much of his personal time is devoted to helping charitable organizations.*

diagnose to diagnose someone's symptoms **as** a particular illness. *They all died from a disease diagnosed as consumption.*

dialect in dialect. *He could recite the Declaration of Independence in dialect... He spoke in Sicilian dialect.*

diameter in diameter. *...bottles 9 inches in diameter.*

dictate /dɪkteɪt/ to dictate **to** someone. *There was no doubt who would be dictating to the generals.*

die 1 to die **of** or **from** a particular disease or illness. *Before he could retire, he died of a heart attack... A man who worked at the nuclear processing plant has died from a rare form of leukaemia.* 2 to die **in** a particular event or accident. *One of her daughters died in the disaster... A leading human rights activist has died in a car crash.* 3 to be dying **for** something. *I'm dying for a cigarette.*

differ to differ **from** something else. *Your position differs from mine in some respects.*

difference 1 a difference **between** two things or people. *She could tell the difference between the snarl of a lion and that of a leopard.* 2 a difference **in** something. *They stood back to back measuring their difference in size.*

different be different **from, to,** or **than** someone or something; a different thing **from, to,** or **than** another thing. *Judy's home was very different from Etta's. ...customs which are different to a Jewish person's customs... The atmosphere was different than our earlier meetings... They clearly had a different perspective from my own.*

differentiate 1 to differentiate **between** two things or people. *...his inability to differentiate between sexual and platonic relationships.* 2 to differentiate one thing or person **from** another. *...the works which differentiate you from your many imitators.*

discriminate

difficult be difficult **for** someone to do something. *It was difficult for me to adjust to the new syllabus... A few precautions can make life difficult for criminals.*

difficulty in difficulty. *He went to the aid of a swimmer in difficulty.*

dilute to dilute one liquid **with** another. *Dilute the milk with water.*

diminution a diminution **of** something or **in** something. *...a diminution of freedom. ...a diminution in contentment.*

dine to dine **on** a particular food. *...dining on a casserole of fresh leeks.*

dip 1 to dip **into** a book or particular subject. *If you want to know more, we suggest you dip into 'The English Legal System' by K.T. Eddey... You only have to dip into Victorian literature to see that this was not the case.* **2** to dip **into** an amount of money. *It is normal for people to dip into their savings from time to time.*

direct 1 to direct someone **to** a place. *The police had directed him to the wrong courtroom.* **2** to direct criticism, anger, threats, and so on **at** someone or **against** someone. *The boos and whistles were directed at the manager, not the team. ...the rising tide of racism directed against immigrants.*

disabuse to disabuse someone **of** an idea or belief. *She longed to disabuse him of this mistake.*

disadvantage 1 be **at a disadvantage:** have a problem that other people do not have. *Once again, the Government has put the less well-off at a disadvantage.* **2 to** the **disadvantage of** someone: giving them problems that other people do not have. *The terms of trade have moved to the disadvantage of the third world.*

disagree 1 to disagree **with** someone **about, on,** or **over** something. *I disagree with them about maintenance... We'll just have to disagree over that... It would be inaccurate to say that they disagree on most issues.* **2** to disagree **with** an action or proposal. *No one would disagree with the first suggestion.*

disagreement a disagreement **with** someone or **between** people. *She dropped out of university after a disagreement with her tutor. ...the public disagreement between Sir Alan and Nigel Lawson is causing embarrassment to the Government.*

disappointed 1 be disappointed **in** someone or **with** someone. *Rudolph had the feeling that she was disappointed in him for not telling her... I'm afraid the children are very disappointed with me.* **2** be disappointed **with** or **at** something. *I know he was disappointed at my reaction.*

disapprove to disapprove **of** something or someone. *Tom disapproved of Sonny's tactics.*

discharge /dɪstʃɑːdʒ/ to discharge someone **from** hospital, prison, or a job. *A few weeks ago I was discharged from the Air Force.*

disconnect to disconnect one thing **from** another. *Disconnect the machine from the electricity supply.*

discontented be discontented **with** something. *She was discontented with the form of Victorian religion.*

discourage to discourage someone **from** doing something. *It is good sense to discourage older people from eating more than they need.*

discourse /dɪskɔːs/ a discourse **on** a particular topic. *They listened politely to his discourse on human relations.*

discrepancy a discrepancy **between** two things. *...the discrepancy between private affluence and public squalor.*

discriminate 1 to discriminate **between** things. *He was unable to* discriminate between colours. **2** to discriminate **against** someone. *Bernstein claimed that teachers discriminate against working-class children.* **3** to discriminate **in favour of** someone. *The landlords tend to discriminate in favour of young childless couples.*

discuss to discuss something **with** someone. *We were willing to discuss the matter with our colleagues.*

discussion under discussion. *...the people who are going to use the items under discussion.*

disdain disdain **for** something or someone. *She was full of disdain for politics.*

disentangle to disentangle one thing **from** another. *He disentangled his head from the netting... Religion cannot be disentangled from Ireland's problems.*

disgrace **1** in disgrace. *His brother had died here in disgrace.* **2** a disgrace **to** a place, profession, or group of people. *...an action condemned as a disgrace to England... These articles can only be described as a disgrace to journalism.*

disguise **1** to disguise something or someone **as** another thing or person. *He disguised himself as a student. ...a laser gun disguised as a pair of binoculars.* **2** in disguise. *I'd come back one day in disguise.*

disgusted be disgusted **with** or **at** someone or something. *I'm absolutely disgusted with Barry; it was a ridiculous idea... Our members are disgusted at this iniquitous situation.*

disillusionment disillusionment **with** something or someone. *...public disillusionment with politics.*

dislike dislike **of** or **for** something or someone. *...a dislike of public expenditure. ...our cat's total dislike for all other cats.*

disloyal be disloyal **to** someone. *We may feel it is disloyal to our parents to recognize how important these other people are.*

dismiss **1** to dismiss someone **from** a place or their job. *He was dismissed from his job in the Press and Publicity Department.* **2** to dismiss something **as** untrue, foolish, or unimportant. *Tim Jones dismissed the policies as 'half-baked and unrealistic'... Her aspirations were dismissed as self-delusion.*

dismount to dismount **from** a horse or a bicycle. *He was dismounting from his horse to greet Luciana.*

disparity a disparity **in** something or **between** two things. *...regional disparities in unemployment. ...the disparity between rich and poor.*

dispense to dispense **with** something. *The job could be done more cheaply by dispensing with safety equipment.*

display on display. *He had all his machines and tools on display.*

displeased be displeased **with** something or **at** something. *She remained obviously displeased with both of us... Philip was not altogether displeased at finding him on the same plane.*

disposal at someone's **disposal**. *...the most intimidating weapons at the state's disposal... He said he remained at Mr Aziz's disposal.*

dispose to dispose **of** something or someone. *Cameron had disposed of some of the gold... Stein will have to be disposed of.*

dispute **1**/dɪspjuːt/ to dispute **with** someone **over** something. *...a neighbour who disputed with them over some land.* **2**/dɪspjuːt/ a dispute **between** people **over** something or **about** something. *The case arises from a dispute between Sir Ian and John Samuels over money... The Committee failed to resolve a dispute about* skyscrapers. **3 in dispute.** *His right to attend is in dispute.*

disqualify 1 to disqualify someone **from** something. *Mr Saunders was disqualified from legal aid... He has been disqualified from sitting in the House of Commons.* **2** to disqualify someone **for** doing something. *He was disqualified for infringing the rules.*

disregard disregard **for** something or **of** something. *...Jefferson's disregard for the constitution... He felt angry at the disregard of his scientific judgement.*

disrespect disrespect **for** something or someone. *He tried to reduce such disrespect for authority among his men.*

dissatisfied be dissatisfied **with** something. *They became dissatisfied with pastries from local bakeries.*

dissent to dissent **from** a proposal or idea. *Our friends would dissent from that description of their labours.*

dissimilar not be dissimilar **from** or **to** something. *His classification is not entirely dissimilar from Goldthorpe's... In appearance, he is not dissimilar to the popular image of Don Quixote.*

dissociate 1 to dissociate yourself **from** someone or something. *They sought to dissociate themselves from the ranchers.* **2** to dissociate one thing **from** another. *Art seemed dissociated from the material conditions of life.*

dissolve 1 to dissolve something **in** a liquid. *...pills which dissolve in water.* **2** to dissolve **into** a particular state. *His relief had dissolved into further anxiety.*

dissuade to dissuade someone **from** doing something. *Intervention might dissuade them from using nuclear weapons.*

distance 1 in the distance or **into the distance.** *He thought he heard new sounds in the distance... He would stare into the distance.*

2 to distance yourself **from** something or someone. *He distanced himself from the Labour Party.*

distaste distaste **for** someone or something. *...his growing distaste for the values of his generation.*

distasteful be distasteful **to** someone. *Any attitude she adopted would have been distasteful to him.*

distinct be distinct **from** something else. *...conventions distinct from the Fine Art tradition.*

distinction a distinction **between** two things. *...the distinction between creative work and servile labour.*

distinguish to distinguish **between** two things; to distinguish one thing **from** another. *...the failure to distinguish between income and capital... Many people found it difficult to distinguish reality from fantasy.*

distract to distract someone **from** something. *Daisy said his presence distracted her from writing.*

distrustful be distrustful **of** someone or something. *It saddened her that he was so distrustful of her.*

diverge to diverge **from** something. *Their views diverge from those of their contemporaries.*

divest to divest someone **of** something. *By doing this they would divest themselves of their status as Christian ministers.*

divide 1 to divide something **into** parts or groups. *...proposals to divide the Nature Conservancy Council into three... The children are divided into three age groups.* **2** to divide something **among** or **between** a group of people. *Diminishing resources will have to be divided among more people... The land was divided between two brothers.*

divided

divided be divided **on** or **over** a particular matter. *Ministers are still divided on whether to go ahead with the plan... Opinions are divided over how many viewers a religious channel would attract.*

divorce to divorce one thing **from** another. *The condition of roads could not be divorced from any other aspect of transport.*

do 1 to do something **about** a problem. *There was nothing he could do about it.* **2** to do away **with** something that you do not want. *Proposals were put forward to do away with air forces and limit military expenditure.* **3** to do **without** something. *It was warm enough to do without a jacket.*

dole on the dole: receiving unemployment benefit from the state. *Most actresses spend more time on the dole than working.*

dominance dominance **over** someone or something. *...man's dominance over his fellow creatures.*

dominion dominion **over** someone or something. *He favoured some sort of dominion over South America.*

donate to donate something **to** a person or organization. *Members were asked to donate their kidneys to the charity after death... Our minibus was donated to us by a local public house.*

doomed be doomed **to** a particular state. *His attempt to achieve this was doomed to failure.*

dose to dose someone **with** a medicine or drug. *Some are reputed to have dosed themselves with pain-killing drugs.*

dote to dote **on** or **upon** someone. *You know how she dotes on you all.*

double to double **as** someone or something. *The living room doubled as an office.*

doubt in doubt. *She may want to ask advice when she is in doubt.*

drain a drain **on** or **upon** someone's energies or resources. *The drain on our resources has already gone too far.*

draped be draped **in** something or **with** something. *I walked out, draped in a blanket... Three sides of the table were draped with Union Jacks.*

draw 1 to draw someone **into** a situation. *He and David had been drawn into a ferocious argument.* **2** to draw **on** or **upon** something that is available for use. *He was able to draw on vast reserves of talent.*

dread a dread **of** something or someone. *...a dread of being alone.*

dream to dream **of** something or **about** something. *I had dreamed of China since childhood... He had once dreamed of being a footballer... When you are young you dream about all sorts of things.*

dress to dress **for** a particular occasion or activity. *...Englishmen who dressed for dinner in the jungle.*

dressed be dressed **in** particular clothes. *I was dressed in slacks and a jersey.*

drill 1 to drill **for** oil or water. *Nor will it be long before we drill for oil on ocean floors.* **2** to drill something **into** someone. *...the training rules that had been drilled into him.*

drink to drink **to** someone or something. *He took a bottle with him to drink to the health of his hosts.*

drive to drive someone **to** or **into** a particular state. *These disasters drove men to desperation... Filling in the form only drove his mind into further confusion.*

drool to drool **over** or **at** someone or something you find attractive. *You were drooling over that idiotic woman.*

drop 1 to drop in **on** someone. *You must drop in on me sometime.* **2** to drop out **of** an institution, agreement, or competition. *Jenny asked me if I would like to drop out of law school. ...the virus that forced him to drop out of the Commonwealth Games.*

drum to drum ideas, knowledge, or behaviour **into** someone. *I have had the fine art of tidiness drummed into me... This knowledge had been drummed into her.*

due 1 be due **to** a particular cause. *Death was due to natural causes.* **2** be due **for** something. *I reckon we're due for a rest.*

duplicate /djuːplɪkət/ **in duplicate.** *...a form which I had to read and sign in duplicate.*

duress under duress: while affected by force or threats. *The statement appeared to have been made under duress.*

duty 1 on duty: working at your job. *She had to be on duty at the hospital.* **2 off duty:** not working at your job. *You can go off duty now.*

dwell to dwell **on** or **upon** a fact or memory. *He had dwelt on the new experiences of the day.*

E

eager be eager **for** something. *He will be eager for advice and information.*

earmark to earmark something **for** a particular purpose. *...the money earmarked for supplies.*

earth on earth. *...the coldest place on earth.*

ease 1 at ease; at ease with someone. *She began to feel more at ease... You will soon feel at ease with your fellow students.* **2 for ease of** something. *For ease of riding, they wore a coat that was cut away in front.*

east east **of** a place. *It is being constructed on a site a few miles east of Liverpool.*

easy 1 not be easy **about** something. *I have never been able to feel easy about being in debt, even temporarily.* **2** be easy **for** someone to do something. *It will not be easy for any newcomer to stay the course.* **3** to go easy **on** something. *For those who want to lose weight, it is best to go easy on the rice and bread.*

eat to eat **into** a substance or resource. *Copper or iron pans are not suitable as vinegar eats into them.*

eavesdrop to eavesdrop **on** someone. *I don't like eavesdropping on people talking on the phone.*

economize to economize **on** something you use or buy. *They had to economize on staff.*

edge 1 an edge **to** someone's voice. *There was a definite sharp edge to his melodious voice.* **2** an edge **over** someone. *He was the eldest, which gave him an edge over the other boys.* **3** be **on edge:** be nervous. *She'd been on edge and had tried not to show it.*

edged be edged **with** something. *...a path edged with round, white stones.*

effect 1 the effect **of** something **on** the thing or person affected. *...the withering effect of welfare on the morale of those receiving it.* **2 in effect:** almost, but not exactly. *Each of the frog's feet is, in effect, a small parachute.* **3 to this effect; to that effect:** with this or that meaning. *I was about to say something to this effect.* **4 for effect:** in order to create a particular impression. *I've never cried, except for effect, since I was twelve.*

elaborate /ilæbərɪt/ to elaborate **on** what you have said. *She would not elaborate on her earlier pronouncements.*

elect

elect to elect someone **as** something or **to** a particular group. *In 1956 he was elected as Senator for the Armed Forces... I was elected to the Assembly.*

elevate to elevate something **to** or **into** something more important. *Fourteen of the colleges were elevated to the status of State Universities. ...where dancing becomes elevated into an art form.*

elicit to elicit a response or a piece of information **from** someone. *They gave up trying to elicit some response from him... Cameron elicited from her the fact that Cal was still sleeping.*

eligible be eligible **for** something. *Students with dependants may be eligible for an extra allowance.*

eliminate to eliminate something undesirable **from** something. *...the desire to eliminate risk from human life.*

emanate to emanate **from** a place, thing, or person. *...as if she could feel the holiness that emanated from them.*

embargo an embargo **on** trade. *...the long-standing US embargo on trade with Cuba.*

embark to embark **on** or **upon** a new project or course of action. *...if you are embarking on a long period of training.*

embarrassed be embarrassed **by** something, **about** something, or **at** something. *I felt embarrassed by all this helpfulness... He seemed terribly embarrassed about what had just been said to us... The two officers seemed embarrassed at such candour.*

embarrassment
1 embarrassment **at** something. *...their embarrassment at walking in on me.* 2 an embarrassment **to** someone. *The prisoners had become an embarrassment to the authorities.*

embedded be embedded **in** something. *...a detailed model embedded in a block of plastic.*

embellished be embellished **with** things. *...simple clothes embellished with hand embroidery.*

emblazoned 1 be emblazoned **with** a design. *...a casket emblazoned with the de Charny crest.* 2 be emblazoned **on** an object. *...a backdrop on which was emblazoned the imperial double-headed eagle.*

emblem an emblem **of** a person or thing. *...a ruler's staff, an emblem of kingship.*

embodiment the embodiment **of** a quality. *She was the embodiment of loyalty.*

embroidered 1 be embroidered **on** cloth. *...black slippers with little flowers embroidered on them.* 2 be embroidered **with** a design. *...Oriental silks embroidered with designs of bamboo and dragons.*

embroil to embroil someone **in** an argument or scandal, or **with** a person or group. *The episode embroiled Benn in a major political storm... He had no intention of becoming any further embroiled with Bill Potter.*

emerge 1 to emerge **from** or **out of** a place, situation, or experience. *...when the two inspectors emerged from the flat. ...the new nations which emerged out of the disintegration of Austria-Hungary.* 2 to emerge **from** an investigation. *One general problem emerged from our discussions.*

emigrate to emigrate **from** the country you leave **to** another country. *...a young man who had emigrated from Germany in the early 1920s... He emigrated to Canada.*

empathize to empathize **with** someone. *...so that they may empathize with the less fortunate.*

emphasis emphasis **on** something. *...our culture's heavy emphasis on the need for beauty in women.*

employ to employ someone or something **as** something. ...*the factory where he was employed as an assistant to a senior salesman... Sexual actions are employed as threatening devices in a large number of species.*

empty be empty **of** something. *The street was empty of cars.*

enamoured be enamoured **of** someone or something. *I was always enamoured of the theatre.*

encased be encased **in** something. *From childhood, our feet are encased in shoes.*

enclose 1 to enclose something **in** or **with** a letter or document sent by post. *The cheque was enclosed in a letter. ...return envelopes enclosed with charity appeals.* 2 to be enclosed **in** something or **by** something. *His nose was enclosed in the mask. ...a tennis court enclosed by wire fencing.*

encounter 1 someone's encounter **with** another person; an encounter **between** two people. *My own encounters with the woman confirmed everything I had heard about her. ...any encounter between the heroine and the man she loved.* 2 someone's encounter **with** something. *It was my first encounter with pure terror.*

encroach to encroach **on** or **upon** something. *A small housing estate had encroached on the slopes.*

encrusted be encrusted **with** something. *The knocker is encrusted with paint.*

encumber to encumber someone **with** things that cause them difficulties. *...passengers encumbered with suitcases.*

end 1 the end **of** a period of time, situation, activity, or object. *...by the end of that year. ...at the far end of the room.* 2 an end **to** a situation: the stopping of it. *An end to civil service secrecy will only come about through intense pressure.* 3 to end **with** particular words. *The letter ended with a curious request.* 4 to end **with** or **in** a particular part, thing, or event. *The meal normally ended with dessert. ...long straight streets, each ending in a piazza.* 5 be **at an end**: be finished. *The romantic years were now at an end.* 6 **in the end**: finally. *He had, in the end, become genuinely fond of her.* 7 **on end**: continuously. *It is designed to fly at well over 65,000ft for days on end.*

endear to endear someone **to** someone else. *It's not an approach that endears him to critics.*

endemic be endemic **in** a place or society. *...the pollution that is now endemic in the Mediterranean.*

endow to endow someone or something **with** a quality or thing. *Sickness endows the mind with a new perceptiveness.*

enemy an enemy **of** a person, group, or thing. *...enemies of the state.*

enfold to enfold someone **in** your arms. *Ginny enfolded him in her arms and rubbed his head.*

engage to engage **in** an activity. *You may not engage in conversation with them.*

engaged 1 be engaged **in, on,** or **upon** an activity or task; be engaged **with** something or someone. *Paul was engaged in a chess game... I shall be engaged on church business on Sunday evening... Mr Smith was engaged with a client.* 2 be engaged **to** someone. *She told us all she was engaged to him.*

engraved 1 be engraved **on** an object. *The date is engraved on the base.* 2 be engraved **with** a design. *...a stone engraved with strange figures.*

engrossed be engrossed **in** something or **with** something. *He was completely engrossed in his book... He was far too engrossed with his task to bother about us.*

engulfed be engulfed **by** something or **in** something.

enlarge

Miraculously, they had not been engulfed by the avalanche... The raging ocean that covered everything was engulfed in total darkness.

enlarge to enlarge **on** or **upon** a subject. *I went on to enlarge on the difficulties of naming a cat.*

enlist to enlist **in** the army, navy, or air force. *Jamie had enlisted in the army at Georgetown.*

enmeshed be enmeshed **in** something. *...at a time when India was enmeshed in turmoil.*

entailed be entailed **in** an action or activity. *...despite the difficulties entailed in establishing what people eat.*

entangled be entangled **in** or **with** something. *Parker had risked becoming entangled in the investigation... Our limbs got entangled with each other.*

enter 1 to enter **into** negotiations or an agreement. *The TUC were not prepared to enter into discussions.* 2 to enter **into** something: be a factor in something. *All sorts of emotional factors enter into the relationship.* 3 to enter someone or something **for** or **in** a race or competition. *I entered her for the race myself... Also entered in this race is Gold Ace.* 4 to enter something **in** a written record. *The grades were entered in a book.*

enthuse to enthuse **over** something or **about** something. *There is plenty to enthuse over. ...as they enthused about the success of their latest campaign.*

enthusiasm enthusiasm **for** something. *...her enthusiasm for new experiences.*

enthusiastic be enthusiastic **about** something. *My parents were not altogether enthusiastic about the theatre as a profession.*

entitle to entitle someone **to** something. *You are entitled to this money, so why not claim it?*

entrance 1 the entrance **to** or **of** a building or place. *...in front of the main entrance to the building. ...the entrance of the cave.* 2 entrance **to** an institution. *There is no examination for entrance to secondary schools.*

entrust 1 to entrust something **to** someone. *I was entrusting my life to them.* 2 to entrust someone **with** something. *At first he will only be entrusted with minor jobs.*

entry 1 the entry **to** a place. *...the entry to the tunnel.* 2 entry **into** or **to** a group or area of activity. *...the qualifications needed for entry into elite occupations... 'A' levels are the basic qualification for entry to higher education.* 3 an entry **in** a written record **for** a particular date. *...the entry in his diary. ...my diary entry for Sunday, 25 May.*

entwine to entwine something **with** or **in** something else. *She entwined her arm with his... One second later, her fingers were entwined in my own.*

envelop to envelop someone or something **in** something. *Our heads were enveloped in smoke.*

envious be envious **of** someone or **of** something they have. *They may be envious of your success.*

epitome the epitome **of** a quality or type of thing. *His wealth of knowledge made him seem the epitome of a philosopher.*

equal 1 be equal **to** something: be the same as something. *His influence is at least equal to that of any politician.* 2 be equal **to** a task. *...as soon as they feel equal to the challenge.*

equality equality **of** something or **in** something; the equality **of** one group **with** another. *...equality of opportunity. ...equality in pay rates. ...the political, social, and economic equality of women with men.*

equate to equate one thing **with** another. *War should on no account be equated with glory.*

equip to equip someone or something **with** useful things or **for** a task or activity. *...huge bulldozers equipped with special blades... We're not equipped for winter travel.*

equivalent 1 the equivalent **of** something. *They would be expected to spend the equivalent of a month's wages on their costumes.* 2 be equivalent **to** something. *The poor had to borrow from the rich, at rates equivalent to 250 per cent a year.*

escape 1 to escape **from** someone or something unpleasant. *She had escaped from two unfortunate marriages.* 2 to escape **from** a place **to** a safer or better place. *Two of the sentenced men escaped from prison... I escaped to a quiet spot under a hedge.*

essence in essence: used when mentioning the basic nature of something. *This was in essence the theory that Lipset and Bendix had advanced to account for their findings.*

essential 1 be essential **to** or **for** the occurrence of something. *The outboard motor was essential for our escape... Calcium is essential to health.* 2 be essential **to** someone or something. *Feathers are essential to a bird.*

establish 1 to establish contact **with** someone or something, or a relationship **between** two people or things. *...the proposal to establish contact with pressure groups. ...the relationship established between the psychiatrist and the patient.* 2 to establish yourself or something **as** something. *It helps him to establish himself as one of the gang.*

estimate /ɛstɪmeɪt/1 to estimate something **at** a particular amount. *The fire caused damage estimated at more than half a million pounds.* 2 /ɛstɪmət/ an estimate **for** the cost of something. *...the enormous estimate for repairing the Mercedes.*

estranged be estranged **from** someone. *He knows I am estranged from my father.*

evict to evict someone **from** a building. *...attempts to evict families from their homes.*

evidence evidence **of** or **about** something. *It was visible evidence of his wealth... Until recently there has been very little evidence about how the brain functions.*

evolve to evolve **into** something new; to evolve **from** one thing **to** another. *Early horses evolved into the forms we know today... The French revolution evolved from the protest of a few lawyers to a popular movement.*

exact to exact something **from** someone. *...his reluctance to exact from the Germans a forfeit they could not pay.*

example for example. *On this farm, for example, we've got very light soil.*

excel to excel **at** or **in** an activity. *He does not excel at games... Athletes devote their lives to excelling in some single sport.*

exception 1 an exception **to** a rule or tendency. *Royal visitors were the one exception to the tendency of the great to travel with fewer people.* 2 **with the exception of** something. *With the exception of Gower, none of the batsmen scored more than 20.*

excerpt an excerpt **from** a piece of writing or music. *...an excerpt from a letter to her mother.*

exchange 1 to exchange one thing **for** another. *...coupons which can be collected and exchanged for goods.* 2 to exchange things of a particular kind **with** someone. *I exchanged letters with these people.* 3 **in exchange for** something. *...the boy who had given him a marble in exchange for a biscuit.*

exclaim

exclaim to exclaim **over** something or **at** something. *They had exclaimed over my volume of Vermeer prints... The guests exclaimed at how well he looked.*

excluded be excluded **from** a place or activity. *I disliked being excluded from foreign policy discussions.*

exclusive 1 be exclusive **to** a particular company or place. *You could try and get some special stuff made, exclusive to us.* 2 be exclusive **of** a particular amount or group. *The Astors had thirty servants in the 1930s, exclusive of three daily cleaners.*

excursion 1 an excursion **to** a place. *...an excursion to the Greek temples at Paestum.* 2 an excursion **into** a new field of activity. *...a relatively rare excursion into contemporary music.*

excuse 1/ɪkskjuːs/ an excuse **for** something. *I was trying to think up an excuse for leaving him.* 2/ɪkskjuːz/ to excuse someone **for** doing something wrong or rude. *Excuse me for interrupting, Professor.* 3 to excuse someone **from** taking part in an activity. *He is to be excused from duty for one year.*

exempt 1 be exempt **from** tax or a duty. *Harold was exempt from military service.* 2 to exempt someone **from** a tax, duty, or obligation. *This system exempted those on low incomes from paying tax.*

exercise 1 an exercise **in** doing something. *This problem was put to me as an exercise in logic.* 2 the exercise **of** power, responsibility, or judgement. *The exercise of judgment is a higher function than the ability to count and calculate.*

exit an exit **from** a place. *...the north exit from the gardens.*

exonerate to exonerate someone **from** blame. *We've promised Captain Imrie a statement exonerating him from all blame.*

expand to expand **on** or **upon** what you have said. *Marx does not expand on the social processes lying behind this situation.*

expel to expel someone **from** a place or organization. *Grigorenco was deprived of his pension and expelled from the party by his local committee.*

experiment 1 to experiment **with** or **on** animals or things. *Professor Skinner is still experimenting with pigeons... I started experimenting on Jonathan's machines and realized I had hit on something unique.* 2 to experiment **with** something new. *We are already experimenting with these strategies.* 3 an experiment **with** or **on** animals or things. *...the results of his experiments with plants. ...her experiments on what diets babies choose.* 4 an experiment **in** a particular kind of activity. *...an experiment in industrial organization.*

expert 1 an expert **on** or **in** a subject; an expert **in** doing something. *...an expert on constitutional law... Professor Hick is an expert in oriental religions... David was an expert in judo and karate.* 2 be expert **at** doing something. *They have to be expert at dealing with any problems that arise.*

explain to explain something **to** someone. *I explained my predicament to the air hostess.*

explanation 1 an explanation **for** or **of** an event or situation. *The most obvious explanation for my lack of success was that I was a bad writer. ...to obtain from Perris an explanation of his extraordinary behaviour.* 2 an explanation **of** something: a detailed description. *The secretary-general proceeded with* an explanation of the WPA's legal position.

exponent an exponent **of** an idea or activity. *Janet Roberts is an exponent of the 'social work' approach.*

export 1/ɪkspɔːt/ to export goods **from** one country **to** another. *Thousands of sheep are being illegally exported from Britain to Europe.* 2/ɛkspɔːt/ the export **of** goods **to** another country. *India earned 4.3 million pounds from the export of frogs' legs to the West in 1976-7.*

expose 1 to expose a person or thing **to** something. *...after a child has already been exposed to the disease.* 2 to expose someone or something as deceitful. *Soon I will be exposed as a fraud.*

expressive be expressive **of** something. *The work seems expressive of pride, power, and sorrowful pessimism.*

extend 1 to extend **to** something. *His radicalism did not extend to the field of economics.* 2 to extend something **to** someone. *He extended his hand to Ellen... I write to extend a welcome to you.*

extent to a particular **extent**. *To a certain extent, dying of a heart attack is related to prosperity and good living.*

extort to extort money or something else **from** someone. *His mother attempted, on several occasions, to extort money from him.*

extract 1/ɪkstrækt/ to extract something **from** a place, person, or thing. *...when you have extracted the juice from the pulp... I'd only used the threat to extract information from him.* 2/ɛkstrækt/ an extract **from** a book, tape, etc. *...in this extract from his diary.*

extrapolate to extrapolate **from** information that you have. *It attempts to extrapolate from established data.*

extreme 1 an extreme **of** circumstance or behaviour. *The root of Ecuador's extremes of poverty and wealth is in land tenure.* 2 **in the extreme.** *Her manner was friendly and welcoming in the extreme.*

extricate to extricate someone **from** a situation or place. *...the effort of extricating myself from those miniature ravines.*

eye an eye **for** something of a particular kind. *You've got an excellent eye for detail.*

F

face to face up **to** a problem or difficult situation. *This will not help offenders face up to their crimes.*

faced be faced **with** a problem or difficulty. *We were then faced with a terrible dilemma.*

fact in fact. *In fact, there is a problem of over-crowded prisons everywhere.*

faculty a faculty **for** doing something. *...people who develop the faculty for looking at things in different ways.*

fail 1 to fail **in** an attempt or area of activity. *She failed in her attempt to swim to France.* 2 **without fail.** *Every afternoon, he would without fail take a nap.*

fair 1 be fair **to** someone or **on** someone. *The situation is just not fair on the children or their parents.* 2 be fair **to** another person. *He always was fair to everybody around him.*

faith faith **in** something or someone. *I've got faith in human nature.*

faithful be faithful **to** someone or something. *They wish to remain faithful to their heritage.*

fall 1 a fall **in** an amount or level. *...a 3 per cent fall in industrial* output. **2** to fall **from** one level or amount **to** another. *He fell from third place to twentieth in the rankings.* **3** to fall **for** someone or something attractive. *Richard fell for her the moment he set eyes on her.* **4** to fall **for** a lie or trick. *Unaware of these tactics, Mr Khan fell for every trap.* **5** to fall **into** an unwanted state. *Their ideas had simply fallen into disuse.* **6** to fall **to** someone: to be their task or duty. *The task of informing Phil Cavilleri fell to me.* **7** to fall back **on** a resource or method. *They may fall back on a variant of the original proposals... This time there was no reserve to fall back on.* **8** to fall behind **with** something that you are doing. *Unfortunately, we have fallen behind with the payments.* **9** to fall in **with** a proposal: to agree with it. *I didn't know whether to fall in with this arrangement.* **10** to fall in **with** a person or group of people: become friendly with them. *Phil fell in with a perky survivor called Ros and started begging.* **11** to fall out **with** a friend or colleague. *I've fallen out with certain members of the band.*

falling-off a falling-off **of** something or **in** something. *There was a definite falling-off of active interest... A falling-off in business was expected.*

familiar 1 be familiar **to** someone: a familiar thing **to** someone. *His name was familiar to me... This is not, or not yet, a familiar term to most voters.* **2** be familiar **with** something. *I am, of course, familiar with your work.*

familiarize to familiarize someone **with** something. *He had to familiarize himself with the ship... In her early puzzles, she wanted to familiarize readers with the idea of a crossword.*

famous be famous **for** something. *The church is famous for the tomb of William Hogarth... The council*

is famous for spending the most amount of money on education.

fan a fan **of** something or someone. *...fans of Elvis Presley.*

fantasize to fantasize **about** something. *She does not dare to fantasize about her novel being widely acclaimed.*

far not far **from** a place. *...a villa not far from Hotel Miranda.*

fascinated be fascinated **by** something or **with** something. *I'm fascinated by the whole world of politics... Babies may become fascinated with one thing for several weeks.*

fashion 1 be in **fashion:** be popular. *Such ideas were now no longer in fashion.* **2** be **out of fashion:** be no longer popular. *Hats are out of fashion.*

fasten to fasten **on** or **upon** something or fasten on **to** something. *A vicious serpent leapt upon him and fastened on his arm... The kids fastened on to their families like iron filings to a magnet.*

fault at fault. *It was 1976, I believe, if my memory is not at fault.*

favour 1 in favour; in favour of something: supporting or helping something. *A national opinion poll in the Daily Mail showed 78% to be in favour... He was in favour of modernising the trade unions.* **2** in someone's **favour:** to their advantage. *The computer seems to be programmed so that the error is always in the bank's favour. ...a series of court decisions in his favour.* **3** in favour of another thing: because that thing is preferred. *He had long ago discarded a horse and cart in favour of a motor truck.* **4** be **out of favour:** be no longer popular. *Their views are very much out of favour now.* **5** a favour **to** someone. *He had persuaded her, as a personal favour to himself, to move her bank account.*

favourable be favourable **to** something. *Most people were favourable to the idea. ...an atmosphere favourable to expansion.*

fear 1 to fear **for** someone or something that you do not want harmed. *Local people fear for her safety... He feared for his brother after hearing about the escape attempt.* **2** someone's fear **of** a frightening thing or person. *She was brought up with no fear of animals.* **3** fear **for** someone or something you care about. *...trembling with fear for the children... They left Beirut because of fears for their safety.* **4 in fear of** experiencing something bad: thinking you might experience it. *Raymond now lived in fear of dismissal.* **5 for fear of** doing something: because you do not wish to do it. *They did not mention it for fear of offending him.*

fearful be fearful **of** something. *...parents who are fearful of letting their feelings take over... The survey showed that women were particularly fearful of crime.*

feast to feast **on** or **off** food of some kind. *Flies feast on rotting flesh. ...feasting off cold roast duck.*

feature 1 a feature **of** something. *Continuous rapid economic growth was never a permanent feature of the system.* **2** a feature **on** a particular topic. *The local newspaper recently ran a feature on drug abuse.* **3** to feature **in** an event or thing. *One athlete who could have been expected to feature in several events was Daley Thompson... This picture features in a show of fine paintings at the Scottish National Portrait Gallery.*

fed up 1 be fed up **with** something or someone. *I'm fed up with people talking to me as if I was an idiot... We met all sorts of people who got fed up with boarding school.* **2** be fed up **of** doing something: used in informal speech. *I'm fed up of waiting for you.*

feed 1 to feed an animal **on** or **with** food of some kind. *I told her to feed the cat on bread and milk... They used to feed it with warmed goat's milk.* **2** to feed food of some kind **to** an animal. *...the root vegetables we feed to cattle.* **3** to feed **on** or **off** food of some kind. *Foxes feed on rodents, beetles, and berries. ...tiny snails which feed off the surface film of algae.* **4** to feed something **into** a machine or appliance. *Vents in the door feed air into the radiators... This new data is fed into the computer.*

feel 1 to feel **like** a type of person: to have the same feelings as that type of person. *I felt like a murderer.* **2** to feel **like** a thing of a particular kind: to seem to be a thing of a particular kind. *It feels like winter.* **3** to feel **like** something or **like** doing something: to want something or want to do something. *I feel like a stroll... I wondered if you felt like coming out for a drink.* **4** to feel in a particular way **about** something. *We feel very positive about the future... They might not be sure of how they feel about this war.* **5** to feel something **for** someone. *I felt desperately sorry for myself. ...the love he felt for his father at this moment.* **6** to feel **for** something you want to find. *His left hand felt for the button under the arm of the chair.* **7** to feel **for** someone in misfortune. *I felt for Byron, but it could have been worse.* **8** a feel **for** something: an instinctive understanding of it. *...his shrewd, intuitive feel for the newspaper business.*

feeling 1 your feelings **for** someone you like. *My feelings for him had grown deeper.* **2** your feelings **about** something. *...negative feelings about computers.* **3** a feeling **for** something: appreciation or understanding. *You have to have some feeling for the quality of the work.*

ferry by ferry. *They crossed the river by ferry.*

festooned be festooned **with** things. *The houses are festooned with posters.*

fetch to fetch something **for** someone. *'Bet, fetch a shawl for your stepmother.'*

feud 1 a feud **between** two people or groups or **with** another person or group. *...the lasting feud between the two families... His father became involved in a feud with another villager.* 2 to feud **with** someone. *He feuded with the formidable Ernest Bevin.*

fiddle to fiddle **with** something or fiddle about **with** something. *Delaney fiddled with the curtain cord. ...fiddling about with a light.*

fidelity fidelity **to** something or someone. *...fidelity to the cause. ...Vita's fidelity to Harold.*

fidget to fidget **with** something. *Mother stood in front of the mirror, fidgeting with her new hat.*

fight 1 to fight **for** something you want to get or achieve or **against** something you want to stop. *Trade unionists have fought for effective laws... You can't fight against progress.* 2 to fight **with** or **against** an enemy or **with** people on your side. *He was always fighting with his brother. ...bandits fighting against each other... He had fought with the 15th Punjab Regiment in Burma.* 3 to fight **about** or **over** something. *They fought about money. ...robbers who start fighting over the profits.* 4 a fight **against** something bad or **for** something desirable. *...the fight against pollution. ...her fight for freedom.* 5 a fight **with** someone or **against** someone; a fight **between** people. *Eight soldiers have been injured in a fist fight with local people... The referee stopped his fight against Watson in the fifth*

round... *There would be fights sometimes between the workers.*

figment a figment **of** someone's imagination. *I thought this man Broum was another figment of your over-active imagination.*

figure 1 to figure **in** something. *Loneliness figures quite a lot in his conversation... None of the accused figured in the report.* 2 to figure **as** a particular thing. *...the many debates in which he figured as a Minister of the House of Commons. ...a photograph which figured as part of the evidence.*

file 1 to file **for** divorce or bankruptcy. *I instructed my solicitor to file for divorce.* 2 **on file.** *We have half a dozen reports already on file.*

fill 1 to fill a container or place **with** something or fill it up **with** something. *She filled the bottle with water... He filled the car up with petrol.* 2 to fill someone **with** a feeling. *This thought filled her with dismay.* 3 to fill in **for** someone. *...to see friends about filling in for him on sentry duty.* 4 to fill someone in **on** something. *'Kleiber's security company' said Stuart. 'Fill me in on that'.*

filled be filled **with** something. *The house was filled with all kinds of books... He was filled with apprehension.*

find 1 to find something **for** someone. *The next step was to find a new job for the cleaner.* 2 to find pleasure or consolation **in** something. *We may find purpose and healing in the love of God.* 3 to find **for** or **in favour of** one of the people in a court case. *The judge had found for the husband... If the court finds in favour of his appeal, Senna may retain his title.* 4 to find **against** one of the people in a court case. *The European Court of Justice may find against the United Kingdom on these issues.*

finish 1 to finish **with** something or **by** doing something. *The day*

flip

had finished with a quarrel... I
finished by describing Jeremy in
some detail. **2** to finish **with**
someone or something: to stop
dealing with them or being
interested in them. *Come and have
a gossip after M's finished with
you... They've both just finished
with their girlfriends.*
finished be finished **with**
something. *He was almost finished
with the puzzle when the phone
rang.*
fire 1 on fire: burning. *His clothes
were on fire.* **2 under fire**: being
attacked. *The radio headquarters
was under fire from interior
ministry troops... This unfair
system has come under fire from
critics.* **3** to fire bullets or
questions **at** someone. *He saw
Germans and Americans firing at
each other in the square.
...suddenly firing at him strings of
words to spell.*
first at first. *At first she was
nervous.*
fish to fish **for** something you are
trying to catch, find, or obtain.
*...the river in which I used to fish
for salmon... Morph fished for the
key to the back door... He was
happy to see her fishing for
compliments.*
fit 1 be fit **for** a person, thing, or
purpose. *...palaces fit for
noblemen... This meat is not fit for
human consumption. ...subjects fit
for serious painting.* **2** to fit **into** a
space or group. *All my clothes fit
into one suitcase. ...odd things that
don't fit into any category.* **3** to fit
a part **to** an object; to fit an object
with a part. *13-amp fuses should
not be fitted to low-powered
appliances... The dinghies had
been fitted with searchlights.* **4** to
fit in **with** an arrangement,
system, method, or idea. *This
would fit in with his theories about
civilisation... They have claimed
that the new tests will fit in with
normal teaching.* **5** a fit **of**

laughter, rage, etc. *He had broken
the door down in a fit of jealousy.*
fitted be fitted **to** or **for** an
environment or task. *He is exactly
fitted to the society that made
him... She is confident that the
laboratory is fitted for the
investigation.*
fix 1 to fix your eyes or thoughts **on**
or **upon** someone or something.
*His eyes were fixed on her... His
attention now appears fixed on the
German question.* **2** to fix **on**
something: to choose it. *We seem
to have fixed on the same day for
supermarket shopping.* **3** to fix
someone up **with** something. *I told
him that I didn't know anyone who
could fix him up with a job as a
taxi-driver.*
flair a flair **for** something.
*...someone who has a flair for
selling a product.*
flames in flames. *Their home was
in flames.*
flanked be flanked **by** or **with**
people or things. *She was
marching along flanked by two
Danish girls. ...green meadows
flanked with towering cypress
trees.*
flash 1 to flash a look or smile **at**
someone. *Maurice flashed a smile
at Ralph.* **2** to flash back **to**
something. *Soshnick's mind
flashed back to the notorious
lipstick murders.*
flaw a flaw **in** something. *...this
obvious flaw in their theory.*
flecked be flecked **with** marks or
things. *Its stem is tall and white,
flecked with brown scales.*
flick to flick **through** a magazine, a
book, or documents. *When he
returned to his office, he flicked
through the mail.*
flinch to flinch **from** something. *Ms
Amiel flinches from the idea of
trials. ...men who would not flinch
from assassinating a president.*
flip to flip **through** a book or
magazine. *...an abandoned*

magazine I flipped through on a train.

flirt 1 to flirt **with** someone. *She saw him flirting with Carol Swanson.* 2 to flirt **with** an idea or something new. *Vice-chancellors flirted with the idea of private fees last year.*

flock to flock **to** a place or event. *Thousands flocked to the slopes of Glencoe and Aviemore.*

flood 1 to flood **into** a place. *...the refugees flooding into Malawi.* 2 to flood a place **with** things. *...to prevent their home markets being flooded with imports.*

flow to flow **from** something. *...the benefits which might flow from my death.*

flower be in **flower.** *At the foot of the trees, the primroses were in flower.*

fluctuation a fluctuation **in** something or **of** something. *...high winds and fluctuations in temperature. ...my mother's wild fluctuations of affection and selfishness.*

fluent be fluent **in** a language. *He was fluent in French.*

flush be flush **with** a surface. *...a slab almost flush with the ground.*

flushed be flushed **with** an emotion or **with** success. *Carlo leaned back, his face flushed with gratification... Mrs Bradley resumed her seat, flushed with success.*

fly 1 to fly **at** someone: to attack them. *She flew at me and slapped me across the face.* 2 to fly **into** a rage or panic. *Ramiro flew into a temper.*

fob to fob someone off **with** something unsatisfactory. *He may try to fob you off with a prescription for pills.*

focus 1 to focus something such as your eyes, your attention, or a camera **on** someone or something. *I propose to focus attention on one resource—fuel... Watson focused his binoculars on the treetops...*

The zoo management intends to focus on education and conservation. 2 the focus **of** attention. *He expected to be the evening's chief focus of attention... By the spring of 1973, the focus of debate had shifted.* 3 a focus **on** something. *...shifting from a concern with the present to a focus on the future.* 4 be **in focus:** be clear or focused. *All he had to do was to keep his mind and his eyes in focus.* 5 be **out of focus:** be blurred or not focused. *...as a result of being photographed out of focus.*

foil a foil **for** something or **to** something. *...a young orator who is a foil for Socrates in this dialogue... Cranberries are a good foil to fat meat.*

foist to foist something unwelcome **on** or **upon** someone. *Goodness knows what type of manager they might foist on us.*

follow 1 to follow one thing or action **with** another. *To follow one crop of wheat with another and another is inviting trouble... She followed her education with a stint at a Swiss finishing school.* 2 to follow **from** a fact. *It follows from all this that many bureaux are resistant to change.*

fond be fond **of** someone or something. *Angela was very fond of her parents... Mr Kinnock is fond of quoting the Italian communist Antonio Gramsci.*

fool to fool around **with** something. *Nino Valenti was sitting at the piano fooling around with the keys.*

foot 1 on **foot:** walking. *I preferred to enter on foot.* 2 **on** your **feet:** standing. *He's been on his feet all day.* 3 **to** your **feet:** into a standing position. *I tried to get to my feet but could not.*

footing on a particular **footing; on** a particular **footing with** someone. *This puts agriculture on a very precarious footing indeed... The school's constitution puts* parents on an equal footing with staff.

forage to forage **for** food or other things. *Squirrels are foraging everywhere for sustenance.*

foray a foray **into** a field of activity. *...in the forty years since his first foray into journalism.*

force 1 to force something unwelcome **on** or **upon** someone. *Their frequent returns to Scheidegg were forced on them by bad weather.* 2 to force someone **into** doing something or **into** a difficult or unpleasant situation. *Mr Hansen was forced into resigning over the affair... The drive for competition has forced thousands of workers into the job queues.* 3 **in force:** existing and valid. *Demonstrations are barred under the emergency regulations still in force.* 4 **in force:** in large numbers. *One of the guards said that they intended to return in force to carry out the order.*

forefront in the forefront of something; at the forefront of something. *American television is in the forefront of telecommunications technology... Some employers were at the forefront of campaigns to extend safety legislation.*

foreign be foreign **to** someone. *The crime had an ingenuity and subtlety foreign to an Englishman... Everything about his life was foreign to her.*

forerunner the forerunner **of** something. *...working class organizations that are the forerunners of workers' councils.*

foretaste a foretaste **of** something in the future. *These pictures were a foretaste of the coming age of space exploration.*

forget to forget **about** something. *The Count had momentarily forgotten about the letter.*

forgetful be forgetful **of** something. *Howard, forgetful of*

the time, was still working away in the library.

forgive to forgive someone **for** doing something. *Forgive me for using these pompous words.*

form 1 a form **of** something. *Stick-fighting was more an art than a form of combat.* 2 **in the form of** something. *...exercise in the form of walks or swimming.*

forward to forward a document **to** someone. *Regional officials forwarded the results to head office.*

founded be founded **on** or **upon** a basis or fact. *...a novel which is doubtless founded on a mass of historical data.*

framed be framed **in** something or **by** something. *Matron was framed in the doorway. ...pictures of mountains framed by trees.*

frank be frank **with** someone **about** something. *Now, Hugh, I want you to be perfectly frank with me... He's quite frank about everything else.*

fraternize to fraternize **with** someone. *...when they saw me fraternizing with the 'lower class'.*

fraught be fraught **with** a quality or **with** things. *This way of life is fraught with danger... These proposals are fraught with explosive social consequences.*

free 1 be free **of** or **from** something unpleasant or unwanted. *They seemed free of racial prejudice. ...ensuring that they are free from harmful bacteria.* 2 be free **with** advice, money, etc. *She is not known for being free with her money... They are pretty free with their comments.* 3 to free someone or something **from** something or **of** something. *...to free the world from hate and misery... He had freed her of the responsibility of feeling guilty.*

freedom 1 freedom **from** something unpleasant or unwanted. *...freedom from hunger.*

fresh

2 freedom **of** speech or action. *Will you allow them freedom of choice?*

fresh be fresh **from** a place. *...bread fresh from the oven... Nick Faldo arrived, fresh from his victory in the U.S. Masters Tournament.*

fret to fret **about** something or **over** something. *She fretted about her appearance... Nothing can be gained by fretting over results.*

friend 1 be friends **with** someone. *You used to be great friends with him, didn't you?* 2 a friend **of** someone or **to** someone. *She has become a close friend of the President and his wife... She became a friend to them for the rest of their careers.*

friendly 1 be friendly **to** or **towards** someone: behave in a pleasant way towards them. *Everyone is so friendly to everyone else... I have noticed that your father is not as friendly towards me as he used to be.* 2 be friendly **with** someone: be their friend. *I became friendly with a young engineer named Sy Glist.* 3 be friendly **to** someone or something: support them. *...a big corporation very friendly to the President.*

friendship someone's friendship **with** someone else; a friendship **between** two people. *I wanted to maintain my friendship with her. ...a study of the friendship between two South London youths.*

frighten to frighten someone **into** doing something. *...a bombing campaign aimed at frightening the Peruvians into boycotting the elections.*

frightened 1 be frightened **of** something or someone. *He felt a little frightened of going back... I have a reputation now and people are going to be frightened of me.* 2 be frightened **for** someone or something you care about. *Only days ago we were frightened for our lives.*

fringed be fringed **with** things or **by** things. *Her eyes were large and fringed with long false eyelashes. ...a bay of blue water fringed by palm trees.*

front in front; in front **of** something. *...a device which computes the speed of the car travelling in front... An actor has to go out every day and prove himself in front of an audience.*

frontier 1 the frontier **between** or **of** two countries; the frontier **of** one country **with** another. *...the frontier between the United States and Canada. ...along the frontier of the two Germanies. ...the north-west frontier of India... Greece was manning her frontier with Bulgaria.* 2 the frontiers **of** knowledge or a field of activity. *...the way in which technology can expand the frontiers of knowledge.*

frown 1 to frown **at** something or someone. *He frowned at his reflection in the mirror... The President frowned at the suggestion that his council had wasted the money.* 2 to frown **upon** or **on** something that you do not approve of. *Television is frowned upon... In the past, the Edinburgh festival committee frowned on prize-giving.*

fruits the fruits **of** someone's work or success. *You are now in a position to enjoy the fruits of your labours.*

frustrated be frustrated **by**, **at**, or **with** something. *They are frustrated by having no outdoor space to play in... They may get frustrated at their own failure. ...frustrated with the slow pace of reform.*

full 1 be full **of** something. *He seemed full of energy. ...a garden full of fruit trees and roses.* 2 **in full.** *The company would be unable to pay its creditors in full... It is worth quoting in full what the chairman said.*

fun for fun. ...*whether you wish to run just for fun or to compete in races.*

function 1 the function **of** a person or thing; a person's or thing's function **as** something. *The function of criticism is to help the student to improve... He could no longer fulfil his function as breadwinner for the family.* **2** to function **as** something. *...a room which had previously functioned as a playroom for the children.*

fundamental be fundamental **to** something. *Close links with suppliers are fundamental to the success of its business.*

furious be furious **at** or **with** someone or something. *Many people are furious at the Duke for going to the funeral... Rubenstein is furious with the decision.*

furnish to furnish someone **with** something. *They did not furnish us with an opportunity to meet as a group.*

furnished be furnished **with** furniture. *It was furnished with ordinary office furniture of the better sort.*

fuss 1 to fuss **over** someone. *Boys don't like a mother fussing over them.* **2** to fuss **about** something or **over** something. *A great many women nowadays fuss about their weight... John Ford didn't like an actor fussing over his role.* **3** the fuss **over** or **about** something or someone: the expression of anger or anxiety. *There was a tremendous fuss about seating arrangements... It was silly to make such a fuss over a woman whom he had only seen half a dozen times.* **4** to make a fuss **of** someone: to pay them a lot of attention. *I hugged her and made a great fuss of her.*

fussy be fussy **about** something. *She was very fussy about pronunciation.*

G

gain 1 to gain **in** a quality or ability. *Barenboim's playing seemed to gain in confidence as time went on.* **2** to gain **on** someone or something that is ahead of you. *She kept gaining on me all the way down the long hill.*

gallop at a gallop. *The dogs would follow at a gallop, yapping and yelping.*

galvanize to galvanize someone **into** doing something. *She embarked on a mini-tour aimed at galvanizing her supporters into turning out to vote... You've got to galvanize people into action.*

gamble to gamble **on** a race or a particular result. *...families ruined by gambling on the horses... The Swapo High Command seems to have gambled on a certainty.*

gamut a gamut **of** something: its full range. *Fulham were capable of putting their supporters through a whole gamut of emotions.*

gap a gap **in** something or a gap **between** two things. *...closing the gap in military technology... A central theme of the report is that the gap between rich and poor has grown.*

gape to gape **at** someone or something. *Crowds gathered to gape at the players.*

gasp a gasp **of** a particular emotion. *A gasp of disbelief rang out.*

gateway a gateway **to** somewhere or something. *Cockermouth is situated at the northern gateway to the English Lake District... Wealth has not proved to be a gateway to happiness.*

gaze to gaze **at** someone or something. *He gazed at me steadily.*

geared be geared **to, towards,** or **for** a particular purpose. *The whole training programme has been geared to this one event...*

general

Policies will be geared towards sustaining the strength of the pound... The team were geared for action.

general **in general:** used when speaking about the main features of something. *In general, they seem to share amply in the prosperity of the Republic.*

get 1 to get **at** something or someone. *The bull was trying to smash the fence to get at me.* 2 to get a particular feeling **from** or **out of** something. *What you get from the culture of Ceylon depends on your attitude... What does anyone get out of acting?* 3 to get **into** an activity, situation, or way of behaving. *I'm going to need a quick start to get into the mood... I'm not going to get into an argument about it.* 4 to get **over** an unpleasant experience, illness, or difficulty. *George did not get over his homesickness for some time... One mother got over this problem by leaving her baby with someone else.* 5 to get **out of** something. *We'll do anything to get out of working.* 6 to get **round** a rule, problem, or difficulty. *The most valuable architect is the one who can get round the planning system.* 7 to get **round** someone: to persuade them. *She could always get round him in the end.* 8 to get **through** a particular task, problem, or unpleasant experience. *It is difficult to get through this amount of work in such a short time... We just hope we can get through the game without any further injuries.* 9 to get **to** someone: to affect them. *The fatigue and backache are getting to me now.* 10 to get along **with** someone. *I get along very well with Donald.* 11 to get away **with** something. *Pupils disrupt classes and get away with unruly behaviour.* 12 to get down **to** something. *The two of them get down to business here tomorrow.*

13 to get in **with** someone. *She takes good care to get in with the people who matter.* 14 to get on **with** someone. *The children have to learn to get on with each other.* 15 to get on **with** something. *...a life spent hiding my feelings and getting on with the job.* 16 to get on **to** a topic. *Somehow we got on to grandparents.* 17 to get on **to** someone. *Get on to my secretary and arrange an interview.* 18 to get round **to** doing something. *Most people take weeks to get round to filling the forms in.* 19 to get through **to** someone. *...words which will get through to a child.* 20 to get up **to** something. *Many see school trips as an excuse for children to get up to mischief.*

gist the gist **of** something. *She strove to catch the gist of our quarrel.*

give 1 to give something **to** someone or something. *I pulled out a packet of cigarettes and gave them to him... Priority will have to be given to unemployment.* 2 to give in **to** someone or something. *I feared she'd think me weak for giving in to him... Jessica refused to give in to self-pity or despair.* 3 to give something over **to** someone. *A whole page had to be given over to readers' letters.* 4 to give up **on** someone or something. *The lifts take so long to reach the ground floor that you usually give up on them.* 5 to give something up **to** a particular thing. *The last afternoon of the Christmas term was given up to a tea-party.*

given be given **to** a particular kind of behaviour. *David was not given to daring acts of bravado.*

glance 1 to glance **at** something or **through** pages or documents. *I glanced at your letters this morning. ...glancing through the job advertisements.* 2 to glance **off** something. *The ball glanced off his foot into the net.* 3 **at a glance.** *He* could tell at a glance that she was upset.

glare to glare **at** someone or something. *We froze, glaring at each other in hatred.*

gloat to gloat **over** something or someone. *It is worth noting how many independent schools gloat over their Oxford entry success rates.*

glory to glory **in** something. *The women were glorying in this new-found freedom.*

glow to glow **with** a particular emotion. *Mrs Volkov glowed with the pride of having produced a child.*

glutton a glutton **for** something. *He never got tired, and he was a glutton for work.*

gnaw to gnaw **at** something. *The insects continued gnawing at the wood.*

go 1 to go **about** a task, activity, or problem. *...those trying to go about their normal business.* 2 to go **against** someone, or their advice or wishes. *The head is only answerable to the governors, who rarely go against him.* 3 to go **against** someone: used of a decision in a court of law. *The verdict went against his brother.* 4 to go **before** a judge or jury. *The measure went before an ecclesiastical committee.* 5 to go **beyond** something. *Mr Baker's warning went beyond Friday's statement.* 6 to go **by** certain information or evidence. *Don't go by what he says.* 7 to go **for** a particular product or method. *Do you go for organization or do you prefer flair?* 8 to go **for** someone: to attack them. *He went for me with a bread knife.* 9 to go **into** a job, subject, or arrangement of some kind. *When you go into a deal, you can't lay down the law. ...training programmes for people wishing to go into business.* 10 to go **on** or **into** something: used of money or

resources. *A fair amount of money goes on research... Most of the aid has gone into urban projects.* 11 to go **over** something: to examine or consider it. *Potential buyers should go over all the details.* 12 to go **through** an unpleasant event or experience. *She had to go through the indignity of travelling in the luggage van.* 13 to go **through** things such as a collection of papers or clothes. *He went through Guy's books to find something about Poland.* 14 to go **towards** a particular scheme or purchase. *The funds will go towards security and educational activities.* 15 to go **with** something. *White wine goes with fish.* 16 to go **without** something: to not have it. *Prisoners may have to go without a bath for a week.* 17 to go ahead **with** a decision or action. *...Sotheby's determination to go ahead with the sale.* 18 to go along **with** someone or something. *We have to go along with whatever government comes to power.* 19 to go back **on** a promise or agreement. *Now you're going back on what you told me earlier.* 20 to go down **with** a disease or illness. *Seven of the English boys went down with influenza.* 21 to go in **for** a particular kind of thing or a competition. *They have decided to go in for information technology.* 22 to go on **with** something. *'Don't interrupt,' he replied, and went on with his tale.* 23 to go out **with** someone. *She goes out with younger men.* 24 to go through **with** a decision or action. *He hoped they would not go through with their treatment.*

good 1 be good **at** doing something. *He was good at hiding his disappointments.* 2 be good **for** someone or something. *Post-war welfare thinking assumed that the arts were good for the people... It's great to see all these people here, it's good for the game.* 3 **for good:**

permanently. *The theatre closed down for good.*

grab to grab **at** something. *He grabbed at the drawer where the pistol was.*

graduate /ˈɡrædjʊɪt/ **1** to graduate **from** a school or institution **in** a particular subject. *Volpin graduated from Moscow University in 1946... She was educated at Edinburgh University and graduated in law.* **2** to graduate **from** one thing **to** another. *There are stadium groups and arena groups, and they have graduated from the latter to the former.*

graft to graft one thing **onto** or **to** another thing. *...modern political structures grafted onto ancient cultural divisions... Cuttings from the fruit tree will have been grafted to another kind of tree.*

grant to grant something **to** someone. *Has his government granted favours to businessmen?*

grapple 1 to grapple **with** someone. *...detectives grappling with an unidentified man.* **2** to grapple **with** a problem or difficulty. *English Victorian novelists were grappling with guilt and melancholy.*

grasp 1 to grasp **at** something. *The specialists had given him some hope, but he was not grasping at it.* **2** be **within** someone's **grasp**: be attainable. *It looked as if Jones had victory within his grasp.*

grass to grass **on** someone. *The rumour started that I had grassed on them.*

gravitate to gravitate **to** or **towards** a particular place, thing, or activity. *Like many a French-speaking Belgian, she inevitably gravitated to the French capital... Jordan resigned from the Communist Party and had since gravitated towards the Labour Party.*

greeting in greeting. *They kissed each other in greeting.*

grieve to grieve **for** or **over** someone or something. *...grieving over the death of someone I loved... His step-mother had grieved for the motherless child.*

grin to grin **at** someone. *Fontane was grinning at his friend.*

grind to grind away **at** a task. *Millions of children are forced to spend precious hours of their lives grinding away at pointless tasks.*

groan 1 to groan **about** something. *...moaning and groaning about his bellyache.* **2** to groan **beneath** or **under** the weight or difficulty of something. *The bed groaned beneath her as she sat down... The fathers of many daughters groan under the weight of paying large sums for marriage ceremonies.*

groom to groom someone **as** something or **for** a particular position. *Barber told me I had been chosen to be groomed as editor... Clive Lloyd has been grooming him for the West Indies captaincy for a long time.*

grope to grope **for** something. *Its citizens are groping for a sense of identity.*

ground 1 to ground an opinion or argument **on** something. *They had grounded their appeal on the common law.* **2** on certain **grounds; on the grounds of** something: used when giving a reason. *Mr Coverly pleaded not guilty on the grounds that cucumbers could not be classed as firearms... They started making cuts, on the grounds of paper shortage.*

grounded be grounded **in** a fact or situation. *...if parental pronouncements are grounded in reality.*

grounding a grounding **in** a particular subject. *It is desired that all instructors have a better grounding in general culture.*

groundwork the groundwork **for** something. *Chairman Mao* provided the groundwork for future economic success by creating full employment.

group a group **of** things or people. ...a group of cancan dancers from East Anglia.

grow 1 to grow **into** something. A small faction may grow into an extremist group. 2 to grow **into** an item of clothing. It's a bit big, but she'll soon grow into it. 3 to grow **on** someone. She was someone whose charm grew very slowly on you. 4 to grow **out of** a type of behaviour or interest. My ambition was to become a comic strip artist but I grew out of it. 5 to grow **out of** an item of clothing. It cost a small fortune and she grew out of it in three months.

grudge a grudge **against** someone. Nor did Churchill harbour any grudge against Miss Cazalet.

grumble to grumble **about** something. A match with nine goals, some of them spectacular, should be nothing to grumble about.

guard 1 to guard **against** something or guard someone **from** something. ...long-standing doubts over how one can guard against cheating... I'm trying to protect him, to guard him from his enemies. 2 **on guard:** alert and ready for action. Police twirled their batons gently, on guard for possible trouble. 3 **under guard:** being guarded by someone. Police have put another serviceman under guard.

guess 1 to guess **at** something. The degree of improvement can only be guessed at. 2 **at a guess.** At a guess, I'd say she must have got lost.

guide 1 a guide **to** a particular subject or place. He published a professional guide to French music. 2 to guide someone **through** something. Mr Lightbody went out of his way to guide me through the red tape jungle.

guilty 1 be guilty **of** a crime. They were both found guilty of causing death by reckless driving. 2 feel guilty **about** doing something that you think is wrong. Perhaps women should be made to feel guilty about wearing furs.

gulf a gulf **between** two things. This is the real gulf between first division and non-league football.

gun to gun **for** someone. I don't want half an army gunning for me.

gunpoint at gunpoint. Twice he was challenged at gunpoint.

H

hack 1 to hack **at** something. We found Charlie hacking at the bacon with a knife. 2 to hack **through** something such as undergrowth. The vegetation is so thick we will have to hack through it.

haggle to haggle **with** someone **over** something. She haggled with the man until the matter had been settled... After haggling over the price all day I was determined to make a deal.

hail to hail someone or something **as** a particular thing. It was hailed as the most spectacular concert in the history of rock.

hand 1 to hand something **to** someone. This bulletin has just been handed to me. 2 to hand something on or over **to** someone. After investigation, the relevant documents are handed over to the DTI... They handed on to their children the only life they knew. 3 **at hand:** near. The day for which they had been fighting was close at hand. 4 **by hand:** manually or in person. They scaled the wall and began tearing it down by hand... Applications can be delivered by hand. 5 **on hand:** near and available. There were no

hang

less than twelve additional musicians on hand.

hang 1 to hang **about** or **around** a place. *I was hanging around the Bush theatre one night waiting for an audition... George was left to hang about the station.* **2** to hang **over** someone or something. *It's awful having a criminal case hanging over you... A question mark hangs over the future of London as a leading financial centre.* **3** to hang **onto** something. *He has only a slim chance of hanging onto power.* **4** to hang **on** something: to depend on it. *At such times, hope or despair hangs on the last phone call.* **5** to hang around **with** someone. *I was becoming more cynical, probably from hanging around with newspapermen.*

hangover a hangover **from** the past. *Their obsession with exports is an obvious hangover from colonial times.*

hanker to hanker **after** something or **for** something. *Lucy had always hankered after a house of her own... They still hanker for the past.*

happen to happen **to** someone or something. *It is a mystery what happened to Dibble; he just collapsed.*

happy be happy **about** or **with** something. *Mr Henderson is not happy about the level of his shares. ...the self-realized woman who is happy with her job.*

hard be hard **on** someone or something. *This sort of presentation can be hard on the listener... These rough roads are hard on the car's suspension.*

hardback in hardback. *I missed it when it was published in hardback.*

harmful be harmful **to** someone or something. *Too much salt can be harmful to a young baby.*

harmonize to harmonize **with** something. *It is absurd to suggest that modern architecture cannot harmonize with its setting.*

harmony in harmony **with** someone or something. *...the ecological importance of learning to live in harmony with the planet.*

harness to harness one thing **to** another. *These aspirations are harnessed to a political or religious programme.*

hatred hatred **for** or **of** someone or something. *...periods of stifled hatred for Daniel's father. ...the widespread fear and hatred of witches.*

hazardous be hazardous **to** someone or **for** someone. *Breathing asbestos-laden air may be hazardous to health... Strong winds are expected to make roads hazardous for drivers today.*

head to head **for** a place. *As the travellers head for Stonehenge, the police are preparing to repel them.*

heap to heap praise or criticism **on** or **upon** someone. *The Chancellor took care last week to heap praise on Bernard.*

heaped be heaped **with** things. *The boy balanced a tray heaped with his wares.*

hear 1 to hear **from** someone. *She had not heard from her sister in Cleveland for many years.* **2** to hear **of** someone or something. *The vast majority of these students had never heard of the Marshall Plan.* **3** to hear **about** something. *I first heard about the shooting on the radio.*

heart 1 at heart: used when indicating someone's true character. *He was, at heart, a kindly and reasonable man.* **2** by heart: used to indicate that something is memorized. *Learn the above conversation by heart.*

heavy be heavy **with** something. *...a voice heavy with scorn.*

hedge to hedge **against** something. *...hedging against inflation.*

heir the heir **to** a throne, property, or a position. ...*M. Fabris, heir to the estate of Utrillo.*

heiress the heiress **to** a throne, property, or a position. ...*his wife Bodil, heiress to a fortune from a leading chemicals company.*

help 1 to help someone **to** something. *Mr Stokes helped himself to rum.* 2 to help someone **with** something. *Grant has spent the last two years of his life helping his wife with her fight against cancer.* 3 be **of** help; be **of** help to someone. *I sat with my head bent forward but this was of no help either.*

heralded be heralded **as** a particular thing. *The miners' strike was heralded as a new weapon in the class struggle.*

hew to hew something **out of** or **from** rock or wood. ...*hewing stone out of the mountain... Small memorials hewn from the rock mark the spot of an earlier massacre.*

hide to hide something **from** someone. *He hid the ignition key from her.*

hiding in hiding. *He has been in hiding for almost a year.*

high be high **on** drugs or alcohol. *There were rumours that one speaker was high on acid.*

hindrance a hindrance **to** someone or something. *Private ownership was either a help or a hindrance to certain goals.*

hinge to hinge **on** or **upon** a particular thing or event. *The immediate future of Poland hinges on more than a new Parliament.*

hint 1 to hint **at** something. *He seemed to be hinting at a coalition between the two parties.* 2 a hint **of** something. *He would rarely give a hint of emotion.*

hire for hire. *Three boxes with a view of the race-course were available for hire.*

hit 1 to hit **on** an idea. *After discussing various methods of escape we hit on the following plan.* 2 to hit back **at** someone. *They have been urging him to hit back at Mr Bush's campaign.*

hold 1 a hold **over** someone. *His hold over the people enabled him to grind down all opposition.* 2 to hold something **against** someone. *His refusal to cooperate will be held against him.* 3 to hold **to** an idea or opinion. *I also hold strongly to the idea that the university should seek funding from industry and commerce.* 4 to not hold **with** a particular activity or practice. *I don't hold with play acting in church!* 5 to hold on **to** something. *Angelica sat staring ahead, holding on to the iron rail... Harry Lodge, from England, held on to third place overall.* 6 to hold out **for** something. *The United States and other countries are holding out for a full settlement.*

holiday on holiday. ...*an idea which grew while she was on holiday in Europe.*

homage a homage **to** someone or something. *'Blue Moon' is a charming romantic homage to Elvis Presley.*

home 1 to home in **on** something. *The shark turned, homing in on the stream of blood.* 2 **at** home. *I find it very difficult to work at home.*

honour 1 an honour **to** someone or something. *His mother was somewhat calmed by this honour to the family.* 2 **in honour of** someone or something. ...*a party given in honour of her arrival.*

hooked be hooked **on** something. *Do we need to worry about the adolescent getting hooked on certain books? ...hooked on drugs.*

hope 1 to hope **for** something. *He could hardly have hoped for a better start to his career.* 2 **in the hope of** doing something. *We should try to spread our ideas in the hope of showing people what is possible.*

horizon

horizon 1 on the horizon. *The domes and minarets of Delhi showed on the horizon.* **2 on the horizon; over the horizon:** in the near future. *...with inflation rising and an election on the horizon. ...the thought that over the horizon is another assignment.*

horseback on horseback. *People waited, watched by policemen on horseback.*

hour on the hour: at 1 o'clock, 2 o'clock, 3 o'clock, and so on. *Buses for London leave every day on the hour.*

howl to howl **with** laughter, pain, or anger. *The students howled with glee as they followed the brothers.*

hub the hub **of** a place or area. *Venice was the hub of the Mediterranean.*

hum to hum **with** a particular activity or feeling: used of a place. *The town was already humming with excitement.*

hunger 1 hunger **for** something. *...this compulsive hunger for victory.* **2** to hunger **for** something or **after** something. *She hungers for contact with her child... What makes people hunger after power?*

hungry be hungry **for** something. *He knows what it is to be hungry for success.*

hunt 1 to hunt **for** something. *Badgers are still about at night, hunting for acorns or beetles.* **2** a hunt **for** someone or something. *Detectives have launched a hunt for the mother.*

hysterics in hysterics. *The audience were in hysterics.*

I

idea 1 someone's ideas **on** something or **about** something. *...traditional ideas on how to feed sick children... He had superficial ideas about politics.* **2** someone's idea **of** a particular thing: what they think it is like. *...Mary Jordache's idea of a normal American family.* **3** an idea **of** something or **about** something: some knowledge of what it is. *...occasionally flashing my torch to get an idea of my immediate surroundings... I had quite the wrong idea about it.* **4** the idea **of** something: the actual concept that it represents. *She cannot bear the idea of parting. ...the idea of freedom.* **5** an idea **for** something new. *I had this idea for a book.* **6** the idea **of** an action or scheme: its purpose. *The idea of these improvisations is to force the actors to find justifications for the way their characters behave.*

ideal be ideal **for** a purpose or person; an ideal thing **for** a purpose or person. *All these oils are ideal for cooking, frying and salad dressings... It's a healthy, interesting holiday—ideal for families... A yellowish-brown is the ideal colour for camouflage.*

identical be identical **to** or **with** something else. *The third diagram is identical to the first... My view is identical with that of Mr Jefferson.*

identify 1 to identify **with** someone. *Do you identify with the working class then?* **2** to identify someone or something **with** a person or thing. *The planets were identified with gods... I was identified with that issue.* **3** be identified **as** a particular person or thing. *The victims have been identified as Hazel Danks and Joan Abbot... The main concerns were identified as a good bus service and a low crime rate... In each case, private contractors were identified as being at fault.*

ignorant be ignorant **of** a fact or **about** a subject. *They were ignorant of his plans. ...if the President is ignorant about major aspects of national policy.*

imbued be imbued **with** a quality or idea. ...*cultivated individuals, imbued with a sense of social purpose.*

immerse 1 to immerse yourself **in** an activity. *I immersed myself totally in my work... All the team had been immersed in the project for several months.* **2** to immerse something **in** a liquid. *The foot was to be immersed in a bucket of the stuff... Pilgrims are supposed to immerse themselves three times in the water.*

immune be immune **to** or **from** something harmful or bad. *We are virtually immune to certain diseases which cause death elsewhere... This renders academics immune from criticism.*

immunity immunity **to**, **from**, or **against** something harmful or bad. *Vaccines generate immunity to a disease. ...immunity from prosecution. ...their natural immunity against pests.*

immunize to immunize someone **against** a particular disease. *...failing to have their children immunized against diphtheria.*

impact an impact **on** or **upon** something. *Higher interest rates will have an impact on profits.*

impale to impale something **on** or **upon** something sharp. *Impaled on the hook was a small shark.*

impart to impart information or a quality **to** someone or something. *The news was imparted to John Curcuas. ...otherwise the kippers may impart their flavour to the raspberry mousse.*

impatient 1 be impatient **with** someone or something; be impatient **at** something; be impatient **of** a kind of behaviour. *He was very impatient with students who did not listen carefully... Most prisoners seemed genuinely impatient with such ideas... They have often made me angry and impatient at their petty faults... Those with real power are*

usually impatient of too much deference. **2** be impatient **for** something you want to happen. *...leaders impatient for results.*

impediment an impediment **to** development. *...those who say that the unions are an impediment to progress.*

impervious be impervious **to** something. *I became impervious to influence of any kind... Slate is impervious to water.*

impinge to impinge **on** or **upon** someone or something. *...as the pressures of change impinge more heavily on the individual.*

implant /ɪmplɑːnt/ to implant something **in** something or someone else. *We might implant tiny sensors in the body... She managed to implant a lot of enthusiasm in me.*

implicate to implicate someone **in** an unpleasant situation. *But was it fair to implicate her in this sort of situation?*

implication 1 by implication: used when mentioning a related fact. *Her policies have failed and, by implication, so has she.* **2** the implication **of** something. *...realising the scandalous implication of the remark.*

implicit be implicit **in** something. *...the sense of shattering defeat implicit in his attitude.*

import /ɪmpɔːt/ to import something **from** another place **into** the place where you are. *...goods imported from abroad... 200,000 parrots are imported into EC countries each year.*

impose 1 to impose a restriction, law, or penalty **on** or **upon** a person or activity. *They immediately imposed a ban on further advertising. ...chafing at the restraint imposed on them by the previous government.* **2** to impose **on** or **upon** someone. *'Would you care to join me?'—'No, I couldn't impose on you.'*

impregnate

impregnate to impregnate something **with** a chemical. ...*softwood impregnated with creosote.*

impress to impress something **on** or **upon** someone. *The authorities impressed on him the need for a psychiatric consultation for his son.*

impressed be impressed **by** something or **with** something. *I was impressed by his self-control... We are highly impressed with the way you have been working.*

impression someone's impression **of** a person or situation. *My first impression of Nigel Lever was a bad one... One man described his impressions of that fateful day.*

improve to improve **on** or **upon** a previous thing. *Our furnace is not perfect, but we are improving on it.*

improvement an improvement **in** something or **of** something. ...*the resultant improvement in health. ...the gradual improvement of relations between East and West.*

impunity **with** impunity. *National distinctions cannot be trampled on with impunity.*

inappropriate be inappropriate **for** or **to** someone or something; an inappropriate thing **for** someone or something. *Dependency is inappropriate for adults. ...foreign ideas, inappropriate to hungry countries... Oddly, it never struck me as being an inappropriate name for him.*

incapable be incapable **of** doing something. *He seemed incapable of expressing his feelings. ...states incapable of self-defence.*

incarnation the incarnation **of** a quality. *He became, in their eyes, the incarnation of evil.*

incentive an incentive **for** or **to** a person or action. ...*an incentive for special effort. ...a real incentive to women.*

incidence the incidence **of** something. ...*the high incidence of disease.*

incidental be incidental **to** something. *Was the killing incidental to the assault?*

incite to incite someone **to** action of some kind. *Had Burr incited others to treason?*

inclination an inclination **towards** something or **for** something. *How could I indulge even the faintest inclination towards self-pity?... The condition of our lives destroys all inclination for culture and refinement.*

inclusive be inclusive **of** something. *The holiday costs around seven hundred pounds, inclusive of the flight.*

incompatible be incompatible **with** something. ...*ideas that are incompatible with scientific knowledge.*

inconsistent be inconsistent **with** something. *The actions of member countries remain inconsistent with their stated ideals.*

incorporate to incorporate something **into** or **in** something new. ...*where societies were not incorporated into more advanced civilizations. ...incorporating Roman tiles in the arch.*

increase /ɪnkriːs/1 an increase **in** something or **of** something. ...*the increase in crime. ...the increase of learning and wisdom among the people.* **2** be **on the increase.** *Poverty is on the increase.*

incumbent be incumbent **on** or **upon** someone. *If you reject my answer, it is incumbent on you to find a better one.*

incursion an incursion **into** a region. ...*after their incursion into Yugoslavia.*

indebted be indebted **to** someone **for** something. *I am indebted to the following individuals for their assistance.*

independent be independent **of** something or someone. *Its finances would be independent of official control.*

index an index **of** a level or amount. *...the value of the pupil-teacher ratio as an index of the quality of teaching.*

indication an indication **of** something. *He gave no indication of what he was thinking.*

indicative be indicative **of** something. *Such symptoms were not in themselves necessarily indicative of recent exertion.*

indict to indict someone **for** a crime. *He had been indicted for printing obscene and indecent advertising.*

indictment 1 an indictment **against** someone **for** a crime. *An indictment against me for murder was being prepared... His closest adviser is under indictment for fraud.* 2 an indictment **of** something or someone bad. *...a matter which the 44 psychiatrists viewed as an indictment of their profession... That elderly people are afraid to leave their homes at night is a shocking indictment of the times we live in.*

indifferent be indifferent **to** something. *She seemed indifferent to insect bites... British children and teenagers are indifferent to politics.*

indignant be indignant **at** something or **about** something; be indignant **with** someone. *The mother bird swooped, indignant at this invasion of her privacy... He wasn't indignant about his low pay. ...pretending to be indignant with Frank.*

indispensable be indispensable **to** someone or something. *I don't regard myself as indispensable to my household... A degree is becoming indispensable to career success.*

indistinguishable be indistinguishable **from** something else. *...a coffee substitute which is almost indistinguishable from real coffee.*

indulge to indulge **in** an activity. *I don't have time to indulge in games.*

ineligible be ineligible **for** something. *...the numbers of unemployed who are ineligible for unemployment benefit.*

inequality inequality **in** something or **of** something; inequality **between** different groups. *...inequalities in housing. ...the basic inequality of strength between workers and their employers.*

infatuated be infatuated **with** someone. *He was for several years infatuated with her.*

infect to infect someone **with** a disease or feeling. *They cannot infect another person with this illness. ...afraid that she would infect him with her own emotional disarray.*

infected 1 be infected **with** a disease. *...people infected with hepatitis.* 2 be infected **by** a quality. *We were infected by their enthusiasm.*

infer to infer something **from** some evidence. *The change in the balance of economic power may be inferred from three developments.*

inferior be inferior **to** someone or something. *He does not feel himself socially inferior to the manager. ...an oxygen mask much inferior to the one being used by the Germans.*

infested be infested **with** or **by** pests. *...a field infested with aphids... The backyard was infested by rats.*

inflict to inflict something unpleasant **on** or **upon** someone. *...the torment which they inflicted on others.*

influence 1 influence **on** or **over** someone or something. *The Catholic church has an enormous influence on them. ...to give people more influence over their own lives.* 2 be **under the influence of** someone or something. *John*

influx

Wilkinson was much under the influence of his brother-in-law. ...driving while under the influence of drugs.

influx an influx **of** people. *...an influx of tourists.*

inform 1 to inform someone **of** something. *Holokov had informed him of the Englishman's death.* **2** to inform **on** someone who has done something wrong. *It can be difficult for a child to inform on someone he knows.*

information information **about** something or **on** something. *...information about the university. ...information on transport and accommodation.*

infringe to infringe **on** or **upon** someone or something. *...when they infringe on our own children's right to freedom.*

infringement 1 an infringement **of** or **on** someone's rights or freedom. *...an infringement of individual liberty. ...an infringement on free speech.* **2** an infringement **of** a rule. *This was not an infringement of the law.*

infuse to infuse someone or something **with** a quality; to infuse a quality **into** someone or something. *His voice was infused with chilling venom. ...to infuse confidence into the buyer.*

ingrained be ingrained **in** people's minds or culture. *The notion that idleness is wrong is deeply ingrained in our culture.*

ingratiate to ingratiate yourself **with** someone. *...guests who wished to ingratiate themselves with their host and hostess.*

ingredient an ingredient **of, in,** or **for** something. *Envy and resentment are not the ingredients of political stability. ...chemical ingredients in cosmetics... It can be used as an ingredient for salads.*

inhabitant an inhabitant of a place. *...the inhabitants of the neighbouring valley.*

inherent be inherent **in** something or someone. *...the dangers inherent in this situation. ...the contradictions inherent in my own personality.*

inherit to inherit something **from** someone. *He had inherited from his mother two houses in Florence.*

inimical be inimical **to** someone or something. *The very nature of society is inimical to freedom.*

initiate /ɪnɪʃɪeɪt/ to initiate someone **into** a type of knowledge or a group. *Certain small groups were initiated into the dominant literary culture.*

inject 1 to inject someone **with** a drug; to inject a drug **into** someone. *Somebody injected her with a lethal dose of morphine... She injected a sleeping drug into my arm.* **2** to inject a particular feeling **into** an event or situation. *Phil injected some of the old energy into the performance.*

injection an injection **of** a liquid, a thing, or money. *...a substantial injection of funds.*

inkling an inkling **of** something. *So you now have some inkling of the importance of the task that confronts us.*

inlaid be inlaid **with** a valuable or beautiful material. *...a box inlaid with pearl shell. ...marble lattice-work inlaid with garnets and turquoise.*

inoculate to inoculate a person or animal **with** a drug **against** a disease. *Elderly patients were inoculated with living cancer cells... The children should be inoculated against serious diseases.*

inquire 1 to inquire **about** something or **as to** something. *We inquired about the precise circumstances surrounding the arrest... He added a reminder to inquire as to the soil analysis.* **2** to inquire **after** someone or their health. *The King seldom inquired after his daughter.* **3** to inquire

into a matter that needs investigation. *The Government does not inquire into the committee's recommendations.*

inscribe to inscribe words **on** an object; to inscribe an object **with** words. *The names of the dead were inscribed on the wall. ...a grave inscribed with a quote from his book.*

insensible 1 be insensible **to** something: be unaffected by it. *...insensible to the call of friendship.* 2 be insensible **of** something: be unaware of it. *...those children that lived and died insensible of their misery.*

insensitive be insensitive **to** people's feelings or thoughts. *Lucy was rude and insensitive to the feelings of others... He gradually became insensitive to the suffering he was causing.*

inseparable be inseparable **from** something else. *Culture is inseparable from class.*

insinuate to insinuate yourself **into** something. *Yet the past invariably insinuates itself into our present life.*

insist to insist **on** or **upon** doing or having something. *He insisted on staying for supper... We insist upon the highest standards of safety.*

inspiration 1 the inspiration **for** something. *The inspiration for the campaign came from Ron Bailey.* 2 an inspiration **to** someone. *...a place which has proved an inspiration to generations of our countrymen.*

inspire to inspire confidence or enthusiasm **in** someone; to inspire someone **with** confidence or enthusiasm. *...a doctor who is particularly good at inspiring confidence in children... Buy a copy of Do-It-Yourself Magazine to inspire you with enthusiasm.*

instance for instance: as an example. *Take advertising, for instance.*

instil to instil a feeling or idea **in** or **into** someone. *...ideas instilled in his mind by his mother... You never know what fears may be instilled into a baby by a loud, angry voice.*

instrument an instrument **of** or **for** a particular activity. *...the power of the media as an instrument of mass control. ...an instrument for managing the economy.*

instrumental be instrumental **in** achieving something. *He was instrumental in foiling a disguised takeover bid.*

insulate to insulate someone or something **from** or **against** something. *He had insulated himself from the world... The industry is not insulated against shocks.*

insurance an insurance **against** something bad that might happen. *A family provides a sort of insurance against isolation.*

insure to insure yourself or your property **against** something bad that might happen. *His neighbour's house is not insured against fire.*

integral be integral **to** something. *The actor is integral to the play.*

integrate 1 to integrate someone or something **into** a larger group. *He has thrown away a chance to integrate himself into the organization... Environmental considerations need to be integrated into the policy paper.* 2 to integrate one thing **with** another. *...the extent to which the planning of education can be integrated with planning for the economy as a whole.*

intended 1 be intended **as** a particular thing. *This last remark was intended as an insult.* 2 be intended **for** a particular person or purpose. *The invitation had really been intended for someone else.*

intent be intent **on** or **upon** something. *They seem intent on*

interact

harassing the players. ...they were so intent on what she was saying.

interact to interact **with** someone or something else. *The creature begins to interact with the world around it... Certain vitamins will interact closely with calcium ions.*

interaction interaction **between** two or more things. *...interaction between children and grandparents. ...the subtle interactions between religions, morality, and politics.*

intercede to intercede **for** someone in trouble **with** someone in authority. *I interceded for him with his employer... Max came to my rescue and interceded with the professor.*

interest 1 an interest **in** something. *...his interest in antiques and architecture.* 2 to interest someone **in** something. *Miss Musson had attempted to interest her in learning to read.* 3 be **in** someone's **interest:** be to their advantage. *It would not be in my interest to entrust the documents to you... The paper should be closed down in the national interest.*

interested be interested **in** something. *Too few people nowadays are interested in literature. ...people interested in buying property overseas.*

interface the interface **between** two things. *...the interface between technology and design.*

interfere 1 to interfere **in** or **with** something: to try to influence it. *I don't want to interfere in your marriage... When you decorate your home, I do not interfere with your schemes.* 2 to interfere **with** something: to have a damaging effect on it. *Get rid of any inhibitions which interfere with your playing.*

interplay the interplay **of** or **between** several things. *...the necessary interplay of theory and practice. ...the interplay between fate, chance, and free will.*

interpret to interpret something **as** a particular thing. *Your silence can upset people who interpret it as dumb insolence... The report was interpreted as reflecting a more cautious attitude.*

intersect to intersect **with** another road or line. *...where the Church road intersected with the Club road.*

interspersed be interspersed **with** things. *...plain white crosses interspersed with cherry trees... His speech was interspersed with catcalls and noise.*

intertwined be intertwined **with** something. *Its history is intertwined with that of the labour movement.*

interval 1 an interval **between** two events; an interval **of** a particular length of time. *...in the intervals between fighting... These seemed to occur at intervals of twenty years.* 2 **at intervals:** regularly. *The supplies were replenished at intervals.*

intervene to intervene **in** a situation. *The State may intervene in disputes between employers and workers.*

intimacy intimacy **with** someone. *Never before had he known such intimacy with another person.*

intolerant be intolerant **of** something. *They tend to be intolerant of anything strange.*

intoxicated be intoxicated **by** or **with** something exciting. *...actors intoxicated by their press cuttings... I felt intoxicated with the desolation of this world of ice and cold.*

introduce 1 to introduce someone **to** someone or something new. *I introduced him to Colonel Burr... He introduced his young friend to romantic poetry.* 2 to introduce something new **into** or **to** a place or system. *...when the fish were first introduced into Britain.*

...*changes which should be introduced into the training programme. ...as new technologies are introduced to the workplace.*

introduction the introduction **to** a book or talk. ...*in his introduction to the report.*

intrude to intrude **on** or **upon** someone or something. *I shall not intrude on your grief.*

inundated be inundated **with** things. *They were inundated with letters.*

invest 1 to invest **in** a business or something useful. *Some companies have invested in so-called 'supercars'. ...families who have invested money in luxury villas.* 2 to invest someone or something **with** a power or quality. *The singer invested the notes with a wealth of feeling and sensitivity... The IBA should be invested with an additional power.*

investigation an investigation **into** something. *Sherman ordered an investigation into her husband's death.*

invisible be invisible **to** someone. *That should make us practically invisible to anyone approaching from the south.*

invite to invite someone **to** an event or place or **for** a meal or activity. *Why did Byrne invite them to his party?... They repeatedly invited me to their apartment for dinner.*

involve to involve yourself or someone else **in** something. *Without thinking, I had involved her in a situation that might become violent.*

involved 1 be involved **in** something or **with** something: take part in it or be interested in it. *I became increasingly involved in politics. ...people directly involved with farming.* 2 be involved **in** something: be present or inevitable. ...*the risks involved in selling a story to the popular press.* 3 be involved **with** someone.

...*being romantically involved with someone in the same profession.*

invulnerable be invulnerable **to** something harmful. *The nuclear submarine is almost invulnerable to attack.*

irrelevant be irrelevant **to** something. *He felt that right and wrong were irrelevant to the situation.*

irritated be irritated **by** something or **at** something; be irritated **with** someone **for** doing something. *She was irritated by this suggestion... He appeared irritated at the delay... I felt irritated with myself for lying there day-dreaming.*

isolate to isolate someone **from** other people. *His force was completely isolated from the rest of the army.*

isolation in isolation. *Health regulations require her to stay in isolation for four months. ...a teacher working in isolation.*

issue 1 to issue someone **with** something; to issue something **to** someone. *The UN office in Maseru had issued us with refugee passports... The Committee issued a statement to the press.* 2 **at issue:** being discussed. *The point at issue here is not the number of trained leaders but their social class.*

J, K

jab to jab **at** something. *He jabbed at me with his finger.*

jar to jar **on** someone. *The harsh, metallic sound jarred on her.*

jealous be jealous **of** someone. *Joseph's brothers were jealous of him.*

jeer to jeer **at** someone. *Boys had jeered at him at school.*

jeopardy

jeopardy be **in jeopardy.** ...when the future of the planet is in jeopardy.

jest in **jest.** It was said half in jest.

join 1 to join **in** an activity. Some passers-by had also joined in the demonstration. 2 to join one thing **to** another. Join one pipe to the other... The two islands are joined to the coast. 3 to join up **with** other people or another thing. The French division joined up with the rest of the Southern Army Group.

joke 1 to joke **about** something; to joke **with** someone. Perhaps I am the only person to joke about the end of the world... Don't joke with me! 2 a joke **about** something. ...jokes about computers.

judge 1 a good or bad judge **of** something. She was gregarious, well-read, and a good judge of style. 2 to judge something **on** or **by** a factor or basis. Each case obviously has to be judged on its merits... She will judge their progress by the extent to which they become fluent. 3 judging **by** or **from** facts or evidence. Judging by its colour, it was no hotter than a glowing coal... I feel that Miss Gray will be our best choice, judging from her application.

judgement someone's judgement **on, about,** or **of** something. His judgement on individuals cannot seriously be taken into account... You have to make your own judgement about what is reality and what is not. ...society's judgement of risk.

juggle to juggle **with** things. ...still juggling with figures and possibilities.

jump to jump **at** an offer or opportunity. I'm sure she'll jump at the chance.

juncture at a particular **juncture.** It was at this juncture that his luck temporarily deserted him.

justification the justification **for** something or **of** something. There's no justification for what they've been doing... What is the social justification of university education?

keen be keen **on** something or someone; be keen **about** something. The headmaster was keen on music... You'd have to be keen about teaching.

keep 1 to keep someone or something **from** doing something. Towels were stuffed in their mouths to keep them from crying out. ...the effort to keep French-speaking Quebec from being isolated. 2 to keep information **from** someone. He was convinced I was keeping some secret from him. 3 to keep something **off** something else. Keep those dogs off her!... It kept his mind off his acute anxiety about his friend. 4 to keep **to** a rule or plan. Try to keep to a routine. 5 to keep someone **out of** a situation. ...keeping them out of trouble. 6 to keep away **from** a place or thing. Keep away from dark alleys. 7 to keep in **with** someone: to stay friendly with them. I ought to try to keep in with him. 8 to keep on **about** something: to talk about it continuously. She kept on about the stupid car. 9 to keep on **at** someone: to say something to them repeatedly. She kept on at the authorities until a visit was arranged. 10 to keep up **with** someone or something. We simply cannot keep up with the demand.

keeping be **in keeping with** something. This extraordinary feat was in keeping with his character.

key the key **to** something. Human ingenuity is the key to the problem.

kind 1 a particular kind **of** thing. ...a new kind of book. 2 something **of** a particular **kind.** He was clearly sensitive to pressures of this kind. 3 be kind **to** someone. Many of the staff were exceptionally kind to me. 4 **in kind:** paying with goods rather

156

than money. ...*repayment in kind of huge debts.*

knack a knack **of** or **for** doing something. ...*her knack of finding good new books... Others seem to have a knack for combining colours and patterns.*

knock 1 to knock **on** or **at** a door or window. *I had been knocking on the door for some time... At dawn, the police came and knocked at his door.* **2** to knock an idea or quality **out of** someone. *Most of the refugees have had the fight knocked out of them.*

know 1 to know **about** something or **of** something. *He did not know about the funeral... Only a handful of people knew of this discovery.* **2** to know **about** a subject. *Tom didn't know much about architecture.* **3** be **in the know:** have knowledge of something. *I heard this from someone who is in the know.*

knowledge 1 to your **knowledge:** as far as you know. *No government, to my knowledge, has yet been able to devise such a scheme.* **2 without** someone's **knowledge:** without their knowing. ...*to photograph them and record them without their knowledge.*

known be known **as** something. *Soon our neighbourhood became known as Dynamite Hill.*

L

label to label a person or thing **as** something. *His behaviour is labelled as eccentric.*

labour 1 to labour **under** a delusion or burden. *I still laboured under the delusion that everyone was a good guy at heart.* **2** be **in labour:** be giving birth. *She was in labour for seven hours.*

lace 1 to lace a drink or food **with** alcohol or a drug. *Food supplies are being laced with pesticides.* **2** to lace a speech or piece of writing **with** language or ideas of a particular kind. ...*plays laced with a mixture of intuition and common sense... The first round of talks was laced with rhetoric.*

lack a lack **of** something. ...*his lack of ambition.*

lacking 1 be lacking **in** a quality or thing: not have it. *Gaitskell thought him lacking in judgement.* **2** be lacking **in** a place or thing: not be in it. ...*a way of finding the love that was lacking in the home.*

laden be laden **with** something. *Their mules were laden with silver.*

land 1 to land someone **in** a particular situation. ...*observations that would have landed him in jail.* **2** to land someone **with** something they do not want to deal with. *I never guessed I'd be landed with all the medieval stuff.* **3 by land.** *Access by land may result in delays.*

lapse to lapse **into** a state or way of doing something. *She lapsed into a deep sleep. ...lapsing into her native tongue.*

large 1 at large: not yet captured. *His kidnapper is still at large.* **2 at large:** used to refer to most of the people in a group. ...*in the interests of the community at large.*

lash to lash out **at** or **against** something or someone. ...*lashing out at them critically in social situations... The slave lashes out against his immediate master.*

last at last: eventually. *At last the day came when his plans were completed.*

latch to latch **onto** someone or something. *She would look for women's liberation groups and latch onto them.*

late be late **for** an event or appointment. *I'm late for dinner as it is.*

laugh 1 to laugh **at** someone or something ridiculous. *I used to laugh at narrow-minded, old-fashioned people.* **2** to laugh **at** or **about** something amusing. *He did not laugh at the joke. ...if parents can admit the feeling and laugh about it together.*

launch to launch **into** an activity. *He launched into an attack on his opponent.*

lavish to lavish attention or money **on** or **upon** someone or something. *His films have deserved the trouble he has lavished on them.*

law 1 be **against the law**: be illegal. *It's against the law to bribe people.* **2** **within the law**: legally, rather than illegally. *Shimanov explained that he had always acted within the law.* **3** **in law; by law; under the law**: according to a legal system. *An employer's right to dismiss his employees is sanctioned in law... Employers were required by law to report these accidents... Homeworkers have few rights under the law.* **4** be **above the law**: not have to obey the law. *...legislation that put the airlines above the law.*

lay 1 to lay an idea or problem **before** someone. *He then went on to lay his own difficulties before them.* **2** to lay blame or a responsibility **on** or **upon** someone. *...laying the blame on others.* **3** to lay stress or emphasis **on** or **upon** something. *The Government has laid great stress on harnessing private enterprise.* **4** to lay **into** someone: to attack them. *Mounted police laid into them.* **5** to lay **off** something: to stop having or using it. *Tom, lay off that sherry—it's terrible.*

lead /liːd/ **1** to lead **to** a situation or event, especially a bad one. *Their efforts had led to disaster... The article led to a heated debate.* **2** to

lead **to** or **into** a different room or place. *...a door that led to the bedroom. ...the door leading into the living room.* **3** to lead **off** a place. *...the rooms leading off the courtyard.* **4** to lead up **to** something. *...in the days leading up to the tour.* **5** **in the lead.** *...the kind of quick thinking that kept Leicester in the lead.*

leaf to leaf **through** a book or magazine. *...surreptitiously leafing through a fashion magazine.*

league be **in league with** someone else. *She is in league with the Devil.*

leak to leak information **to** someone. *Sir Patrick's comments were leaked to the Press Association.*

lean 1 to lean **towards** a belief or practice. *...parents who naturally lean towards strictness.* **2** to lean **on** someone: to threaten them gently. 'I leaned on him a tiny bit,' I admitted.* **3** to lean **on** someone: to depend on them. *Dr Lieberman leaned on her more each day.*

learn 1 to learn **of** the existence or occurrence of something. *Reporters in Maseru soon learned of our arrival.* **2** to learn **about** a subject. *...students who want to learn about modern society.*

lease to lease something that you own **to** someone; to lease something **from** the person who owns it. *96% of the available space has been leased to small companies... Jōhn Rich leased the site from the Duke of Bedford.*

least 1 **at least**: used when mentioning a minimum. *At least three people were killed.* **2** **at least**: used when mentioning something you are pleased about. *At least he was safe.* **3** **in the least**: used to intensify 'not'. *I am not in the least perturbed that I was found guilty.*

leave 1 to leave **for** a particular destination. *Kathy is leaving for*

Vienna in a fortnight. **2** to leave something **with** someone. *Leave your phone number with the secretary.* **3** to leave a matter **with** or **to** someone to deal with. *I will put the matter right—you leave it with me... It was a difficult decision, and I left it to her... I'm happy to leave the rest to your imagination.* **4** to leave someone **with** a feeling or problem. *That left me with an agonizing problem.* **5** to leave property or money **to** someone in your will. *The wife left all her property to her husband.* **6** **on leave.** *Hayward was on leave from his regiment.*

lecture a lecture **on** something or **about** something. *Adam had been going to lectures on philosophy. ...a lengthy lecture about Lithuanian history.*

leer to leer **at** someone. *Karen could see the prisoners leering at her.*

left be left **with** the remainder of something. *I was left with only a mattress.*

legislation legislation **on** something; legislation **for** or **against** something. *...legislation on immigration. ...legislation for the reform of the House of Lords. ...legislation against unofficial strikes.*

lend **1** to lend something **to** someone. *...the additional money lent to you.* **2** to lend a quality **to** something. *Tradition lends order to the world.*

length **1** **at length:** after a while. *The coroner waited courteously and at length I resumed.* **2** **at length:** for a long time. *They talked at length about the farm.*

let **1** to let someone **into** or in **on** a secret. *I can let you into a little-known fact about Colin... They are going to let all of us in on their happy secret.* **2** to let someone **off** a duty. *He is let off domestic chores.*

letter **1** a letter **of** inquiry, thanks, resignation, and so on. *His father wrote a letter of congratulation.* **2** **by letter.** *...whether arrangements are made by letter or phone.*

level **1** be level **with** something else. *Vulkan's knee was level with the top of my head.* **2** be **on a level with** something else. *Her eyes were on a level with his.* **3** to level criticism **at** or **against** someone or something. *More serious charges were levelled at television during the Sixties. ...criticisms he has levelled against gangsters and the police.* **4** to level a look **at** someone. *A number of unfriendly glances were levelled at him.* **5** to level **with** someone: to tell them the truth. *It was decent of her to level with me about her intentions.*

liable be liable **for** a debt or accident. *The solicitor will be liable for all costs incurred.*

liaise to liaise **with** another person or group. *We have been liaising with neighbouring police forces.*

liaison liaison **with** another person or group; liaison **between** different people or groups. *...better liaison with regional water authorities... The Government has been encouraging liaison between colleges and industry.*

liberate to liberate someone or something **from** something bad. *...a group determined to liberate their country from oppression.*

liberty be **at liberty** to do something. *...someone whose name I am not at liberty to disclose.*

lie **1** to lie **to** someone **about** something. *She never ever lied to us... Why had Waddell lied about giving Carlin the money?* **2** to lie **behind** a situation or event: to be a cause or reason for it. *...a detailed analysis of what lay behind the near disaster.* **3** to lie **with** someone: used of a choice, duty, or fault. *In many cases, the decision lies with the doctor.* **2**

light

light 1 to light **upon** something: to find it. *I could, I immediately realized, have lighted upon a more fortunate turn of phrase.* 2 **in the light** of something: as a result of considering it. *In the light of subsequent events, this was obviously a sound decision.*

liken to liken one person or thing **to** another. *One newspaper had likened him to Hitler.*

likeness 1 a person's or thing's likeness **to** someone or something else. *Her likeness to her son was startling.* 2 a likeness **of** someone: a picture of them. *...a charming likeness of a radiant young queen.*

liking 1 a liking **for** something. *I can't understand my children's liking for white bread.* 2 be **to** your **liking.** *...watching to see whether this fragrant dish was to his liking.*

limit 1 a limit **to** something. *There is a limit to the obligation we have to protect others.* 2 a limit **on** something; a limit **of** a particular amount. *There was a three-dollar limit on what we could buy. ...an upper limit of two hundred pounds.* 3 the limit **of** an area or thing. *The helicopter flew to Bantry Bay, the limit of its range. ...a job that would extend me to the limit of my talents.* 4 to limit yourself or something **to** a particular thing. *You must read round the subject, not limit yourself to one book... The number of future universities is to be limited to thirty-six.* 5 **within limits:** used to qualify a statement. *Betting, within limits, can be an acceptable form of entertainment.* 6 be **off limits:** be forbidden. *Moscow and Petrograd were off limits.*

limitation 1 the limitations **of** something. *...a doctor so patently aware of the limitations of medical skill.* 2 a limitation **to** something or **on** something. *...physical limitations to growth. ...the limitations on trade union leaders' powers.*

limited be limited **to** a particular place or group. *Some slang expressions are limited to certain small areas... This concession is limited to those on lower incomes.*

line 1 **along the line:** during the course of something. *Somewhere along the line they had gone wrong.* 2 **in line; in a line.** *We had to wait in line at the counter... The prisoners sat in a line and toyed with their food.* 3 **in line:** behaving as you should. *You need a very strict director to keep you in line.* 4 be **in line for** promotion, an award, or a job: be likely to get it. *His handling of the controversy has put him in line for promotion.* 5 **in line with** something else: similar to it. *The results were in line with City expectations... Tax allowances are being increased in line with inflation.* 6 be **on the line:** be at risk. *We should be prepared to place our jobs on the line, if need be.* 7 be **out of line:** behave badly or be different. *They were severely punished for stepping out of line... His views are out of line with those of most City economists.* 8 **on the lines of** something; **along the lines of** something: resembling it. *...an economic union, on the lines of the EEC. ...experiments along the lines of those used in the laboratory.*

lined be lined **with** things. *The roads out of Prague are lined with cherry trees.*

linger to linger **over** something or **on** something. *...lingering over their meals... She was too busy to let her mind linger on alternatives.*

link 1 a link **between** two things; a link **with** something else. *...the link between love and fear... The university has always had close links with industry.* 2 to link one thing **with** another or **to** another.

...armaments industries intimately linked with national governments. ...reports linking the bombing to Middle East terrorists. **3** to link up **with** someone else. *We have no plans to link up with anyone else—we're determined to go it alone.*

listen 1 to listen **to** someone or **to** a sound. *She was sitting listening to the radio.* **2** to listen **for** a sound that might come. *...listening for feet on the stairs.*

littered be littered **with** things. *The table is littered with dirty pans.*

live /lɪv/ **1** to live **by** a principle or belief. *I know a man who really tries to live by the Ten Commandments.* **2** to live **for** something: to regard it as very important. *She had lived for meal-times.* **3** to live **off** a source of income. *They have lived off the thriving tourist trade.* **4** to live **on** a particular amount of money or kind of food. *If you put it in the bank, you could live on the interest... Some birds live on meat.* **5** to live **through** an unpleasant or exciting time. *He lived through the Civil War.* **6** to live **with** an unpleasant situation that cannot be changed. *They have to live with the consequences of their decision.* **7** to live up **to** someone's expectations. *The team just have not lived up to their early promise.*

living for a living. *...men who play this game for a living.*

loaded be loaded **with** or loaded down **with** things. *...a cart loaded with explosives... Their Volkswagen was plainly loaded down with supplies.*

loan 1 a loan **to** someone; a loan **of** a particular amount. *...loans to Third World nations. ...a bank loan of two hundred thousand pounds.* **2** the loan **of** something. *He has been offered the loan of Jonathan's yacht.* **3** to loan money or property **to** someone. *The money was loaned*

to Hall during the summer. **4 on** loan **to** a borrower; **on loan from** the owner. *This painting was originally on loan to the National Gallery of Scotland. ...a shotgun on loan from his father.*

locked be locked **in** a disagreement with someone. *The two sides were locked in political arguments about the new tax... Mr Yeltsin is locked in a power struggle with the authorities.*

long to long **for** something. *I longed for a bath.*

look 1 to look **at** someone or something. *She kept looking at Rudolph... We shall be looking at ways of achieving a closer working relationship.* **2** to look **for** something or someone that you want to find. *She helped me look for a law firm which would take me on... Well, aren't you going out to look for him?* **3** to look **like** something: to resemble or seem to be something. *The main hall looks like an aircraft hangar... This play looks like a winner.* **4** to look **after** someone or something. *...women looking after young children.* **5** to look **into** a matter. *In 1959 a working party was set up to look into the problem... They do not seem to have looked into the facts of these cases.* **6** to look **on** or **upon** someone or something **as** a particular thing. *I no longer looked on him as my guide.* **7** to look **through** a collection of things such as clothes or documents. *I made a few telephone calls and looked through the post.* **8** to look **to** someone **for** something. *...a public which still looked to the state for the protection of its environment.* **9** to look **to** the future. *We're looking to April 1992 for the big comeback.* **10** to look back **on** something in the past. *When I look back on these incidents, I feel furious with myself.* **11** to look down **on** someone or something. *You make*

lookout

people look down on the school.
12 to look forward **to** something pleasant. *I'm very much looking forward to interviewing her... I always looked forward to those meetings.* **13** to look out **for** something that you might see. *Doctors and midwives have to look out for abnormalities.* **14** to look up **to** someone. *I was happier in John's company because I looked up to him.*

lookout be on the lookout; be on the lookout **for** something. *Everyone is on the lookout for extra work.*

loose be on the loose. *...a fear that the assassin may still be on the loose.*

loss **1** be at a loss; be at a loss for something. *He was at a loss without his familiar office... I've never been at a loss for an excuse.* **2** at a loss: not making a profit. *The zoo was running at a loss when he took over in July.*

lost **1** be lost **on** someone. *Sarcasm was always quite lost on John... The importance of this policy has clearly not been lost on politicians.* **2** be lost **without** someone or something. *I am lost without him... Schmidt admits he would have been lost without my advice.*

love **1** someone's love **for** a person. *Their love for each other is genuine.* **2** someone's love **of** something. *...his love of poetry.* **3** be **in** love; be **in** love **with** someone. *Our only crime was to fall in love... I was madly in love with Steve.*

loyal be loyal **to** someone or something. *In the long run they will remain loyal to the party.*

luck **1** be **in** luck: be lucky on a particular occasion. *I was in luck: somebody had left their vehicle unlocked.* **2** be **out of** luck: be unlucky on a particular occasion. *They were out of luck because there was really little for them to take.* **3** **with** luck: used to say

what you hope might happen. *I might with luck never have to live with anyone again.*

lull to lull someone **into** feeling safe. *...having lulled them into thinking what an amiable person he was... With Rick around, I had been lulled into a false sense of security.*

lumber to lumber someone **with** something that is not wanted. *New families were unwilling to lumber themselves with too much land.*

lust **1** a lust **for** something or someone. *My lust for praise was inordinate.* **2** to lust **for** or **after** something or someone. *Before, I had lusted for revenge... She had lusted after other men.*

luxuriate to luxuriate **in** something. *I luxuriated in her affection.*

M

mad **1** be mad **about** something: be enthusiastic about it. *She was mad about the cinema.* **2** be mad **at** someone or something: be angry with them. *I guess they're mad at me for getting them up so early.*

made **1** be made **of** a substance. *...a figure made of clay.* **2** be made up **of** things. *Our bodies are made up of millions of cells.*

mainstay the mainstay **of** something. *The short story has been the mainstay of science fiction.*

make **1** to make something **from** or **out of** a substance or thing. *...making soup from wild mushrooms. ...making a shelf out of cardboard boxes.* **2** to make something **into** something else. *You can make the leaves into soup.* **3** to make something **of** someone. *Harold's made fools of us all.* **4** to make something **of** something: to have an opinion or theory about it.

I wondered what they made of my decision. **5** to make **for** a destination. *Peter had picked up his coat and was making for the door.* **6** to make **for** something: to result in it. *Disappointment makes for bad manners.* **7** to make off **with** something: to steal it. *The dog tried to make off with one of his sausages.* **8** to make a cheque out **to** someone. *...a cheque made out to 'Lloyds Bank plc'.* **9** to make property over **to** someone. *You should make the business over to me.* **10** to make up **for** something that has been lost, missed, or damaged. *We'll make up for the adventure you missed.*

making 1 in the making: developing. *He had the ability to smell out a story in the making.* **2** be **of** your own **making:** be caused by yourself. *The effect of Dutch Elm Disease has been partly or wholly of our own making.*

mania a mania **for** something. *My father had a mania for gardening.*

margin a margin **of** something or **for** something. *...to create a margin of safety by building stockpiles... They have allowed a large margin for error.*

mark 1 a mark **of** a quality or situation. *To be able to ask for another version is a mark of status.* **2** to mark someone **as** a particular kind of person. *My skill at typing marked me as a girl who had once had to work for a living.* **3** to mark someone down **as** a particular kind of person. *Gillian and I were marked down as troublemakers.*

market 1 the market **for** a product or type of thing: people willing to buy that thing. *...the once booming market for natural cereals.* **2** a market **in** a product or type of thing: trade in that thing. *...an international market in drugs.* **3** be **in the market for** something: be wanting to buy something. *I wasn't really in the market for a pony.* **4** be **on the market:** be available for people to buy. *There are far too few creative toys on the market.*

married be married **to** someone. *I haven't been married to her for long.*

marvel to marvel **at** something. *I never ceased to marvel at their deftness and precision.*

masquerade to masquerade **as** someone or something else; to masquerade **under** a false name. *...quick-dried peas masquerading as fresh garden peas. ...where he might even now be masquerading under an assumed name.*

master be master **of** a situation or type of activity. *Vermeer was also master of the science of perspective.*

masterpiece a masterpiece **of** a quality. *...a speech which was a masterpiece of ambiguity.*

mastery 1 mastery **of** a skill. *Mastery of the game depends upon practice.* **2** mastery **over** something or **of** something. *It gave him a sense of mastery over time. ...mastery of the sea and air.*

match 1 a match **with** or **against** an opponent; a match **between** two people or teams. *We should win the match with Yugoslavia... The previous match against Coventry was a draw. ...a match between two novices.* **2** be a match **for** someone or something. *In the matter of muscle, he was a match for any two of them.* **3** to match yourself **against** an opponent. *Many amateurs were matching themselves against the professionals.* **4** to match one thing **with** or **to** another; to match one thing up **with** another. *...matching the skills and needs of the applicant with vacancies advertised by employers... The approach and methods should be matched to his previous experience... They will match up* the decision with others of a similar nature. **5** to match up **to** an idea or description. *Very rarely does that person match up to expectation.*

mate to mate **with** another animal. *The dominant males mate with every female in the tribe.*

mean 1 to mean a particular thing **by** a word or expression. *What do we mean by prosperity?* **2** to mean something **to** someone. *My medal may be a joke to you but it means a great deal to me.* **3** be mean **with** money. *He's mean with cash.* **4** be mean **to** someone. *Don't be mean to him.*

meant be meant **for** a particular person, thing, or purpose. *These children had simply no idea that books were meant for them... The beds were evidently not meant for comfort.*

meantime in the meantime. *I will persuade Dr Ford to come; in the meantime, you must sleep.*

measure 1 to measure something **by** a particular factor. *The grandeur of a house could be measured by the number of chefs in the kitchen.* **2** to measure one person or thing **against** another. *It would be hard to measure the gains against the losses.* **3** to measure up **to** a standard or someone's expectations. *...people who fail to measure up to even the minimum standards.*

mechanics the mechanics **of** something. *...the government's concern over the mechanics of the election campaign.*

meddle to meddle **in** something or **with** something. *Benjamin said that he refused to meddle in such matters... I don't let anyone else meddle with my kitchen.*

mediate to mediate **in** a dispute; to mediate **between** the people or groups involved. *...when he tried to mediate in a school fight. ...mediating between the author and his critics.*

meditate to meditate **on** or **upon** something. *He was left alone for half an hour to meditate on his sins.*

meet 1 to meet **with** or be met **with** a particular reaction. *The recommendation met with a storm of local protest. ...when her opening move was met with silence.* **2** to meet up **with** someone. *I met up with Mick Burke in the camp site.*

melt to melt **into** a crowd. *He melted into the sea of faces.*

member a member **of** a group or organization. *...working as members of a team.*

memento a memento **of** a person, event, or time. *...as a worthy memento of my visit.*

memorial a memorial **to** someone. *...an elaborate memorial to Sir Walter Mildmay.*

memory 1 someone's memory **of** something in the past. *The memory of hunger was fading from their minds.* **2** someone's memory **for** a type of thing. *I have an almost photographic memory for what I read.* **3 from memory:** remembering something rather than reading it. *He quoted the poem from memory.* **4 in memory of** someone who is dead: as a sign of respect for them. *...the Austin Prize, founded in memory of the late W.H. Austin.*

mention to mention something **to** someone. *She had mentioned the book to a few friends.*

mercy be **at** the mercy of someone or something. *Men are at the mercy of forces which are cruelly vindictive.*

merge to merge **with** or **into** something else. *Now they too can merge with the urban landscape if they choose... In practice, these categories merge into each other.*

merger a merger **between** two organizations or **with** another organization. *...the merger between the Council and the*

Commission... *We need to work out a merger with Boeing.*

mess 1 be **in a mess**. *The US economy is now in a mess.* **2** to mess about **with** something or mess around **with** something. *It's silly to mess about with the one thing everyone agrees on.*

metamorphose to metamorphose **into** something. *Soon, respectable bank clerks were metamorphosing into hippies for two weeks.*

metaphor a metaphor **for** something else; the metaphor **of** something that is used as an image. *In the work of many writers, nature becomes a metaphor for God... I have used the metaphor of the sea to express this.*

mete to mete out punishment **to** someone. *Exclusion is the sentence girls mete out to rule-breakers now.*

mid-air in mid-air. *The bird did a crazy half-turn in mid-air and darted away.*

middle in the middle of a place, time, or thing. *They were squatting in the middle of the road. ...the slam of car doors in the middle of the night.*

midst in the midst of a situation or group. *We were in the midst of a violent thunderstorm. ...if Ernest sees her sitting alone in the midst of all these people.*

militate to militate **against** something. *Family tensions can militate against learning.*

mind 1 not to mind **about** something. *He didn't mind about not reaching Konya.* **2** be **out of** your **mind**: be crazy. *Have you gone out of your mind?*

mindful be mindful **of** something. *Mindful of Ashok's warning, Kairi no longer spoke to him in public.*

mingle 1 to mingle or be mingled **with** something else. *Smells of petrol and oil mingled with those of turpentine and paint.* **2** to mingle **with** other people. ...*flying*

in to Heathrow Airport in order to mingle with diplomats.

minister to minister **to** people or their needs. *...ministering to the needs of her husband.*

miracle a miracle **of** a quality or action. *I have been told that I was a miracle of goodness. ...a miracle of perception.*

mirrored be mirrored **in** something or **by** something. *Inequalities between the sexes were mirrored in life in general... Diversity in animals and smaller plants is mirrored by the trees themselves.*

miserable be miserable **about** something. *I was still feeling a bit miserable about the canary.*

misgivings misgivings **about** something. *I had some misgivings about turning up unannounced.*

mislead to mislead someone **into** doing something. *Make sure Nature hasn't misled you into thinking you know something you don't actually know.*

miss to miss out **on** something. *...resentment about missing out on an important part of life.*

missing be missing **from** something. *The letter is missing from our files.*

mistake 1 by mistake. *...the British diplomat they had killed by mistake.* **2** to mistake one person or thing **for** another. *...young lecturers concerned not to be mistaken for students.*

mistaken be mistaken **about** something or **as to** something. *How could she have been mistaken about a thing like this?... He suggested hopefully that she might be mistaken as to her condition.*

misunderstanding a misunderstanding **between** people **about** something or **over** something. *This often led to misunderstandings between the press and Marine officers. ...misunderstandings about* discipline. ...the misunderstanding over the government's plans.

mix to mix one thing **with** another. *Mix the baking powder with the flour... We seek to mix serious debate with humour.*

mixed up 1 be mixed up **in** a situation or activity. *I was getting mixed up in a conspiracy.* **2** be mixed up **with** something else. *The computer had got the man's seat number mixed up with someone else's.*

mixture a mixture **of** things. ...*a mixture of cement and sand. ...a mixture of contempt, envy, and hope.*

moan to moan **about** something. *They're always moaning about how long they've waited for the bus.*

mock to mock **at** someone or something. *They mocked at the respectable middle class.*

mode a mode **of** something. ...*more conventionally acceptable modes of life... Consider the tricycle as a mode of transport.*

model 1 a model **of** an object. ...*a model of a sailing ship.* **2** a model **of** a quality: a fine example of it. *Sophia now became once again a model of efficiency.* **3** to model something **on** something else. *Mary had modelled her handwriting on Sister Catherine's.*

moderation in **moderation.** *Salted and smoked foods should be eaten in moderation.*

modification a modification **to** something or **of** something. *It recommended a number of modifications to the previous design. ...unable to make rational modifications of their positions.*

moment 1 at the **moment:** now. *I'm sorry, but she's not in at the moment.* **2** for the **moment:** temporarily. *The project seems to have been shelved for the moment.* **3** of the **moment:** used to describe what exists or what is important now. *Everything is decided according to the mood of the moment.*

monopoly a monopoly **of** something or **on** something. ...*the Communist Party's monopoly of power... Neither sex has a monopoly on thought or emotion.*

monument 1 a monument **to** someone. *So we built this monument to our dead.* **2** a monument **to** something or **of** something. *The scheme is a monument to bad planning. ...a precious monument of Parisian life.*

mood be in the mood **for** something. *He was in the mood for a chat.*

moratorium a moratorium **on** something. ...*a ten-year moratorium on whaling.*

most at **most;** at the **most.** *My job will only last two years at most... I only have fifteen minutes or twenty minutes at the most.*

motion 1 in **motion.** ...*the idea of seeing an atom in motion.* **2** to motion **to** someone. *Kleiber motioned to him and he unlocked a wine-cellar door.*

mourn to mourn **for** someone or something. *I mourned for that lost labour.*

move 1 be on the **move.** *The normal method is for the angler to keep on the move.* **2** to move **from** one place or home **to** another; to move **into** a new home or area. *They moved from Dundee back to Glasgow... Later he moved to Manchester... We'd just moved into a new apartment.* **3** to move in **with** someone. *He virtually moved in with the family.* **4** to move in **on** a place or person. *The guards were about to move in on the little crowd.* **5** to move on **to** another thing that needs dealing with. *Jimmie moved on to the more tricky matter of protocol.*

muck to muck about **with** something. *She was mucking about with a jug of flowers.*

multiply to multiply one number **by** another. *I had multiplied seventeen by ten and then doubled it.*

mumble to mumble **to** yourself. *She is still mumbling to herself in a vague way.*

murmur to murmur **to** someone. *'Poor chap,' Miss Darke murmured to Miss Craig.*

muscle to muscle in **on** something. *They may resent the way you are muscling in on their territory.*

muse to muse **on**, **over**, or **about** something. *I fell to musing on the revolution that is spreading through the land... I began to muse over a boyhood incident connected with the club... I was musing about the water.*

mutter to mutter **to** yourself. *I heard him muttering to himself.*

N

nag to nag **at** someone. *Eva had made his life a misery by nagging at him... Thoughts of Conrad constantly nagged at her.*

name 1 a name **for** a type of thing or person. *Every language has a name for them.* **2 by name.** *He mentioned you by name.* **3 by the name of** something: called something. *...an English criminal by the name of James Griffiths.* **4** to name a person or thing **after** someone, or, in American English, to name a person or thing **for** someone. *I hope that one day we will name something on Mars after him... Hayman Creek was named for Charles Hayman.* **5** to name someone **as** the person who did or will do something. *Lin Biao had been named as Mao's successor.*

native 1 a native **of** a particular country or region. *He is a native of Northern Ireland.* **2** be native **to** a particular country or region. *Both*

these species are native to America.

nature 1 by nature: naturally. *We are by nature forgetful.* **2 by** its **nature:** inevitably, because of its nature. *Equality is contagious. By its nature, it cannot be contained.* **3** be **in the nature of** something: be characteristic of it. *It is in the nature of state visits that the host country receives lavish praise from the visitors.*

necessary be necessary **for** something; a necessary requirement **for** something. *The forest maintains the conditions necessary for its own existence. ...space for play and the necessary peace for reading.*

necessity 1 the necessity **for** something or **of** something. *They are coming to realize the necessity for reform. ...its judgement as to the necessity of the investigations.* **2 of necessity.** *He has, of necessity, been careful in his treatment of white farmers.*

need 1 the need **for** something or **of** something. *He saw the need for change... The party would have no need of such an arrangement.* **2 in need; in need of** something. *Should those in need rely on the good will of their fellow men?... We are badly in need of a rest.*

negative in the negative. *The controller replied in the negative.*

neglectful be neglectful **of** something. *He had been neglectful of his duties.*

negotiate to negotiate **with** a person or group **for** something that you want. *...negotiating with the Government... He was no longer negotiating for the lives of a few prominent people.*

nervous be nervous **about** something or **of** something. *I began to get nervous about crossing roads... I have always been nervous of the sea.*

new 1 be new **to** an activity, situation, or place. *...the growing* *number of enthusiasts new to auctions.* **2** be new **to** someone. *...a story that was new to me.*

news 1 news **of** something or **about** something. *The Coast Guard called her with the news of Hooper's death. ...more encouraging news about England's cricketers.* **2** be **in the news.** *South Africa has been much in the news recently.*

next door next door **to** a building or the people who live there. *...Mrs Morris, who lives next door to Simon's parents.*

nibble to nibble **at** something. *I saw squirrels nibbling at the moist red berries.*

nice be nice **to** someone. *Find time to be nice to babies.*

night 1 at night: when it is night or during the night. *At night the streets are brilliant with neon signs. ...if he were to have a car accident at night.* **2 in the night:** at some time during the night. *He woke in the night with a dreadful pain.*

nod 1 to nod **to** someone or **at** someone, in greeting. *I nodded to them and sat down... They smiled and nodded at us.* **2** to nod **at** something or someone, in order to indicate them. *She nodded at the pictures of herself on the wall.*

nominate to nominate someone **for** an award or post, or **to** a body; to nominate someone **as** something. *She was four times nominated for an Oscar... Trade unions nominate representatives to public bodies. ...when Stevenson was nominated as democratic candidate.*

north north **of** a place. *Last year, a London furniture-maker opened a factory north of Newcastle.*

nostalgia nostalgia **for** the past. *...nostalgia for the sure values of faith and family.*

notable be notable **for** something. *The feature was notable for the brilliant quality of the writing.*

note be **of note:** be important or worth mentioning. *Raman's only previous score of note on this tour was 55.*

noted be noted **for** something. *...a man noted for his sense of humour.*

notify to notify someone **of** something; to notify something **to** someone. *...his failure to notify his colleagues of the contract... The ship's master did not notify the losses to the authorities.*

notorious be notorious **for** something. *...across the Bay of Biscay, which was notorious for bad weather.*

numb be numb **with** a painful or unpleasant emotion or sensation. *They look haggard and numb with grief... His legs were numb with cold.*

numbered be numbered **among** a group of people or things. *One of his wins this week will be numbered among the classics.*

O

oath on oath; under oath. *Witnesses sometimes lie on oath... He has been under pressure to testify before MPs under oath.*

obedience obedience **to** a person or rule. *...steadfast loyalty and obedience to our captains.*

object 1 /ɒbdʒɪkt/ the object **of** an action. *The object of these regular management meetings is to raise morale.* **2** the object **of** a feeling or reaction. *He became the object of considerable hero-worship.* **3** /əbdʒɛkt/ to object **to** something. *...those who object to killing animals for food.*

objection an objection **to** something. *I have a great objection to publishing private correspondence.*

obligation someone's obligation **to** someone or something. *Their sense* *of obligation to the child is so intense that they are not thinking enough of each other.*

oblivious be oblivious **to** something or **of** something. *They were seemingly oblivious to the sights and sounds around them... She seemed oblivious of the attention she was drawing to herself.*

obscure to obscure something **from** someone or something. *The cap of the man in front obscured most of the screen from Claude.*

obsessed be obsessed **with** or **by** someone or something. *She was obsessed with the past... I was obsessed by all sorts of doubts and fears.*

obstacle an obstacle **to** something. *The main obstacle to the extension of talks was the employers.*

obtain to obtain something **from** someone or something. *We suggest you obtain advice from your bank manager.*

occasion 1 the occasion **for** an action or thing. *The crisis will be the occasion for fundamental change.* **2 on occasion; on occasions.** *Suspension from school has an uneven effect but on occasion it has to be used.*

occupied be occupied **in** or **with** an activity; be occupied **with** someone or something. *She was occupied in examining the gift... Belinda seemed far too occupied with George.*

occur 1 to occur **in** a type of thing or person. *Most cases of stuttering occur in tense children.* **2** to occur **to** someone: to come into their mind as an idea. *It occurred to me that the time will come when we are all dead.*

odds 1 be **at odds with** someone or something: disagree with them. *The Prime Minister appeared to be at odds with the Environment Secretary.* **2 against the odds; against all odds:** when something seems difficult or impossible.

...when a Liberal wins a by-election against the odds... Against all odds, this story had a happy ending.

off-chance on the off-chance. *Should we preserve all our millionaires on the off-chance that one of them may fight an occasional battle for freedom?*

offend to offend **against** a law, rule, or principle. *It offends against a well-established principle of family life.*

offer 1 to offer something **to** someone. *He had thought about offering his help to the police... Catherine Parr offered apples to the young girl in the orchard.* **2 on offer.** *I ran my eye over the other belts on offer.*

office 1 in office: in an official position of authority. *The new president is not yet in office.* **2 out of office:** no longer in an official position of authority. *They decided on a campaign to throw all the United Party councillors out of office in the election.*

offset be offset **against** or **by** something else. *Such costs cannot be offset against income tax... The formal politeness of her curtsy was offset by her captivating smile.*

old of old: belonging to former times. *We were like treasure hunters of old who had stumbled upon a fabled emperor's jewel vaults.*

onslaught an onslaught **on** someone or something. *The bulldozers are mobilizing for their onslaught on some of the best countryside in the world.*

open 1 be open **to** something. *She is tolerant and open to new ideas.* **2** be open **to** someone. *The gardens are open to the public at lunch time... There is only one course of action open to you.* **3** be open **with** someone. *He was so kind and open with me.*

opening an opening **for** someone or something. *There is an opening*

operate to operate **on** someone. *The doctor advised him to have the hand operated on by a top surgeon.*

opinion someone's opinion **of** something or **about** something. *What is your opinion of social workers?... One seldom heard his opinion about anything in those days.*

opponent an opponent **of** someone or something. *...sensational propaganda from opponents of the party.*

opportunity an opportunity **for** achieving something. *Existing opportunities for profit are shamefully unexploited.*

opposed be opposed **to** someone or something. *The rest of the team were opposed to staying at Base Camp.*

opposite 1 the opposite **of** or **to** someone or something. *In many ways, passion is the opposite of love... Think of a word that means the opposite to work.* 2 be opposite **to** someone or something; the opposite thing **to** something else. *The other type of education system is entirely opposite to that... Lying down, roll your head in the opposite direction to your legs.*

opposition opposition **to** someone or something. *...her opposition to his plan of joining the army.*

opt 1 to opt **for** something. *Some defendants opt for trial by jury.* 2 to opt **out of** something. *...schools that opt out of local authority control.*

optimistic be optimistic **about** something. *We are extremely optimistic about Sky Television.*

option the option **of** doing something. *...offering more people the option of part-time employment.*

orbit **in orbit; into orbit.** *The astronauts of Apollo 9 had spent Christmas Day in orbit round the moon... Sputnik II had gone into orbit.*

order 1 **in order:** satisfactory. *I am in the process of putting my own affairs in order.* 2 be **out of order:** be broken. *Residents said the public telephone system was out of order last night.*

orientated be orientated **to** something or **towards** something. *The new movement was strongly orientated to gaining power.*

origin **in origin.** *Most health problems are environmental in origin.*

ornamented be ornamented **with** something. *...a booklet ornamented with sketches of flowers and baby birds.*

oscillate to oscillate **between** two things. *His mood had oscillated between gentle co-operation and physical violence.*

outcome the outcome **of** a situation or event. *A fierce battle was taking place, the outcome of which would be critical.*

outcry an outcry **against, about,** or **over** something. *He predicted an imminent outcry against collective investment... There was a public outcry about selling arms to the rebels. ...a growing public outcry over the frequency of kidnappings.*

outline 1 the outline **of** an object. *I could see the outline of the cliffs.* 2 an outline **of** a situation, plan, or idea. *The Government seeks an outline of future plans.* 3 **in outline.** *The tale has already been referred to in outline.*

outlook 1 someone's outlook **on** something. *What is new in human history is the power to change our outlook on time.* 2 the outlook **for** someone or something. *The outlook for food and energy prices is good.*

outpouring an outpouring **of** something. *...a massive outpouring of friendliness.*

outset 1 at the outset: at the beginning. *Both men resolved at the outset to tell the truth.* **2 from the outset:** from the beginning. *The conference was beset by controversy from the outset.*

outskirts the outskirts **of** a city or town. *The hospital was on the outskirts of town.*

overflow to overflow **with** something. *Her eyes overflowed with tears.*

overgrown be overgrown **with** plants or weeds. *A little path, overgrown with weeds, led to the bridge.*

overlap 1 to overlap **with** something else. *This land overlaps with land which is earmarked for acquisition.* **2** an overlap **between** things. *There is an overlap between attempted suicides and those who succeed in killing themselves.*

overloaded be overloaded **with** something. *Large parts of the ocean are overloaded with toxic waste.*

overview an overview **of** something. *...a broad overview of existing research.*

owe to owe something **to** someone. *We all owe a great debt to Dr Whitefeet... Many famous men have said they owe their success to their wives.*

own to own up **to** doing something wrong. *No-one owned up to taking the money.*

P, Q

packed be packed **with** things. *The room was packed with toys.*

pad to pad out a speech or piece of writing **with** something. *She has a habit of padding out her essays with a lot of long quotes.*

padded be padded **with** something. *The saddles were nicely padded with sheepskins and blankets.*

painted be painted **with** something. *...porcelain painted with intricate designs.*

pair to pair up **with** someone; to pair off **with** someone. *Disabled women have a greater chance of pairing up with able-bodied men... They show no inclination to pair off with each other.*

palm 1 to palm somebody off **with** an excuse or lie. *Don't let them palm you off with half answers.* **2** to palm something unwanted off **on** someone. *See what kind of cement those crooks palmed off on me.*

panacea a panacea **for** a problem or illness. *Nationalisation is no panacea for bad relations.*

pander to pander **to** someone or **to** their wishes. *...pandering to his guests' tastes.*

pang a pang **of** a feeling or emotion. *She felt a pang of regret that she had given up the theatre.*

panorama a panorama **of** things or people. *We stood looking at the panorama of trees and tiny meadows.*

paper 1 to paper **over** a problem or difficulty. *The Prime Minister was trying to paper over the crisis in the cities.* **2 on paper:** in theory, if not in reality. *My financial position was good, on paper.*

par on a par with something. *These recordings are nearly on a par with standard cassettes.*

parallel 1 be parallel **to** something or **with** something. *...a section of School Road running parallel to Thayer Street... The mystery of her family ran parallel with the mystery of the past.* **2** a parallel **between** two things. *White's article drew a parallel between Chiang and Stalin.* **3** parallels **with** someone or something. *His career and attitudes have interesting parallels with Pareto's.*

paralysed

paralysed be paralysed **by** something or **with** a feeling. *I was paralysed by that sight... Jimmie is nearly paralysed with tiredness and worry.*

paraphrase a paraphrase **of** something written or spoken. *His remarks sounded suspiciously close to a paraphrase of the Olympic motto.*

pardoned to be pardoned **for** doing something. *Women must be pardoned for being less than enthusiastic about such a gift.*

parity parity **with** something or **between** two things. *The women went on strike for parity with men... The aim is to create parity between private and public tenants.*

parody a parody **of** someone or something. *He spoke in a parody of the local dialect.*

part 1 to part **with** someone or something. *We were miserable at the prospect of parting with her.* 2 someone's part **in** an event. *He was arrested for his part in the demonstrations.* 3 **in part:** not completely. *In part, the relaxed atmosphere reflected new attitudes by the clergy.* 4 **on** someone's **part:** by or from someone. *Pointless malice on her part is revealed as envy of your success.*

partake 1 to partake **of** something. *He did not partake of either meal.* 2 to partake **in** an activity. *I was made to partake in a good deal of menial work.*

parted be parted **from** someone or something. *He would not be parted from his only weapon.*

partial be partial **to** something. *The vicar is very partial to roasted pheasant.*

partiality a partiality **for** something. *...a child's partiality for splashing through mud and puddles.*

participant a participant **in** an activity, action, or system. *...an active participant in the political guidance of the country.*

participate to participate **in** an activity, action, or system. *The students enjoy participating in the music and drama activities on offer.*

particular 1 be particular **about** something. *Hamsters are not especially particular about their food.* 2 **in particular:** especially. *...a remorseless campaign against crime and, in particular, violent crime.*

partnership a partnership **of** or **between** two people or groups; a partnership **with** one or more people or groups. *...forging a partnership between government and industry. ...Britain's move towards partnership with Europe.*

party be party **to** a plan, agreement, or action. *They simply wouldn't be a party to such a ridiculous exercise.*

pass 1 to pass something **to** someone. *He took the ball from Dan and passed it to Graham.* 2 to pass **for** or **as** a particular person or thing. *Tonight, he wanted to pass for a gentleman... If Ashton were to grow a moustache they could almost pass as brothers.* 3 to pass **over** a subject. *He passed over the events of that week.* 4 to pass something off **as** something else. *The painting had been passed off as early Flemish, or Dutch.* 5 to pass something on **to** someone. *I was to pass the information on to her.*

passion a passion **for** someone or something. *He had a passion for detective movies.*

passionate be passionate **about** something. *He is intensely violent and passionate about everything.*

passport a passport **to** something desirable. *Is education to be a passport to privilege?*

patient be patient **with** someone or something. *Rudolph was patient with the old man.*

patrol be **on patrol**. *They were constantly on patrol, ready for war.*

patterned 1 be patterned **on** something. *The Daily Dispatch was patterned on the British press.* **2** be patterned **with** designs of some kind. *...ties patterned with flowers.*

pay to pay **for** something. *He often leaves a cafe without paying for his drink.*

payable be payable **to** a particular person or organization. *It enables you to withdraw money by writing cheques payable to yourself.*

peculiar be peculiar **to** a person or thing. *...a disease peculiar to modern civilisation.*

pelt to pelt someone **with** things. *...pelting the actors with custard pies.*

peopled be peopled **by** or **with** people. *...a criminal world that seems to be peopled by businessmen rather than crooks... Britons still thought the American west was peopled with cowboys and Indians.*

perceive to perceive someone or something **as** doing or being a particular thing. *It is important that the president should be perceived as moving the country forward.*

persevere to persevere **with** something. *Almost any 'cure' can claim to be effective if you persevere with it long enough.*

persist to persist **in** something or **with** something. *Why did you not persist in your inquiries?... He persisted with his policy of mediation.*

perspective 1 a perspective **on** something or **of** something. *As an infant you gain a strange perspective on time. ...a shared perspective of the way in which society is organized.* **2** the perspective **of** a particular person. *This study looks at things from the perspective of an individual purchaser.* **3 in perspective; into perspective.** *We must keep the whole problem in perspective.*

pertain to pertain **to** someone or something. *...matters pertaining to education.*

phobia a phobia **about** something that frightens you. *Later, she developed a phobia about water.*

phone 1 by phone. *The ticket had been booked the previous Saturday by phone.* **2** be **on the phone**: be speaking to someone by telephone. *After speaking to the secretary on the phone, I never heard another word.* **3** be **on the phone**: have a telephone in your home or office. *I wish Elizabeth was on the phone, it's so hard to get in touch with her.*

pick 1 to pick **at** food: to eat only a small amount. *His mother just picked at her food.* **2** to pick **on** someone. *The stronger people would always pick on the ones who were quiet.*

picture a picture **of** someone or something. *In an oval frame was a picture of Guy's grandmother.*

piled be piled **with** something. *...an apparently endless counter piled with food.*

pin 1 to pin the blame for something **on** or **upon** someone. *The Court was unable to pin responsibility upon any one person.* **2** to pin your hopes or faith **on** someone or something. *The Treasury pinned its hopes on a sharp cut in borrowing.*

pine to pine **for** something or someone. *He had been pining for a moment like this.*

pivot to pivot **on** something. *Success or failure pivoted on a single exam.*

place 1 to place responsibility or pressure **on** or **upon** someone. *The responsibility placed upon us is too heavy to be borne.* **2 in place of** someone or something. *Oil can be used in place of the margarine if preferred.*

plagued be plagued **by** someone or something; be plagued **with** something. *...a cold, wet, disagreeable land plagued by constant winds... The young romance was plagued with constant separations.*

plan 1 to plan **for** a particular thing or event. *A commission was established in Tokyo to plan for the needs of the city.* **2** to plan **on** doing something. *I plan on staying in London for the foreseeable future.* **3** to have not planned **on** a particular thing. *I hadn't planned on the bad weather.*

plane by plane. *Robert and I have decided to go by plane.*

plastered be plastered **with** something. *Her face was plastered with white powder and her lips were bright red.*

play 1 to play **against** a person or team. *He is confident of playing against Scotland in the Calcutta Cup.* **2** to play **at** doing or being something. *When they were little girls they had played at being grown-ups.* **3** to play **on** or **upon** someone's feelings, attitudes, or weaknesses. *He used to play on their prejudices and their fears.* **4** to play **with** a toy or a child. *It is normal for little boys to want to play with dolls.* **5** to play along **with** someone or something. *I wouldn't play along with his plan to drop the union agreement.* **6** to play around **with** someone or something. *We spent the whole afternoon playing around with bits of string.* **7** to play people off **against** each other. *Here was an example of one section of workers being played off against another.*

pleased 1 be pleased **with** someone or something. *His employers were pleased with his efforts.* **2** be pleased **at** something or **about** something. *Hamo was pleased at this praise of his great-uncle... He tried to feel pleased about the acceptance of his article.*

plot to plot **against** someone. *They plotted against him and decided to kill him.*

plough ! to plough **into** something. *The car skidded before ploughing into the bank.* **2** to plough money **into** something. *...huge sums of money which could be ploughed into computing.* **3** to plough **through** a meal or a piece of work. *They must be given time to plough through their meals.*

plump to plump **for** something. *Few gentlemen would now care to plump for an army career.*

plunge to plunge **into** an activity or subject. *He has a half-hour sleep before plunging into work.*

ply to ply somebody **with** food, drink, or questions. *They had plied him with too much drink.*

point 1 to point **at** or **to** someone or something. *Lebel pointed at the door lock with his forefinger... Brody pointed to the table near the other side of the bed.* **2** to point something **at** someone or something. *I found him pointing an air-gun at a chicken.* **3** to point **to** someone or something: used of evidence. *All the evidence points to him being the killer.* **4** be **beside the point**: be irrelevant. *My actual guilt or innocence seems beside the point here.* **5** be **to the point**: be relevant. *Make sure that your memos and letters are intelligible and to the point.*

poke 1 to poke **at** someone or something. *Gretchen poked at his cheek with two fingers.* **2** to poke **through** something or **out of** something. *...a wet armchair with a rusty spring poking through the fabric... His huge hands poked out of a bright red silk smoking jacket.*

ponder to ponder **on** or **upon** something. *Mary pondered bitterly upon the meaning of life.*

poor be poor **in** a quality or substance. *Their food was poor in nutritional value.*

popular be popular **with** a person or group of people. *She is very popular with the general public.*

populated be populated **by** or **with** people or things. *The town is heavily populated by immigrants. ...huge gardens populated with marble statues.*

pore to pore **over** something. *He was sitting in a corner, poring over the accounts.*

portrait a portrait **of** a person. *...that vivid portrait of the Queen.*

pose to pose **as** someone else. *Two police officers managed to infiltrate the drugs syndicate by posing as yachtsmen.*

positive be positive **about** a fact or thing. *I am trying to persuade them to be more positive about the future.*

possessed 1 be possessed **of** a thing, quality, or ability. *...a young man possessed of exceptional ability, character and courage.* 2 be possessed **by** someone or something. *Alexander was possessed by terrible sadness.*

possession be **in** possession **of** something. *MacDonald has been in possession of the letter for some weeks.*

possibility the possibility **of** an event or result. *There was now no possibility of success.*

post **by** post. *Winners will be notified by post.*

potter to potter **about** or **around** a place. *He spent the Saturday afternoon pottering about his garden.*

pounce to pounce **on** or **upon** someone or something. *Three men wearing stocking masks pounced on Mr Terence Culshaw... His colleagues were ready to pounce upon any slip he made.*

power 1 the power **of** a person or thing. *His opponents were well aware of the power of his propaganda.* 2 power **over** someone or something. *For once*

parents see a chance to wield real power over their children's future.

pray 1 to pray **to** a god. *He knelt down and prayed to Allah.* 2 to pray **for** someone. *They prayed for him in church on Sundays.* 3 to pray **for** something you want to have or to happen. *Lerwick was still praying for his friend's recovery three weeks later.*

preach 1 to preach **to** a group of people. *There were only ten people in the congregation, but when I preached to them I felt faint and helpless.* 2 to preach **against** someone or something you disapprove of. *He came to preach against the heretics.* 3 to preach **at** someone. *I've had enough of you preaching at me all the time!*

precondition a precondition **of** something or **for** something. *Economic growth is a precondition of any kind of human advance... A sense of loyalty to the planet is a precondition for our survival.*

precursor a precursor **of** something or **to** something. *The railways were the precursor of what was to come... Learning the Highway Code was a precursor to any actual driving.*

prediction a prediction **of** something or **about** something. *A prediction of the likely outcome of the next election was made by Alan Taylor. ...a number of alternative predictions about the future of higher education.*

predilection a predilection **for** something. *Why do the British have such a predilection for expelling Soviet spies?*

predispose to predispose someone **to** a particular belief, way of life, or attitude. *The stranger's role predisposes him to a distinctly 'objective' attitude.*

preface 1 a preface **to** a book. *Granville-Barker had written a fine preface to the play.* 2 to preface an action or activity **with**

something. *Each girl who spoke prefaced her remarks with 'sorry'.*

prefer to prefer one thing **to** another. *There are men who prefer death to dishonour.*

preferable be preferable **to** something else. *Gradual change is preferable to sudden, large-scale change.*

pregnant 1 be pregnant **with** a child; be pregnant **by** a man. *My mother was pregnant with me at the time... Sarah was pregnant by another man.* 2 be pregnant **with** meaning or significance. *She kept a silence which was pregnant with indications of how much more she could say.*

prejudice prejudice **against** someone or something. *Prejudice against women is becoming less severe.*

prejudiced be prejudiced **against** someone or something. *An increasing number of people believe the police are prejudiced against coloured people.*

prejudicial be prejudicial **to** someone or something. *Such conduct would surely be prejudicial to the interest of the union.*

prelude the prelude **to** an event. *The speech has been hailed by his friends as the prelude to his return to office.*

premonition a premonition **of** an event. *His hand shook violently and he had a premonition of failure.*

preoccupied be preoccupied **with** a particular idea or problem. *Ike seemed completely preoccupied with his own thoughts.*

prepare to prepare **for** an event or situation. *Police in Wiltshire are preparing for a hippy invasion of Stonehenge.*

prepared be prepared **for** something. *Be prepared for power-cuts by buying lots of candles.*

prerequisite a prerequisite **for, of,** or **to** something. *Freeing the press was a necessary prerequisite for full democracy. ...educated skills that are the prerequisite of progress for our country... A full stomach is the prerequisite to self-respect.*

prescription 1 a prescription **for** something. *...an analysis of the nature of the crisis or a prescription for its cure.* 2 **on prescription.** *...pharmaceutical products supplied on prescription.*

present 1 /prɛzənt/ **at present:** now. *I don't want to get married at present.* 2 **for the present:** now and until a later time. *That's all for the present, Miss Livingstone.* 3 /prɪzɛnt/ to present something **to** someone. *The Princess of Wales presented a special award to Sir Alec Guinness.* 4 to present someone **with** something. *I closed our meeting by presenting him with a signed copy of my book.* 5 to present yourself **at** a particular place. *The visitor presented himself at the vicarage.*

preside 1 to preside **at** or **over** a formal gathering. *He presided at Saturday's meeting alone... He was the sixth judge to preside over the pre-trial hearings.* 2 to preside **over** an event. *He presided over the rapid expansion of the company.*

press 1 to press something **on** or **upon** someone. *They were flattered enough by the gifts that were pressed on them.* 2 to press **for** something you want. *He continued to press for a peaceful solution.* 3 to press someone **into** doing something. *The expedition to capture Brighton fishermen and press them into national service had been a total failure.* 4 to press ahead **with** or press on **with** an activity or task. *The Commission will continue to press ahead with its controversial demands... They courageously pressed on with their vital repair work.*

pressurize to pressurize someone **into** doing something. *The West continued to pressurize the Prince into cutting his ties with the Khmer Rouge.*

pretence a pretence **of, at,** or **to** something. *The industry has abandoned any pretence of restraint... Gone, now, was all pretence at sociability... She has never made any pretence to ladylike behaviour.*

pretensions pretensions **to** something. *He was a modern man with no pretensions to education at all.*

prevail 1 to prevail **on** or **upon** someone. *Security staff prevailed upon the crowd to move back from the crash barriers.* 2 to prevail **over** someone or something. *Political arguments had prevailed over economic sense.*

prevent to prevent someone or something **from** doing something. *A storm was preventing rescue aircraft from landing.*

pride 1 pride **in** someone or something. *Everything Rattle says confirms his overwhelming pride in his Birmingham orchestra.* 2 to pride yourself **on** doing or being something. *Cricket prides itself on being a gentlemanly game.*

principle 1 **in principle:** as a probability but not yet officially. *The Government has agreed to this measure in principle.* 2 **on principle:** in accordance with a belief or rule. *Subordinates must be kept waiting on principle.*

prise to prise something **out of** someone. *They hoped that growing publicity would prise more money out of the California State Legislature.*

privy be privy **to** something. *Very few of them were privy to the details of the conspiracy.*

probability The probability **of** an event or result. *Such radio-telescopes would greatly increase the probability of success.*

probe 1 to probe **into** something. *Humming birds gather nectar by probing deep into the blossoms with long thin tongues.* 2 to probe **for** something. *He went ahead in the first car, probing for road blocks.*

proceed 1 to proceed **with** something. *They were having difficulty in trying to decide how to proceed with the project.* 2 to proceed **against** a person or organization. *Subsequent police investigation found no grounds for proceeding against him.*

proceeds the proceeds **of** an event or activity. *The land was bought out of the proceeds of the Exhibition.*

procure to procure something **for** someone. *He offered to procure extra comforts for the prisoner.*

produce 1 to produce evidence or an argument **for** or **against** something. *He produces no evidence for his beliefs... They had produced all kinds of arguments against her.* 2 to produce something **from** a place or thing. *We are capable of producing the same amount of food from less and less land.*

product the product **of** something. *Strikes are the product of the society in which we live.*

profession by profession. *By profession she was a stewardess.*

proffer to proffer something **to** someone. *He helped himself from the sauce boat proffered to him.*

proficient be proficient **in** something or **at** something. *You must be proficient in the language to gain equal opportunities... Do you think calculators stop children being proficient at mathematics?*

profile a profile **of** someone. *She wanted to write profiles of the leaders of the party.*

profit to profit **from** something or **by** something. *Businessmen are seeking to profit from the Single European Market... They have* *profited by their experience with me.*

progress 1/ˈprəʊgrɛs/ to progress **to** something new. *From there we progressed to a discussion on politics.* 2/prəʊgrɛs/ progress **towards** something. *...rapid progress towards ending the civil war.* 3 progress **with** a task. *...if you are making no progress with your training schedule.* 4 **in progress:** happening. *Change is already in progress.*

prohibited be prohibited **from** doing something. *Banks are prohibited from dealing in securities.*

project /ˈprɒdʒɛkt/ to project someone or something **as** a particular thing. *They are projecting the farmer as a rural entrepreneur.*

promise 1 a promise **to** someone. *I hope you will be able to keep your promises to that poor old man.* 2 a promise **of** something. *...her endless waiting for Rossetti to honour his promise of marriage.*

promote to promote someone **from** one job **to** a more important one. *He was promoted from corporal to sergeant.*

prone be prone **to** something. *Large families are usually poorer and more prone to sickness than small ones.*

pronounce to pronounce **on** or **upon** something. *He is expected to pronounce on every moral and social issue.*

proof 1 proof **of** something. *Every day was bringing him further proof of Gertrude's love.* 2 proof **against** someone. *...the absence of proof against the three defendants.* 3 be proof **against** something. *We can design a system that's proof against accident and stupidity.*

proportion 1 in proportion **to** something; **in proportion with** something. *Schoolchildren expend far more energy in proportion to their size than adults do... Western cities expanded in proportion with the growth of industry.* 2 be **out of proportion to** something: be too large or small in comparison with that thing. *Their significance is out of all proportion to their size.*

proportional be proportional **to** something. *As a rule the suicide rates are proportional to the size of the city.*

prospect /ˈprɒspɛkt/ 1 the prospect **of** something. *Many people are horrified at the prospect of learning new skills.* 2 the prospects **for** something. *The prospects for revolution are remote.*

protect to protect a person or thing **from** or **against** a danger. *The ozone layer protects the Earth from harmful radiation... Babies are protected against some diseases by their mother's milk.*

protective be protective **of** or **towards** someone or something. *Daniel had become protective of his privacy... Molly felt very protective towards her sister.*

protest /prəˈtɛst/ to protest **at, about,** or **against** something. *...a leaflet protesting at animal experiments... Both players protested about some of the decisions. ...hundreds of marchers protesting against the planned construction of a nuclear power plant.*

proud be proud **of** someone or something. *Somerset Maugham was proud of his prowess as an avocado farmer.*

provide 1 to provide someone **with** something. *The Army has provided US troops with combat exercise facilities.* 2 to provide something **for** someone or something. *The company spends the bulk of its funds on providing training for executives.*

pry to pry **into** something. *Don't go prying into my affairs or you'll get hurt.*

public in public. *Meetings previously held in public will now take place in closed session.*

pull 1 to pull **on** something or **at** something. *The driver pulled on a lever... Margaret pulled at Dixon's sleeve.* 2 to pull **out of** an event or situation. *John McEnroe has pulled out of the United States tennis team's forthcoming match.*

punctuated be punctuated **by** or **with** particular things. *...a night of terror punctuated by the roar of shells and rockets... Many of us have had a school career punctuated with exams, marks and tests.*

punish to punish someone **for** doing something wrong. *They discovered his crime and punished him for it.*

punishable be punishable **by** something. *...a criminal offence punishable by six months in jail.*

purge to purge someone or something **of** a particular thing. *I tried desperately to purge myself of these dangerous desires.*

pursuit in pursuit of something. *It was in pursuit of these very ideals that hundreds of people have died.*

push 1 to push **for** something you want. *The Transport Department is clearly pushing for further privatization of ports.* 2 to push someone **into** doing something. *...their determination not to be pushed into acceptance of nuclear missiles.* 3 to push something **on, onto,** or **upon** someone. *...an insurance salesman persistently trying to push an unwanted policy on him.* 4 to push ahead **with** or push on **with** a task. *Michael Ward is pushing ahead with loans and help for projects... I must push on with these enquiries as fast as I can.*

put 1 to put an idea or question **to** someone. *I half agreed and so I put the idea to Gillian.* 2 to put one thing **above** another or **before** another. *He is prepared to put the interests of his profession above that of the Conservative Party... British Rail admitted that it had put passenger convenience before safety.* 3 to put something **before** someone for them to consider. *The Bill was put before Parliament in December.* 4 to put a bad or unpleasant experience **behind** you. *The company appears to have put its troubled past behind it.* 5 to put someone down **as** something. *I put him down as a loutish member of the Socialist Workers Party.* 6 to put something down **to** a particular cause. *It seemed unsafe to put anything down to coincidence.* 7 to put up **with** something. *Maybe Sally was not able to put up with that much stress.* 8 to put someone up **to** doing something. *Julia had probably put them up to it herself.*

qualify 1 to qualify **for** something. *Only a very small proportion of people who qualify for benefit draw it for any length of time.* 2 to qualify **as** something. *He's coming home to try and qualify as an estate agent.*

quarrel 1 to quarrel **with** someone **about** something or **over** something. *...quarrelling with landlords about foreign coins in the gas meter... They have ceased to quarrel over the repeal of such laws.* 2 a quarrel **with** someone or **between** people **about** something or **over** something. *Jefferson gave his version of the quarrel with Adams. ...a quarrel between a bus driver and his passengers. ...quarrels about words and their meanings. ...quarrels over land ownership.*

quest 1 a quest **for** something. *...the fundamental human quest for understanding.* 2 in quest of something or someone. *So he set off in quest of immortality.*

question

question 1 a question **about** something. *...questions about the future of the environment.* 2 a question **of** a particular thing: used to say what topic you are talking about. *It's all a question of your attitude... I have no views on the question of subsidies.* 3 to question someone **about** something. *She was questioned about the subject of her latest book.* 4 **beyond question:** definitely. *The survey has shown beyond question a real and dramatic improvement.* 5 be **in question:** be doubted *His ability to lead his country in difficult times has never been in question.* 6 **in question:** used when referring to the thing involved. *A copy of the bulletin in question was received by my department.* 7 be **out of the question:** be impossible. *A cut in interest rates is out of the question.* 8 **without question:** undoubtedly. *They are without question the best team in Europe.*

quibble to quibble **with** someone **about** or **over** something. *Was the president of the student council quibbling about representation on the committee?... I will not quibble with him over his evaluation of the situation.*

quick be quick **at** something. *You're quick at learning aren't you?*

quiet on the quiet: secretly. *They've been building up quite a large shareholding on the quiet.*

quotation a quotation **from** a book, play, film, and so on. *...a direct quotation from Burton's journals.*

quote 1 to quote **for** doing a particular piece of work. *Ask the refuse department to come and quote for removing the stuff.* 2 a quote **from** a book, play, film, and so on. *...a quote from the American magazine Business Week.*

R

racked be racked **by** or **with** an unpleasant or painful feeling. *During the last five days Anne was racked by delirium from typhus... So you see, we are all racked with guilt.*

radiate 1 to radiate **from** a particular point. *The roads radiating from the circuit are expected to be jammed.* 2 to radiate **from** someone. *A sense of enjoyment radiates from the players.*

radio on radio; on the radio. *Mr Li Xiannian's speech was broadcast on radio this morning. ...the suggestion made on the radio by Douglas Hurd.*

rage a rage **for** something. *All over England there was a great rage for bell-ringing.*

raid a raid **on** a place. *They wrote to protest about police raids on members' homes.*

rail to rail **against** or **at** something. *MPs railed against the inhumanity of such a steep increase... Rather than railing at fate, it would be better to re-examine the relationship.*

raise to raise a subject **with** someone. *His next most likely step is to raise the issue with the Bishop of Chicago.*

ramble to ramble on **about** something. *Just babble—ramble on about nothing, basically.*

random at random. *Juries are selected at random from men and women aged between 18 and 65.*

range 1 a range **of** things. *...a wide range of audio-visual aids.* 2 to range **between** two things, or **from** one thing **to** another. *Performances range between the dull and the hysterical... Symptoms range from a mild flu to the brain disease meningitis.* 3 **at** a particular **range.** *They shot him several times at close range.*

rapport a rapport **with** someone or **between** people or things. *Mrs Thatcher, for all her rapport with Mr Gorbachov, is sceptical. ...the rapport between human values and the goals of socialism.*

rat to rat **on** someone or **on** an agreement you make with them. *So you ratted on Gertrude?... I hope you're not thinking of ratting on the deal.*

rate 1 at any rate: used to qualify a statement. *Steve, at any rate, seems to be a satisfied customer.* **2 at this rate:** if things continue as they are doing. *At this rate, we cannot see how Britain can begin to reach the targets for carbon-dioxide reduction.* **3** to rate someone **as** something. *How do you rate her as a photographer?*

ration to ration someone **to** a particular amount of something. *I'm going to ration you to one cigarette a day.*

rationale the rationale **for** something or **of** something. *Religious belief provides a rationale for altruistic behaviour... The rationale of the social services is to promote social equality.*

rattle to rattle on **about** something. *Some of the women there would rattle on about sex.*

ravages the ravages **of** something harmful, dangerous, or unpleasant. *He restored the Academy after the ravages of the revolution.*

rave 1 to rave **against** something or **at** someone. *He raved against the horrors and brutality of war... He sat and raved at me for half an hour.* **2** to rave **about** someone or something. *We don't go and rave about anybody, or celebrate or destroy them.*

reaches the reaches **of** a river or area of land. *...the farthest reaches of the war zone.*

react 1 to react **against** something. *They are likely to react against the identity card scheme.*

2 to react **to** something. *Whether by accident or design, Mrs Thatcher reacted promptly to the call.* **3** to react **with** a particular response or emotion. *Clough reacted with the dignity and graciousness characteristic of his team.* **4** to react **with** a chemical substance. *The water reacts with the ferrous iron.*

reaction 1 a reaction **against** something. *...a widespread reaction against post-war realism.* **2** a reaction **to** something. *We were chatting about his reactions to the paintings.* **3** a reaction **of** one substance **with** another one, or **between** them. *...the reaction of the blades with the water. ...the reaction between methane and steam.*

read 1 to read **about** something. *I had read about the process in novels.* **2** to read something **as** a particular thing. *This drawing could be read as an exemplar of classical expression.* **3** to read a meaning or quality **into** something. *It was possible to read an admission of defeat into his words.* **4** to read up **on** a particular topic. *You can read up on the theory and be ready for it.*

readjust to readjust **to** a situation. *...the problem of readjusting to normal life.*

ready be ready **for** something. *The electronics industry will get bigger and we're not even ready for that... Their crops would soon be ready for harvesting.*

real for **real**. *It was done. I was on my own for real.*

reality in **reality**. *In reality, it's a dreary little town.*

reason 1 a reason **for** something. *The caller gave no reason for the choice of McDonald's as a target.* **2** to reason **with** someone. *I'll have to reason with him to take a smaller amount.* **3** by **reason of** something. *They seem likely, by reason of political expedience, to*

rebel

move to the right. **4 within reason:** not excessively. *You could buy as many letters as you wanted, within reason.*

rebel /rɪbɛl/ to rebel **against** something. *In 1956, Ian Smith rebelled against the British Government.*

rebound 1 /rɪbaʊnd/ to rebound **on** or **upon** someone. *His temper and resentment rebounded on Cal.* **2** /riːbaʊnd/ **on the rebound; on the rebound from** someone: starting a new relationship too soon. *She showed affection—was she on the rebound from Gareth?*

rebuke to rebuke someone **for** doing something. *Was she rebuking me for the things she had grown to condemn?*

receive 1 to receive something **from** someone. *One morning I received a startling letter from him.* **2** to receive someone **into** an organization or society. *According to custom, he had been received into his mother's tribe.*

receptive be receptive **to** something. *Members should be more alert and receptive to the day's business.*

recipe a recipe **for** a particular outcome. *Add to this the traffic problems, and you have a recipe for disaster.*

recipient a recipient **of** something. *He was the recipient of five honorary degrees.*

reckon 1 to reckon **on** or **upon** something. *They had not reckoned on such a fight.* **2** to reckon **with** something. *Le Pen proved he was still a force to be reckoned with.* **3** to reckon **without** something. *But they had reckoned without Margaret's determination.*

recognize to recognize someone or something **as** a particular thing. *They are asking for Ukrainian to be recognized as an official language. ...movements in the womb which most mothers recognize as kicking.*

recoil to recoil **at** or **from** something. *Parents may recoil at this behaviour... He recoiled from me and uttered a sound of disgust.*

recommend to recommend someone or something **as** something, or **for** a particular purpose. *The Cambrian Mountains in central Wales are recommended as candidates for park status in the report... They are unlikely to recommend students for unsuitable positions.*

reconcile 1 to reconcile one thing **to** or **with** another thing. *It was only this which reconciled him to his accident... The difficulty of reconciling the needs of development with concern over the expatriate community.* **2** be reconciled **to** or **with** something. *They were reconciled to higher interest rates... Such views are not easily reconciled with long-standing tradition.* **3** be reconciled **with** someone. *They had gone back to their home towns and had been reconciled with their families.*

record /rɛkɔːd/ **1** be **on record as** saying something. *The employers were on record as supporting the decision to scrap the scheme.* **2** be **off the record:** used of information given unofficially. *Now that remark was off the record, understand?* **3 for the record:** used to make a point emphatically. *For the record, I'd just like to say that I totally disagree with this decision.*

recourse recourse **to** something. *They would give up democratic methods and take recourse to violence.*

recover to recover **from** an illness, disease, or unpleasant experience. *He never recovered from Vita's death... He's still recovering from glandular fever.*

recovery recovery **from** an illness, disease, or unpleasant experience. *Her recovery from fatigue had been rapid.*

reinforce

recruit to recruit someone **for** a particular purpose. *It is becoming harder to recruit lively youngsters for the farms.*

recuperate to recuperate **from** a disease or illness. *He is recuperating from serious health problems.*

reduce 1 to reduce something **from** one level **to** another. *The number of dancers was reduced from 48 to 32.* 2 to reduce something **to** a particular state. *Any survivors would be quickly reduced to the life of a hunter-gatherer.*

reduction a reduction **in** something or **of** something. *Very few people agreed with a reduction in fees. ...the reduction of the prison population.*

reek 1 to reek **of** something or **with** something. *...a small airless theatre crammed with children and reeking with popcorn. ...members of the bench who pass down sentences reeking of racial bias.* 2 a reek **of** something. *The reek of paraffin met her nostrils.*

refer 1 to refer **to** someone or something; to refer **to** someone or something **as** a particular kind of person or thing. *The speeches that followed referred to the Icelandic strike... Jim, on more than one occasion, referred to Alec as 'just plain daft'.* 2 to refer someone **to** someone else. *If necessary, students are referred to a specialist.*

reference 1 reference **to** someone or something. *She made no further reference to Florida.* 2 **with reference to** something. *Candidates should select their options with reference to their future courses.*

reflect 1 to reflect **on, over,** or **upon** something: to consider it. *...reflecting on the political scene back at home... Rodin reflected long over Casson's argument.* 2 to reflect **on** someone or something in

a particular way. *Any lapse in her efficiency would reflect badly on him.*

reflection 1 a reflection **of** something. *The group's title was an accurate reflection of what they stood for.* 2 a reflection **on** or **upon** someone. *...a depressing reflection on the standard of our game.* 3 **on reflection.** *On reflection, I suppose his tales are just too old-fashioned.*

refrain to refrain **from** doing something. *A biographer should refrain from judgement.*

refusal someone's refusal **of** something. *The refusal of a pardon ended with sinister words.*

regale to regale someone **with** stories, jokes, anecdotes, and so on. *The woman regaled the child with stories of poisoned spindles, glass slippers, and malevolent step-sisters.*

regard 1 to regard someone or something **as** a particular thing. *She regarded Mr Gorbachov as a man of great political courage... These museums ought to be regarded as being a unique case.* 2 to regard someone or something **with** a particular feeling. *The plan was regarded with considerable suspicion.* 3 regard **for** someone or something. *The terrorists who planted the bomb showed little regard for the local population.* 4 **with regard to** a particular thing; **in regard to** a particular thing. *Great care needs to be taken with regard to his coaching role. ...differences between nations, especially in regard to the presence of troops on their territory.*

regress to regress **to** a particular state. *She had to get out before she regressed to infancy.*

reimburse to reimburse someone **for** something. *Only a few schools reimburse the chairman for his or her expenses.*

reinforce to reinforce an object **with** something. *I had not thought* *of reinforcing the handles with leather.*

rejoice to rejoice **in** something. *Halifax can rejoice in a convincing victory.*

relapse /rɪˈlæps/ to relapse **into** a particular state. *He relapsed into dreamy silence.*

relate 1 to relate one thing **to** another. *Pupils need to relate what they learn at school to their own experiences.* 2 to relate **to** a particular subject. *...a question that relates to electricity... A thick black line was drawn through words and passages relating to Sylvia.* 3 to relate **to** people. *Children must learn to relate to other children... Patients need to feel that they can relate to the outside world.*

related be related **to** someone or something. *One member of the Government was related to a senior member of the ICRC... Russian art was closely related to social and political change.*

relation 1 relations **with** someone or **between** two groups of people. *...your relations with the opposite sex... Relations between the two countries were badly strained.* 2 the relation **of** one thing **to** another. *...the relation of music to the emotions.* 3 **in relation** to a particular subject; **with relation to** a particular subject. *...research in relation to food consumption. ...a system of cause and effect with relation to parental approval.*

relationship a relationship **with** someone or something, or a relationship **between** two people or things. *The effects on Britain's relationship with Spain could only be positive. ...the relationship between parents and children.*

relaxation the relaxation **of** a rule or law, or a relaxation **in** a rule or law. *Captain Imrie felt he could permit himself a slight relaxation of attitude. ...a general relaxation in child discipline.*

relay 1 /ˈriːleɪ/ to relay an idea or opinion **to** someone. *They have relayed their views to Members of Parliament... I relayed Ali's assurances about safety to them.* 2 /ˈriːleɪz/ **in relays.** *The children at our school have to be fed in two relays.*

release 1 to release someone **from** a place or duty. *He was released from custody in February... This releases them from personal responsibility.* 2 release **from** a place or duty. *...an old woman's release from a mental hospital... Provision was made for a release from employment.* 3 **on release:** used of films being shown at cinemas. *...Geoff Brown's selection of films in London and on release across the country.*

relegate to relegate someone or something **to** a particular state. *This relegated the clergy to the status of amateurs... The supremacy of the Afrikaner is being relegated to a chapter in history.*

relevant be relevant **to** a particular subject. *One speech stands out as being highly relevant to the poll tax.*

reliance reliance **on** or **upon** something. *...reliance on nuclear energy.*

reliant be reliant **on** or **upon** something. *The police are reliant on the goodwill of the public.*

relief relief **from** something unpleasant. *...such practical activity was a light relief from academic work.*

relieve to relieve someone **of** something. *We must relieve them of the burden of debt.*

rely to rely **on** or **upon** someone or something. *They rely on firewood for cooking.*

remains the remains **of** something. *...the remains of a medieval priory... Firemen discovered the remains of a human body.*

remand on remand. *We have one client on remand at a local prison.*

remark to remark **on** or **upon** something. *Miss Ryan remarked on the excellence of his English.*

remedy a remedy **for** a disease, illness, or problem. *...a remedy for arthritis... Military support no longer supplies a remedy for political dissent.*

remember to remember someone **to** another person. *Don't forget to remember me to your father.*

remembrance 1 remembrance **of** something or someone. *...a pictorial remembrance of our trip.* 2 **in remembrance of** someone who is dead. *People tried to throw tributes in remembrance of their dead relatives.*

remind 1 to remind someone **of** someone or something. *Zasi's picture immediately reminded me of you... The damp grey skies reminded me of Manchester.* 2 to remind someone **about** something. *He spent five minutes reminding one speaker about his last speech.*

reminisce to reminisce **about** something. *Among those reminiscing about the early years was Keith Topley.*

reminiscent be reminiscent **of** something or someone. *...a smell reminiscent of cats. ...a solo piece that was reminiscent of Copeland.*

remonstrate to remonstrate **with** someone. *David could not believe it, and remonstrated with her.*

remote be remote **from** something or someone. *The organization has become remote from the members.*

remove to remove someone or something **from** a place. *He removed a card from his pocket.*

removed be removed **from** something. *He is far removed from Catholic teachings... The scene was some way removed from the idyll he'd imagined.*

rendezvous a rendezvous **with** someone. *She failed to keep a rendezvous with him earlier in the evening.*

rendition a rendition **of** something. *An uncertain rendition of The Internationale was drowned by the loudspeakers.*

renege to renege **on** an agreement or promise. *After only three months, he has reneged on all his commitments to reform.*

renowned be renowned **for** something. *Sir Peter is renowned for his charm and sense of humour.*

rent for rent. *Twenty-five per cent of the houses are for rent.*

renunciation the renunciation **of** a belief or method. *...a formal renunciation of terrorism. ...the renunciation of the formalist tradition.*

repair beyond repair. *They need money to restore the church before it is damaged beyond repair.*

repay to repay someone **for** doing something. *We only hope we can repay you for the pleasure you have given us.*

repeal the repeal **of** a law. *...the repeal of the Corn Laws in 1846.*

repent to repent **of** something. *God, how she repented of her self-righteousness.*

repentance repentance **for** something. *...asking repentance for his blasphemous utterances.*

replace 1 to replace one thing **with** another thing; to be replaced **by** another thing. *...plans to replace a forest with an airport... The bell-pull had been replaced by a buzzer.* 2 to replace someone **as** something. *Vaclav Havel is to replace Dr. Husak as president.*

replacement a replacement **for** something or someone. *...potential replacements for fossil fuels... I don't see him as a replacement for David.*

replica a replica **of** an object. *We have a replica of his death mask.*

reply 1 to reply **to** someone or **to** something that they have done, written, or said. *He would reply to* the letter later in the week. **2** a reply **to** a question or challenge. *There was no specific reply to the question.* **3** to reply **with** a particular response. *He shot Adam a glance, who replied with a shrug of the shoulders.* **4 in reply; in reply to** someone or something. *I received a muffled shout in reply... I have nothing to say in reply to your question.*

report 1 to report **on** or **upon** a particular subject; to report back **on** a particular subject. *She had reported on covert activities against her government... Attend the meeting and report back on their activities.* **2** to report someone or something **to** someone else. *He reported his friend to the Inland Revenue for not paying his taxes... More crime is now reported to the police.* **3** to report **to** someone; to report back **to** someone. *The consultant psychiatrist reported to the board on his conduct... He asked his officials to report back to him.*

represent to represent one thing **as** another. *He was represented as being a foreigner... The state can be represented as the enemy.*

representation a representation **of** a person, thing, or event. *...a brilliant theatrical representation of the events leading up to the war.*

representative be representative **of** something. *Are party members representative of Labour voters?*

reproach to reproach someone **for** something or **with** something. *She reproached him for the tactics he used... She would sometimes reproach me for being too mild... Did you come here just to reproach me with my tactlessness?*

reprove to reprove someone **for** something. *She reproved Darrell for his part in the affair.*

repugnant be repugnant **to** someone. *The idea is repugnant to British notions of fair play.*

repute of repute. *He was one of only 17 doctors of international repute.*

request 1 a request **for** something. *...urgent requests for help.* **2 on request.** *We will provide clients with transfer forms on request.* **3 at** someone's **request.** *The building going up now will be named, at the donor's request, the Margaret Thatcher Centre.*

require to require something **for** a particular purpose. *...a list of qualifications required for entrance.*

resemblance a resemblance **to** something or **between** two things. *Gary bears a strong resemblance to his father.*

reservation 1 with reservations; with reservation. *I would treat with reservation anyone's work when they have an interest in what they are promoting.* **2 without reservation.** *Essex University would be one of the options I would recommend without reservation.*

reserve in reserve. *...hundreds of police, with troops in reserve.*

reside to reside **in** a place or thing. *Real power resides in the workshop and on the office floor.*

residence in residence. *His band is in residence at Ronnie Scott's all week.*

resident be resident **in** a place. *...the prosecution of war criminals resident in this country.*

resign 1 to resign **as** someone who has a particular job; to resign **from** a particular job, position, or organization. *Sixty per cent thought it was time she resigned as leader of the Party... Mike was asked to resign from the committee.* **2** to resign yourself **to** something unpleasant. *Sunderland can resign themselves to staying in the Second Division.*

resigned be resigned **to** something unpleasant. *They seem resigned to queueing for vegetables and fruit.*

resistance resistance **to** someone or something. *...resistance to changes in government... Stress can cause lower resistance to infection.*

resolve to resolve something **into** different parts. *What I did was resolve this force into its components.*

resort to resort **to** an unpleasant or unpopular action. *The party officials resorted to more drastic action.*

resound to resound **with** noise. *After the recital. the hall resounded with applause.*

respect respect **for** someone or something. *One grows to have the highest respect for these three artists.*

respite a respite **from** something unpleasant. *...a brief respite from the daily artillery attacks.*

resplendent resplendent **in** a particular outfit or style. *...Tony Greig. resplendent in boater, blazer. and tie... The stable was resplendent in decorative Yorkshire stone.*

respond to respond **to** someone **with** something or **by** doing something. *No matter how experienced you are. you respond to an enthusiastic crowd. ...responding with delight when he tickles her under the chin... The militia responded by shooting and throwing tear-gas.*

response in response or **in response to** something. *May I make two points in response to William Hudson's letter?*

responsibility responsibility **for** an event, situation, or decision. *A new organization has claimed responsibility for the bomb. ...responsibility for covering emergencies.*

responsible 1 be responsible **for** something or someone. *...the person responsible for his death... She feels responsible for the girl's moral welfare.* 2 be responsible **to** a person or group. *Ought the Press to be in some way responsible to the public?*

responsive be responsive **to** someone or something. *The objective is to make the health service more responsive to patients.*

rest 1 be **at rest:** be resting. *The interchange of oxygen is twenty times greater when the body is at rest.* 2 to rest **on** or **upon** a person or thing. *The whole emphasis rested upon the need for a small. closely-knit Party... England's wealth rested on wool.* 3 to rest **with** someone: used of a responsibility or choice. *Authority rested with the doctors of the University, not the teachers.*

restore 1 to restore something **to** someone. *They called for steps to restore Soviet citizenship to Aleksandr Solzhenitsyn.* 2 to restore something **to** a previous state or condition. *...a Charter which will restore pensioners to a position of equality.*

restrain to restrain someone **from** doing something. *...an order restraining the council from re-advertising the post.*

restrict to restrict someone or something **to** a particular activity or thing. *...orchestras which restrict themselves to Mozart and Haydn... Don't restrict your diet to a single kind of food.*

restriction a restriction **on** something or someone. *...restrictions on personal freedom.*

result 1 to result **in** a particular outcome. *The talks resulted in an agreement.* 2 to result **from** a particular action or event. *Four-fifths of the fire damage resulted from incendiary bombing.*

retail to retail **at** a particular price. *These shoes normally retail at £18.50.*

reticent be reticent **about** something. *Five years later she returned, reticent about her adventures.*

retreat 1 to retreat **into** an attitude or belief. *People with eating disorders retreat into their compulsion.* 2 to retreat **from** something. *Mr Parkinson seems to have retreated from this option for the moment.*

retrospect in retrospect. *Was that, in retrospect, really wise?*

return 1 to return something **to** someone. *One man returned his copy to the company.* 2 to return something **to** a particular place, or to return someone **to** a particular post or position. *The yaks were returned to the wild... The electorate returned Mr Mugabe to power in the elections.* 3 to return **to** a particular place, activity, or subject. *He faced dismissal if he returned to Australia. ...the number of women returning to a career.* 4 the return **of** something. *The mother made an emotional plea for the return of her child.* 5 a return **to** a particular subject or activity. *Mr Mazilu promised there would be no return to communism... There will be a return to concern for European security.* 6 in return. *He appreciated my friendliness and liked me in return.*

reunited be reunited **with** someone. *She was treated at hospital, where she was reunited with her mother.*

reveal to reveal something **as** a particular thing. *His gaiety had revealed itself as a manic fear of solitude.*

revel to revel **in** a situation or activity. *He revelled in his new role as photographer.*

revelation a revelation **to** someone. *It was a revelation to those of us who did not think he had it in him to attack.*

revenge 1 to revenge yourself **on** someone. *She will revenge herself on those who helped him escape.* 2 revenge **against** someone **for** something. *...spontaneous revenge against the police. ...intent on getting revenge for her defeat in the semi-final.*

reverse 1 the reverse **of** something. *The delays were the reverse of the situation which used to exist.* 2 in reverse; into reverse. *The trend for free-range eggs has gone into reverse.*

reversion reversion **to** a particular method, activity, or subject. *...a reversion to pre-scientific attitudes.*

revert to revert **to** a former state, condition, or subject. *The European Parliament will revert to a consultative assembly... Can I revert to one other point before you continue?*

review under review. *They agreed to keep these developments under review.*

revolt to revolt **against** someone or something. *He urged the public to revolt against food rationing.*

revolve to revolve **around** something or **round** something. *The talks revolved around problems, real and invented.*

rhyme to rhyme **with** another word. *She called him Guppy, to rhyme with puppy.*

rich be rich **in** something or **with** something. *The leaves contain little protein but are rich in fibre. ...a stone patio rich with the scent of lavender and roses.*

rid 1 to rid someone or something **of** something. *It is difficult to rid clothes of cooking smells... The party still needs to rid itself of anti-Semitic tendencies.* 2 be rid **of** someone or something. *It was wonderful to be rid of their company at last.*

riddled be riddled **with** something. *...a city riddled with racial tensions.*

rife be rife **with** something bad or unpleasant. *'The academic world,'* he said bitterly, *'is rife with jealousy and ingratitude.'*

rifle to rifle **through** a collection of things. *...the task of rifling through the piles of rubbish to find the fortune.*

rift 1 a rift **with** someone or a rift **between** two people or groups. *...trying to heal the rift with their followers... It had been nine years since she had seen her brother, as a result of a rift between them.* 2 a rift **in** a group. *...the growing rift in the party.*

right be right **for** someone or something; the right thing for someone or something. *The course he had chosen ten years ago had proved to be right for him... The decision was certainly the right one for Allan Lamb.*

rigours the rigours **of** something. *...the rigours of Army life.*

ring 1 to ring **for** someone or something. *He rang for Tracy and asked, 'What's wrong with Davis?'* 2 to ring **with** a sound. *...a barn that rang with the cries of geese and turkeys.*

rip to rip **through** something. *The first explosion ripped through the ship's cabin.*

ripe be ripe **for** a change of some kind. *The republic was ripe for a violent uprising.*

ripple a ripple **of** sound or a particular emotion. *The audience registered its interest with a ripple of applause... The tour caused a ripple of speculation.*

rise 1 to rise **above** something. *I was able to rise above the depressing and threatening solitude.* 2 to rise **from** a group of people. *Cheers and shouts of alarm rose from the spectators.* 3 to rise **from** one level **to** a higher level. *Inflation rose from 5.5 per cent to 6.3.* 4 a rise **in** the rate or amount of something. *This allowed a slow rise in house prices.* 5 the rise **of** a

particular thing. *...the rise of a huge managerial class.*

risk at risk; at the **risk of** something. *The level of demand will fall, putting more jobs at risk. ...ensuring short-term survival at the risk of long-term ruin.*

road 1 by road. *A new radar was despatched by road.* 2 the road **to** a particular place or state. *...the road to unity.* 3 on the road: travelling. *I was stiff after seven hours on the road.* 4 be **on the road to** a particular place or state. *Roberts was on the road to recovery.*

roar to roar **with** an emotion or feeling such as pain or laughter. *The crowd roared with expectancy.*

rob to rob someone **of** something. *Nothing can rob him of his place in history as the winner.*

room 1 to room **with** someone. *At first I roomed with Lani, but then she moved to a single flat.* 2 room **for** someone or something. *The results showed there was room for improvement... He resigned to make room for a younger man.*

root to root **for** someone: to support them. *Our editorial friends were all rooting for us.*

rooted be rooted **in** a particular tradition or belief. *Education cannot be rooted in sentiment and good wishes.*

rope to rope one thing **to** another. *Heavy stones were roped to a flimsy iron roof.*

rough to be rough **on** someone. *The past two years have been awfully rough on him.*

round to round **on** someone. *He rounded on critics of the health service reforms.*

rouse to rouse someone **to** a particular action. *Western opinion was only roused to action by the enslaving of Christians.*

row /raʊ/1 to row **with** someone **about** something or **over** something. *She never rowed with her mother about it... The last* *thing most of them want to do is row over money.* **2** a row **with** someone or **between** two people **about** something or **over** something. *After a row with his parents, his father locked him out of the house. ...a backstage row between critic and author. ...a row about leaks to an American newspaper... On Saturday there was a row over Mr Yeltsin's broadcast.*

rudiments the rudiments **of** a subject. *Lo had plenty of time to pick up the rudiments of driving.*

rule **1** to rule **over** a country or group of people. *An old man ruled over the valley.* **2** to rule **on** a particular problem or situation. *The Athletics Association has yet to rule on his eligibility.* **3** to rule **against** someone or something. *The judge is about to rule against the Government identity card scheme.*

rumour a rumour **of** something or **about** something. *The mother had heard a rumour of inappropriate sexual behaviour. ...a rumour about unauthorized bombings.*

run **1** to run **at** a particular level. *Inflation is running at 10 to 14 per cent.* **2** to run **across** someone: to meet them unexpectedly. *I keep running across my old students.* **3** to run **after** someone or something. *People threw sticks at the troop carriers and ran after them on foot. ...always the same, always running after success.* **4** to run **into** problems. *Officials said the talks had run into difficulties.* **5** to run **into** a particular amount. *Exact casualty figures are not known, but they run into hundreds.* **6** to run **over** someone. *We almost ran over a fox that was crossing the road.* **7** to run **through** a list, task, or amount of money. *He proceeded to run through his list of reforms... Arabella ran through a polished repertoire of songs.* **8** to run away

with someone: used of feelings or emotions. *Don't let your emotions run away with you.* **9** to run out **of** something. *English Heritage have run out of funds to restore old churches.* **10** to run **to** someone **for** help or protection. *We must learn to trust our own judgement and not always run to the experts for easy solutions.* **11** to run up **against** problems or difficulties. *Economic growth would sooner or later run up against insurmountable problems.* **12** the run **of** a place. *An expert on energy efficiency is to be given the run of the house to advise on fuel costs.* **13** on the run. *After 17 months on the run, he is behind bars again.* **14** at a run. *The stretchers were carried at a run from the helicopter to the medical tent.*

rush **1** to rush someone **into** doing something; to rush **into** something. *British Steel have made it clear that they are not going to be rushed into a deal... The only advice the experts agree on is not to rush into anything.* **2** a rush **for** something. *...the rush for oil shares.* **3** in a rush. *Chancellor Kohl is in a rush to finalize the details.*

S

sabbatical on sabbatical. *They were biochemists on sabbatical.*

sacred be sacred **to** a god or person. *Among the plants sacred to Dionysus were the myrtle, the fig and the ivy... Her savings were sacred to her.*

saddle to saddle someone **with** something that is a burden. *The last thing I want is to saddle myself with a wife.*

safe **1** be safe **for** someone to use or have. *Zinc stearate powder is not* considered safe for babies, because it can irritate the lungs. **2** be safe **from** someone or something harmful. *...a place where they ought to be safe from attack... On such beaches the eggs were safe from sea-dwelling marauders.* **3** be safe **with** someone. *Muller's notes were safe with old Halliday.*

safeguard a safeguard **against** something harmful. *He argued that the participation of the military in the government acted as a safeguard against the abuse of power.*

sail to sail **through** something. *He sailed through the tests.*

sake for the sake of something or someone. *But Isobel had not married for the sake of money or ambition. ...to be ready to endure hardships and even death for the sake of the tribe.*

sale be for sale. *I butted in to inquire if the horse was for sale.*

salute a salute **to** a person or achievement. *...a salute to the first great English master of classic architecture.*

salvage to salvage something **from** a wreck or disaster. *Men salvaged equipment from the wrecks.*

same be the same **as** something else; the same thing **as** something else. *Animal teeth are not the same as human teeth... By the end of 1974 three others had suffered the same fate as Taverne.*

sanctions sanctions **against** or **on** a country, organization, or group. *They would have imposed sanctions against South Africa. ...penal sanctions on trade unions.*

sated be sated **with** something. *...sated with fresh air and hard exercise.*

satellite by satellite. *It is called Sky Television and is transmitted by satellite.*

satire a satire **on** something. *...'The Election', a satire on democracy in action.*

satisfied be satisfied **with** something. *...if you are not satisfied with the service you get.*

saturate to saturate a place or object **with** something or **in** something. *Teams saturated the community with literature about the attack. ...pads which must be kept saturated in salty or soapy water.*

save 1 to save someone or something **from** an unpleasant or difficult situation. *I rushed into his room just in time to save our kitten from strangulation... He used all reasonable endeavours to save the Talisman from sinking.* **2** to save **on** money, time, and other useful things. *Farmers are introducing machinery to save on labour costs.*

savour to savour **of** something. *To do a good deed a day consciously savours of priggishness.*

say 1 to say something **to** someone **about** something. *Billy Graham, the television evangelist, said farewell to Britain yesterday... Mr McGregor's remarks are far worse than what Edwina Currie said about eggs.* **2** a say **in** something. *If I had any say in it I'd keep them out.*

scared be scared **of** someone or something. *He's scared of horses.*

scathing be scathing **about** something. *She was scathing about extra-marital difficulties.*

scavenge to scavenge **for** food or other things you can use. *The fish and crabs scavenge for decaying tissue and waste products.*

sceptical be sceptical **about** something or **of** something. *He has always been sceptical about nuclear power... I had become a little sceptical of their existence.*

schedule on schedule. *The Government wants to keep its privatization programme on schedule.*

scholarship a scholarship **to** a school or university. *Pete had got a scholarship to Oxford.*

scoff to scoff **at** something or someone. *Many critics scoff at artists such as Mondrian and Kandinsky.*

scold to scold someone **for** doing something wrong. *I had to scold Vita severely for being so thoughtless.*

score to score **over** someone else. *...anxious to score over the opposition.*

scornful be scornful **of** someone or something. *...puritanically scornful of its flamboyance.*

scourge the scourge **of** a place or group of people. *...Steven Berkoff, the scourge of the theatre world.*

scowl to scowl **at** someone or something. *He scowled at me and returned to his work.*

scramble to scramble **for** something. *Throughout Britain, primary schools are scrambling for staff.*

scrape to scrape **through** something. *I just scraped through my exams.*

scream to scream **at** someone. *Hagen started to protest and she screamed at him in Italian.*

sea at sea. *The ships would be at sea for approximately six months each.*

search 1 to search **for** something. *Once again they were homeless and hunted and must search for a safe hiding place.* 2 **in search of** something. *They all left early each day in search of work.*

secondary be secondary **to** something. *The lesson of the game was to make competition secondary to friendship.*

secret 1 the secret **of** doing something. *The secret of sticking is to select the most suitable adhesive for the job.* 2 **in secret.** *The old man met him in secret and said 'Leave me alone.'*

secure to secure a person or thing **against** something or **from** something. *What mattered now was to secure herself against the time when she would not be beautiful any longer... Enough remained to secure us from the threat of invasion.*

seduce to seduce someone **into** something. *They destroy and corrupt and seduce men into their service.*

see 1 to see **through** someone or something. *Lewis would see through her at once.* 2 to see someone **through** something. *...the loan that was to see Britain through the post-war years.* 3 to see **to** something that needs attention. *Karin would see to the olives and cheese straws.*

seize to seize **on** something. *Picasso seized on anything and everything that came to hand.*

self-sufficient be self-sufficient **in** something. *Other discoveries will ensure that Britain is self-sufficient in oil until the next century.*

sell 1 to sell something **to** someone. *They churned out their products and sold them to wholesalers.* 2 to sell something **for** an amount of money, or **at** a particular price. *The Our Price record chain was sold for 43 million pounds... These products are imported and sold at a lower price than their UK equivalents.* 3 to sell an idea **to** someone; to sell someone **on** an idea. *You've got 10 minutes to sell it to me... He was totally sold on the American ethic of free enterprise.* 4 to sell **out of** something. *Shops almost immediately sold out of the advertised goods.* 5 to sell out **to** someone or something. *All but my landlady gradually sold out to the other side.*

semblance a semblance **of** something. *...a cynical contempt for truth, justice or any semblance of decency.*

send 1 to send something **to** someone. *I had written a book and sent a copy to Sheldon.* 2 to send

for someone. *Otto sent for his three fellow directors, Goin, Heissman and Stryker.* **3** to send **for** something or send off **for** something. *Keep on trying, and send for nomination forms... We need more time to note down where to send off for them.*

senior be senior **to** someone. *The appraiser must be senior to the teacher being appraised.*

sense 1 the sense **of** something that is said or written. *In the strict sense of the word, knowledge can only be about the past.* **2** a sense **of** something. *The sense of achievement was extraordinary.*

sensitive 1 be sensitive **to** something. *If your skin is sensitive to detergent, wash your clothes in soap... He was unduly sensitive to criticism.* **2** be sensitive **about** something. *Ministers are sensitive about Britain's bad reputation for international co-operation.*

sentence to sentence someone **to** punishment. *They sentenced 19 year old dissenters to 30 years imprisonment.*

sentimental be sentimental **about** something or someone. *He often felt sentimental about China, and could not resist the lure to return.*

separate 1/sɛpərət/ be separate **from** something; a separate thing **from** something else. *Rosa had remained separate from us, asking finally for a room by herself... He inhabited separate apartments from the others.* **2**/sɛpəreɪt/ to separate one person or thing **from** another. *It is becoming common to separate babies from their mothers after birth... The poor provinces wish to separate from the rich.*

sequel a sequel **to** something. *Mark Twain nearly wrote a sequel to Huckleberry Finn... There was a sequel to the battle of Majuba in 1900.*

sequence 1 in sequence: correctly ordered. *These recordings are in sequence and continuous.* **2 out of sequence:** incorrectly ordered. *This is out of sequence, there's a span of about ten years missing.*

serious be serious **about** something. *You needn't become a professional musician to be serious about music.*

serve 1 to serve **as** something. *Moscow's tactic appears to be to let the congress serve as a safety valve.* **2** to serve a legal document **on** someone; to serve someone **with** a legal document. *A House Committee tried to serve a subpoena on Harry Truman... The court served her with an enforcement notice.*

session be **in session:** be meeting and working. *The public galleries hold a limited audience when the courts are in session.*

set 1 be set **in** or **into** something. *...a brilliant mosaic of porphyry and glass blocks set in marble.* **2** be set **with** jewels. *The crown is set with diamonds and rubies.* **3** be set **for** a future action or experience. *Marsh is set for a return to the boxing ring.* **4** be set **on** doing something. *The boy was obviously set on preparing a defence for himself.* **5** to set a way of behaving, aim, or task **for** someone to achieve. *She had set a half-hour composition for her pupils... Their music set the fashion for a generation of young people.* **6** to set a high value **on** something. *He sets a great deal on loyalty to the company.* **7** to set animals or people **on** or **upon** someone. *We were afraid they might set the dogs on us.* **8** to set **about** doing something. *The terrified sailors and passengers set about saving their own skins.* **9** to set one fact or argument **against** another. *Chamberlain's one mistake can be set against four good saves.* **10** to set an amount of money **against** tax. *It is possible to*

settle

set against tax the costs of raising finance. **11** to set one person **against** another. *The conflict set the mainstream of the organization against the more 'corrupt' and maverick elements.* **12** to set someone apart **from** other people. *These badges set their owners apart from all other groups until the day they die.* **13** to set someone off **on** something. *My cool-headed posture set him off on a tirade that was even more vitriolic than the first.*

settle 1 to settle **for** something or **on** something. *Too many athletes had settled for a quiet life, he said... After taking a variety of jobs, he settled on journalism.* **2** to settle **with** someone or settle up **with** someone. *I'll settle with you on Friday... As soon as the money arrived I was able to settle up with him.* **3** to settle down **to** something or **for** something. *Later in the morning they settled down to a history test... At eight o'clock he settles down for supper.*

shade 1 shades **of** a particular colour. *The coat was patterned in marine shades of blue and green.* **2** to shade **into** something. *As the pressures mount, tension shades into irritability, anger, and violence.*

shake to shake something **at** someone. *She shook her fist at us and told us to stop.*

shame to shame someone **into** doing something or **out of** doing something. *Mother shamed us into hiding. ...horrific living conditions that would shame councillors out of their complacency.*

shape to shape something **into** a different form. *Shape the dough into balls and put on a baking sheet.*

share 1 to share something **with** someone. *I left my attic in Clerkenwell to share a room in Maida Vale with an unemployed actor... Now and then some lucky boy was allowed to share a journey with his father, uncle, or grown-up brother.* **2** to share **in** doing something. *Both partners share in preparing for and rearing their family.* **3** to share something or share something out **among** or **between** a group of people. *I shared out her baggage among the others... Share the sweets between the children.* **4** a share **in** something or **of** something. *His prosperous brother offered him a share in a new automobile agency... In some places they inherit an equal share of family property.*

sheathed be sheathed **in** something. *Skeleton trees, sheathed in ice, glittered against the fronts of the palaces.*

shelter to shelter **from** something unpleasant. *They were trying to shelter from the worst of the fires... The clods help to shelter the young plants from the wind.*

shield 1 a shield **against** danger or damage. *The marriage licence is not so much a bond or shackle as a shield against adversity or a change of heart.* **2** to shield a person or thing **from** danger or damage. *Crane always walked ahead of Peter, to shield him from whatever might menace him.*

shine to shine **at** something. *...the idea that they're sensitive souls who shine at the arts.*

ship by **ship**. *A further 1,000 were due to leave by ship overnight.*

shock a shock to someone. *It came as a shock to Castle to realise how little he had been trusted.*

shoot to shoot **at** a person or thing. *Griffiths took his rifle to the common and started shooting at people there.*

short 1 be short **with** someone. *The judge was very short with her.* **2** be short **of** something. *We were now running short of food.* **3** in **short**: used when giving a summary. *In short, the more*

rapidly changing the environment,
the more information the
individual needs to make
decisions.

shot 1 a shot at something. *...a
serious shot at breaking three
hours in the marathon.* **2** be shot
with something or shot through
with something. *...that special
wonder, shot with awe... This
gloom became shot through with
irritations.*

shout to shout **at** someone. *As we
were leaving, a strange woman in
a trilby hat shouted at me.*

show 1 to show something **to**
someone. *I found it hard to resist
the temptation to show Caine's
book to my father.* **2** to show a
particular emotion or quality **to** or
towards someone. *One would
suppose that in such a case, the son
would show increased tenderness
to his mother... This is a time for
parents to show their
thoughtfulness and generosity
towards each other.* **3** to show
someone **around** or **round** a
place. *She only wanted a little
money to show me around the
church... He said he would make
an exception, and show me
personally round the castle.* **4 on
show.** *The document will go on
show in the manuscript room of
the British Library.*

showdown a showdown **with**
someone. *President Bush faces his
first showdown with unions after a
strike over pay cuts.*

shower 1 to shower someone **with**
things. *The demonstrators were
driven back, but still showered the
police with bricks and rocks...
They are inclined to shower her
with presents and treats.* **2** to
shower something **on** or **upon**
someone. *It is the thwarted love for
parents that is showered on the
teacher.*

shriek 1 to shriek **in** or **with** fear,
surprise, or excitement. *Her head
jerked back and she shrieked in*

alarm... *The crowd shrieked with
gleeful horror.* **2** a shriek **of** a
particular feeling. *His voice rose to
a shriek of terror.*

shrink to shrink **from** something.
*It's a sad truth most of us
amateurs shrink from admitting.*

shrouded be shrouded **in**
something. *In the early morning
light the beaches of Normandy
were shrouded in mist... 'Its
origins', he said, 'are shrouded in
mystery.'*

shudder to shudder **at** something;
to shudder **with** or **in** a particular
emotion. *She shuddered at the
thought of that dark shape moving
towards her... Kunta shuddered
with fear... The sight made her
shudder in primitive distaste.*

shut to shut someone **in** a room.
*She shut herself in the bathroom
and wept.*

shy to shy away **from** something.
*For 26 years, Italy's foremost
opera house had shied away from
staging La Traviata.*

sick be sick **of** something annoying
or tedious. *It was clear that the
members were heartily sick of the
whole issue.*

side 1 be **on** someone's **side:** be
supporting them. *You will then
have a powerful friend on your
side.* **2** to side **with** someone
against someone else. *He sided
with the majority of his advisers
and overruled the die-hards... Her
supporters sided against me.*

sift to sift **through** something. *A
computer could sift through
records and come up with a short-
list.*

sigh to sigh **with** a particular
emotion. *She sighed with
contentment.*

sight 1 in sight: visible. *There was
no-one else in sight.* **2 out of
sight:** not visible. *They waited
until the guard was out of sight.*
3 on sight: as soon as someone is
seen. *She hated him on sight.*

sign

sign 1 a sign **of** something. *The fact that they are risking their lives is a sign of their desperation.* 2 to sign **for** something. *The chief gave me all the money that was due, and I signed for it.*

signal 1 the signal **for** an action. *The plot was for Snowball, at the critical moment, to give the signal for flight.* 2 to signal **to** someone. *I signaled to the waitress for the check.*

silence in silence. *They ate in silence.*

silhouetted be silhouetted **against** a background. *I could see deep patches of cloud silhouetted against the glitter of the stars.*

similar be similar **to** something else; a similar thing **to** something else. *The charter would be similar to a Bill of Rights... The Agency would have similar status to that of existing nationalised bodies.*

similarity 1 a similarity **between** two or more things; a similarity **to** or **with** something else. *There was little similarity between the dull grey English sea and the turquoise Indian Ocean... The situation bears some similarity to my own circumstances... Any similarity with your routine is purely coincidental.* 2 a similarity **in** or **of** a particular feature or quality. *There is some similarity in their educational and occupational achievements. ...the similarity of weapons.*

sin to sin **against** someone or something. *Father, I have sinned against heaven.*

single to single someone out **as** something or **for** particular attention. *The United States is usually singled out as the prime culprit in this indictment... Why should this trait be singled out for such exceptional treatment?*

sink to sink **into** a particular state or situation. *I sank into a state of deep depression.*

sit 1 to sit **for** an artist or photographer. *She had sat for famous painters like Rossetti.* 2 to sit **on** a committee. *He sat on committees relating to the future of the aircraft industry.* 3 to sit **through** something. *The spectators sat through the drama as though watching some horror movie.* 4 to sit in **on** a meeting or discussion. *I was allowed to sit in on the deliberations of the board.*

skate to skate **around, round,** or **over** a difficult subject or problem. *They prefer to skate around the issue of sex... Her phrasing tended to skate over the arrangements in hurried bursts.*

skill skill **in** or **at** doing something. *...their skill in making clothes. ...his evident skill at basketball.*

skim to skim **through** a piece of writing. *I thought I would skim through a few of the letters.*

skirt to skirt **around** or **round** a difficult subject or problem. *The reviewer skirted around the most ferocious criticism.*

slash to slash **at** something. *He slashed savagely at the meat with his knife.*

slight a slight **on** someone. *Advice is too often taken as a slight on the recipient.*

slip to slip **into** different clothes or **out of** clothes that you are wearing. *Slipping into something loose, I went down to dinner... She slipped out of her working clothes.*

slow be slow **in** doing something. *The response was slow in coming.*

slump a slump **in** something such as demand, price, or amount. *...a dramatic slump in holiday bookings.*

slur a slur **on** something or someone. *This is probably an unfair slur on womanhood.*

sly on the sly. *...sitting in the toilets smoking on the sly, just like kids do in school.*

smack to smack **of** something. *Oliver was irritated by this* *suggestion, which smacked of frivolity.*

smart to smart **from** or **under** something unpleasant that has happened to you. *The home team is still smarting from their defeat at Rochdale... He began to smart under the pain of being a minor member of the orchestra.*

smell 1 to smell **of** something. *The laundry smelled of carbolic soap.* **2** the smell **of** something. *I love the smell of new-mown grass.*

smile to smile **at** someone or something. *People think you are weird if you smile at them during a Tube journey.*

smitten be smitten **by** or **with** something or someone. *Surviving in garrets in Paris is bearable because he was smitten by the French... I was smitten with her.*

smother to smother something **with** something. *They were able to extinguish the bombs by smothering them with sand.*

smothered be smothered **in** something or **with** something. *The path was smothered in snow... Climbing roses grew up the side of the house, their tendrils still smothered with late blossoms.*

snap 1 to snap **at** someone. *Do you snap at your partner and then regret it?* **2** to snap **out of** a sad mood. *I snapped out of this melancholy the moment a friend called.*

snatch to snatch **at** something. *The wind snatched at my dress and hair... Etta snatched at the little privacy that this afforded.*

sneer to sneer **at** someone or something. *They sneered at the girlish enthusiasms of their fellow students.*

socialize to socialize **with** people. *I socialized with the philosophy students.*

solution the solution **to** or **for** a problem, question, or puzzle. *Researchers want to know whether the solution to the riddle will*

involve new theories... The plan for polytechnics was meant to be a solution for this problem.

sorry 1 be sorry **about** something or **for** something. *I tended to dominate the conversation and I'm sorry about that... We are all sorry for what happened.* **2** be sorry **for** someone. *I felt desperately sorry for myself.*

sort 1 a particular sort **of** thing. *This sort of argument can go on for ever.* **2** something **of** a particular **sort.** *He will present no evidence of that sort.*

sound the sound **of** something. *This small beetle imitates the sound of a dentist's drill.*

source 1 a source **of** something. *Wood is an inefficient source of energy.* **2** **at source.** *We need to tackle nitrate pollution at source.*

south south **of** a place. *...a fine wine made by a co-operative just south of the Loire.*

sow /sǝʊ/ to sow an area of ground **with** seeds. *Soil cleared of winter vegetables may be sown with rye or field beans.*

spar to spar **with** someone. *Within weeks, he was sparring with the toughest boys in the gym.*

sparing be sparing **with** something. *Aunt Tossie is sparing with the affection Nicandra longs for.*

speak 1 to speak **to** someone or **with** someone. *He never spoke to Captain Baker again... Stein wasn't there. I spoke with his son.* **2** to speak **about** something or **of** something. *On television, Jonathan Porrit spoke about his involvement with the advertising community... Travellers spoke of fighting and shooting at night.* **3** to speak **for** a person or group of people. *'Do we have to go on living here?' she wailed. She spoke for many of us.* **4** to speak **with** a particular accent or style. *She spoke with a very pronounced Scottish accent... 'Are you the*

spec

painter?' She spoke with abrupt formality.

spec on spec. *He turned up yesterday on spec.*

specialize to specialize **in** a particular thing or subject. *Buy dried herbs from a shop which specializes in herbs... The majority had specialized in electronic engineering.*

speculate to speculate **about** something or **on** something. *...the futility of speculating about hypothetical Martian life forms... Energy analysts speculated on further increases in fuel prices.*

speechless be speechless **with** a strong emotion. *Turi was almost speechless with delight.*

spend to spend money or time **on** something. *He spent all his savings on the project... Her time would be better spent on research.*

spin-off a spin-off **from** something or **of** something. *A programme to develop new energy sources could occur as a spin-off from the space effort. ...a spin-off of America's present obsession with personal health.*

splash to splash out **on** something. *We splashed out on a colour television.*

split 1 a split **between** two people or groups or a split **in** or **within** a group. *...a split between hardliners and democrats... The plan has led to a split in the ranks. ...the split within Nato.* **2** to split away or off **from** a group of people. *The more radical intellectuals threatened to split away from the Council... They warned them not to split off from the national party.* **3** to split up **with** someone. *I'd just split up with Paul, the father of my youngest son.*

sponge to sponge **off** someone or **on** someone. *The young unemployed are not simply layabouts who sponge off the Welfare State... She found it distasteful the way Clarissa sponged on them.*

spring 1 to spring **from** a particular cause. *His own doubts sprang from his English education and marriage.* **2** to spring something **on** someone. *He sprang a surprise on all of us by winning.*

springboard a springboard **for** something. *He had hoped to use his election as a springboard for wider and grander political ambitions.*

spy to spy **on** someone. *The policemen who spied on dissidents are to be sacked.*

square 1 to square **with** an idea, statement, or situation. *His interpretation of the rule is not likely to square with the new guidelines.* **2** to square up **with** someone. *I've got to square up with the bank before I can pay you.* **3** to square up **to** a problem, person, or situation. *Truculently, they squared up to each other but kept just out of fighting distance.*

squint to squint **at** someone or something. *She opened her eyes and squinted at him.*

stab 1 to stab **at** something. *She was typing in a fury, her fingers stabbing at the keys.* **2** a stab **at** something. *It was back in 1964 when he had his first stab at conducting this great work.*

staff on an institution's **staff**. *I can say categorically that no-one on the White House staff was involved in this bizarre incident.*

stage on **stage**. *He feels as comfortable on stage as in the studio.*

stake 1 to stake something valuable **on** or **upon** the result of something. *He has staked his leadership claim on this peace initiative.* **2** at **stake.** *There are two prizes at stake in the competition.* **3** a stake **in** a business, property, or industry. *He has a 50 per cent stake in the Hyatt Hotel chain.*

stamp 1 to stamp yourself **on** or **upon** something. *Like all chancellors, he will want to stamp his own personality on the Government's policies.* 2 to stamp something **as** being a particular type of thing. *The recent win stamped him as a useful member of the team.*

stance a stance **on** a particular matter or problem. *She is prepared to recant her stance on women's rights.*

stand 1 to stand **at** a particular level or amount. *The world record stands at 2 hours 57 minutes and 30 seconds.* 2 to stand **by** someone. *If they try to make you resign, we'll stand by you.* 3 to stand **by** a decision or agreement. *It is a very clear law, and I stand by it.* 4 to stand **for** something: to tolerate it. *I won't stand for any more of your disobedience.* 5 to stand **for** something: to represent it. *T.E.C. stands for Technical Education Certificate.* 6 to stand **for** an idea or belief: to support it. *We stand for a single, undivided Russia.* 7 to stand **for** a particular post or position: to apply for it. *Anthony is standing for election as an independent candidate.* 8 to stand in **for** someone. *Howe's big moment comes tomorrow when he stands in for Margaret Thatcher.* 9 to stand out **against** something you disagree with or **for** something you approve of. *The major banks are standing out against raising the limit... The union decided to stand out for its original claim.* 10 to stand up **for** someone or something. *...a profession which has a duty to stand up for the citizen.* 11 to stand up **to** a lot of use, damage, pressure, criticism, and so on. *The charge that we had ignored them just does not stand up to scrutiny.* 12 to stand up **to** someone. *Will he make a name for himself by standing up to the Prime Minister?*

stare to stare **at** someone or something. *John was staring at me in horror and disbelief.*

start 1 to start **as** something or start off **as** something. *It started as an experiment... We started off as a shelving business in the U.K.* 2 to start **by** or start off **by** doing something. *Any business executive should start by considering the job that needs to be done... I started off by buying young pigs.* 3 to start **with** something or start off **with** something. *We start with basic ideas such as trust... We wanted to start with a win.* 4 to start **on** a particular task. *She has already started on her next novel.* 5 the start **of** something. *Interests rates were lowered at the start of last summer.* 6 **for a start**: used to show that there are many more things you could say. *I don't think Bruno will win—he can't take a punch for a start.*

starve to starve **for** something. *Even as they look, their eyes starve for more.*

starved be starved **of** something. *...people who have been starved of culture.*

statute by statute. *These powers were conferred on the court by statute.*

steeped be steeped **in** a particular characteristic or quality. *His works, though steeped in Indian culture, have universal appeal.*

stem to stem **from** a particular situation. *His illness stemmed from bottling up his emotions.*

step 1 **in step**: walking with exactly the same steps as someone else. *They marched in step.* 2 **out of step**: walking at a different rate from someone else. *They occasionally bumped each other, and fell out of step.* 3 be **in step with** an opinion or idea: have a similar opinion. *This government is not in step with informed public opinion.* 4 be **out of step with** an opinion or idea: have a different or unpopular opinion. *It showed the judge was out of step with recent developments.*

stick 1 to stick **at** a particular point or level. *Inflation is likely to stick at about 6 per cent... We tend to stick at asserting the general principle without discussing the details.* 2 to stick **by** someone. *Despite her husband's appalling life of crime, she had stuck faithfully by him.* 3 to stick **by** a law, rule, or principle. *She is determined that they should stick by the policy.* 4 to stick **to** something. *There was no way he could hope to stick to his original plans now.* 5 to stick **with** something or someone. *We would prefer to stick with our own labelling system... Stick with me and you'll be okay.* 6 to stick out **for** something you want. *He stuck out for twice the usual salary, and got it.* 7 to stick up **for** someone or something. *He should have thanked his father for sticking up for him that way... I was too small to stick up for my rights.*

stock 1 to stock up **on** goods or **with** goods. *They stocked up on petrol and sugar before the price rises came. ...houses carefully stocked up with food.* 2 **in stock.** *Phone the office first and see what they have in stock.* 3 **out of stock.** *He wanted cigarettes, but the cafe had run out of stock.*

stop 1 to stop **at** a place. *They were shot after they had stopped at a checkpoint.* 2 to stop someone **from** doing something. *This did not stop their supporters from travelling to the match.*

store be in store: be going to happen in the future. *The whales seemed aware of the threat that lay in store.*

street 1 **on the street:** homeless. *...young teenage mothers left to fend for themselves on the street.* 2 **in the street:** outside. *When people meet a clergyman in the*

street, they cross over to avoid him. 3 **off the streets:** busy and not causing trouble. *We've got to keep youngsters off the streets.*

strength 1 the strength **of** something. *The employers have underestimated the strength of feeling in the docks... See whether it exceeds the strength of steel.* 2 **on the strength of** something: using it as a justification. *She wants to be able to join them on the strength of a British passport.* 3 **in strength:** in large numbers. *They are expected to attend Goodwood in strength.* 4 **below strength:** weak or insufficient. *The UN monitoring force is well below strength.*

stress 1 stress **on** something. *...a greater stress on the humane treatment of psychiatric patients.* 2 **under stress.** *The family cannot cope under stress.*

stricken be stricken **by** something or **with** something. *...the squalor of a society stricken by poverty... They were stricken with fear that they might have been seen.*

strictly be strictly **for** a particular person or purpose. *The race is strictly for amateurs. ...supplies intended strictly for medical purposes.*

strike 1 **on strike.** *Drivers at the bus depot went on strike for twenty four hours.* 2 to strike **at** something or someone. *...a calculated act to strike at the root of religion.* 3 to strike **on** a solution, plan, or idea. *He had for once struck on a shrewd judgement.*

strip to strip a person or thing **of** something. *The Praesidium of the Supreme Soviet had stripped him of his citizenship... He stripped his speech of all references to his wound.*

strive to strive **for** something. *You strive for fame, and that is all part of the deal.*

strong be strong **on** something. *The University is strong on outdoor activities... He is strong on personal morality and family values.*

struck be struck **by** something or **with** something. *I was so struck by the terrible conditions of our neighbours that I had to do something about it... Her continental counterparts were struck with her change of style.*

struggle 1 to struggle **for** something. *We have a great history of struggling for freedom.* 2 a struggle **for** something. *...the struggle for Russian unity.* 3 to struggle **with** or **against** someone or something. *The United States continues to struggle with external deficits... They see themselves as struggling against insuperable odds.* 4 a struggle **with** something or **against** something. *...his well-publicized struggle with drink in his thirties. ...the struggle against loneliness and destitution.* 5 a struggle **between** two people or things. *...the struggle between Gorbachev and Yeltsin. ...the struggle between hope and scepticism.*

studded be studded **with** something. *The hut was studded all over with stones... This ballad is studded with references to rock and roll.*

student a student **of** a particular subject. *...a student of philosophy and law.*

study 1 the study **of** something: learning or research about it. *...the study of German culture and language.* 2 a study **in** something: a detailed description or depiction of it. *His last book was 'At Duty's Call', a study in patriotism.* 3 to study **for** something. *She is studying for a law degree at Keble College.*

stuffed be stuffed **with** something. *The boxes were stuffed with ballot papers. ...pastry stuffed with curd cheese.*

stumble 1 to stumble **across, on,** or **upon** something or someone. *In the course of their search they may stumble across something quite different... We thought we had stumbled on an IRA arms boat.* 2 to stumble **over** something. *...parents who have stumbled over toys left on the floor... He stumbled over the words.*

style 1 **in** a particular **style.** *They all worked in the same style... The present abbey is a smaller building in the perpendicular style.* 2 the style **of** something. *There is growing bitterness at his style of government.*

subcontract to subcontract work **to** a particular firm or organization. *Mintech increasingly subcontracted its growing civil programme to the private sector.*

subdivide to subdivide something **into** smaller areas, sections, or parts. *The school had been subdivided into eleven flats... We now subdivide knowledge into two parts.*

subject 1/sʌbdʒɪkt/ be subject **to** something. *The deal is subject to approval by the Office of Fair Trading.* 2/səbdʒɛkt/ to subject someone **to** something. *One teacher said she would rather break the law than subject her pupils to a test.*

submerge to submerge yourself **in** a particular subject, or be submerged **in** it. *I was eager to submerge myself in the feminist movement... His interests were totally submerged in a personal obsession.*

submit to submit **to** something. *They had to submit to a thorough body search at the airport.*

subordinate 1/səbɔːdɪnət/ be subordinate **to** someone or something. *All other questions are subordinate to this one.* 2

subscribe

/sǝbɔːdɪneɪt/ to subordinate one
thing **to** another. *...an ideology
that subordinates the individual to
the cause.*

subscribe 1 to subscribe **to** an
opinion or belief. *Today, he still
subscribes to the need for more
research.* **2** to subscribe **to** a
newspaper, magazine, or television
channel. *This will enable you to
subscribe to powerful electronic
services.*

subservient be subservient **to**
someone or something. *The unions
are still considered to be
subservient to management.*

subsist to subsist **on** a particular
amount of money or type of food.
*...a man who can subsist on a diet
of rice and fried eggs.*

substance 1 the substance **of**
what someone says or writes. *...the
style and substance of the debate.*
2 in substance. *His Lordship had
no doubt that the submission was
in substance correct.*

substitute 1 to substitute one
thing **for** another. *A stretch of
piano wire was substituted for one
of the ordinary strings.* **2** a
substitute **for** something. *There is
no substitute for real talent.*

subsumed be subsumed **under** or
within a larger group or class.
*...products subsumed under the
anonymous label of 'British
meat'... The other two big firms
have been subsumed within
Barclays.*

subtract to subtract one thing
from another. *They will have to
subtract appropriate sums from
their budgets.*

succeed 1 to succeed **in** doing
something. *All countries are
expected to succeed in bringing
down inflation this year... To an
extent, they have succeeded in
their aims.* **2** to succeed someone
as something. *Lord Young
succeeded him as party chairman.*

succession a succession **of** things
or people. *They missed a

succession of good opportunities...
We had a succession of temporary
designers.*

succumb to succumb **to**
something. *Some succumb to the
temptation to doze off during
seminars... There is some evidence
that pigs can succumb to brain
disease.*

suck to suck up **to** someone. *He's
been sucking up like mad to the
boss.*

sucked be sucked **into** an event or
situation. *She found herself sucked
into one of the dirtiest legal battles
of the 1980s.*

sue 1 to sue someone **for** a civil
offence such as libel. *...Crawley's
attempt to sue a publisher for
libel... The company is being sued
for wrongful dismissal.* **2** to sue
for money or a divorce. *He sued for
maintenance of £53,000 a month...
You must sue for divorce without
delay.*

suffer to suffer **from** a disease or
illness. *He suffered from an
unacceptable level of night
blindness.*

sufficient be sufficient **for** a
particular purpose. *A majority of
seven jurors was sufficient for a
verdict to be reached.*

suffused be suffused **with** light,
colour, or feeling. *Tolstoy wrote
novels suffused with a sense of the
ultimate triumph of divine love.*

suggestion a suggestion **of**
something. *He resists any
suggestion of ill-treatment.*

suggestive be suggestive **of**
something. *It makes a sound
which is suggestive of a mouth
organ.*

suitable be suitable **as** something
or **for** a particular purpose; a
suitable thing **for** a particular
purpose or person. *Its own
products are mainly desktop items
suitable as gifts for men. ...one of
the last 18th century houses in the
City suitable for private
occupation... It did not seem to be

suitable attire for an appearance in court. ...a suitable entertainment for a sick boy.

suited be suited **to** or **for** a particular job or purpose. *He was best suited to casual labour... The Eastern bloc forces are particularly suited for surprise.*

superimpose 1 to superimpose a word, drawing, symbol, or sound **on** another. *...a T-shirt with a clenched fist superimposed on a Union Jack.* 2 to superimpose the features or characteristics of one situation **on** another situation. *It would be wrong to superimpose the pattern of the East-West conflict on the present problems.*

superior be superior **to** someone or something. *The doctor considered himself superior to most of the people around him... Her sporting knowledge was vastly superior to that of the other guests.*

supervision under supervision. *They will have the opportunity to put these skills into practice under supervision.*

supplement 1 a supplement **to** something. *We can only provide our service as a supplement to international services.* 2 to supplement one thing **with** another. *I supplemented my diet with vitamin pills.*

supply 1 to supply something **to** someone. *...contracts to supply electricity direct to companies... The note was supplied to the Press but not the public.* 2 to supply someone **with** something. *They supplied the criminals with facts about him.*

support in support of someone or something. *...meetings in support of Lithuanian independence.*

sure 1 be sure **about** something or **of** something. *The only thing we're sure about is that it's a boy... Lamb is one who can be sure of his place in the team.* 2 **for sure.** *She said that her mother was Irish, but nobody knew for sure.*

surfeit a surfeit **of** something. *They became insensitive to suffering through a surfeit of violence.*

surge a surge **in** something or **of** something. *The eighties saw a surge in military technology. ...a surge of enthusiasm.*

surprised be surprised **at** something or **by** something. *She was surprised at Hugo's vehemence... I was surprised by her reaction.*

surrender 1 to surrender **to** someone or something. *They were allowed to return provided they surrendered to the security forces.* 2 the surrender **of** something. *...an unwitting surrender of pension rights.*

surround to surround a person or thing **with** something. *The guards surrounded him with a barrage of umbrellas to protect him... The river broke its banks, surrounding the hotel with water.*

surrounded be surrounded **by** something. *The whole cake is surrounded by a thick coat of jelly.*

survive to survive **on** something. *The crew had survived on ship's biscuits and six quarts of rum... Events of this scale cannot survive on ideals and fantasies alone.*

susceptible be susceptible **to** something *There are two strains of tropical fish that are susceptible to cancer.*

suspect /ˈsəspekt/ to suspect someone **of** something. *He is one of several who suspects them of having links with the IRA.*

suspend to suspend someone **from** a particular position or job. *Twelve police officers were suspended from duty after being accused of corruption.*

suspicion 1 under suspicion. *He was under suspicion for dishonest conduct.* 2 above suspicion; beyond suspicion. *The permanent secretaries are above suspicion. ...young and determined* lads who are morally beyond suspicion. **3** a suspicion **of** something. ...*a perfumed broth with chrysanthemum leaves and a suspicion of lemon grass.*

suspicious be suspicious **of** someone or something. *She had been suspicious of the man who had managed Mr Heath's campaign... The refugees refused to jump down, suspicious of officialdom.*

swamped be swamped **by** something or **with** something. *His question was swamped by the general merriment of his colleagues... We become swamped with many religions and so do not attach importance to any of them.*

swap 1 to swap one thing **for** another. *She recently swapped her Nik Kershaw posters for Matisse, Modigliani and Vermeer.* **2** to swap something **with** someone else. *Charlotte swapped stories with another elderly lady.*

swarm to swarm **with** people or animals. *Many parts of Kiev are swarming with police.*

swathed be swathed **in** something. *His head was swathed in bandages.*

swear 1 to swear **at** someone. *I was old enough to swear at my mother.* **2** to swear **by** something. *Tourists swear by Swiss Army socks.*

switch 1 to switch **from** one thing **to** another. *79 per cent favoured switching from atomic to wind power.* **2** to switch **with** someone. *I'm on duty on Saturday but I'll switch with one of the other men.*

symbol a symbol **of** something or **for** something. *The bishop is a symbol of Christ... Children will be asked to identify the symbols for rain and snow.*

symbolic be symbolic **of** something. *It was symbolic of Finland's growing importance.*

sympathetic be sympathetic **to** or **towards** someone or their ideas, opinions, or beliefs. *It seems that many troops are sympathetic to the popular insurrection... She had ceased to feel sympathetic towards Helen.*

sympathize to sympathize **with** someone or their ideas, opinions, or beliefs. *He sympathized with her about the way reporters had harassed her... She sympathized with the stand taken by the directors against the strikers.*

sympathy 1 sympathy **for** or **with** someone or something; sympathy **between** people. *Most of us will feel sympathy for all three causes... You have to have sympathy with the Football Association because of the lack of finance... Clearly, there was some strange sympathy between this boy and the bees.* **2 in sympathy; in sympathy with** someone. *Mainland workers might strike in sympathy... The decision was made in sympathy with local residents.*

symptom a symptom **of** something. *The row was a symptom of public anxiety over education.*

symptomatic be symptomatic **of** something. *These problems are symptomatic of the failure of care within the community.*

synchronize to synchronize one thing **with** another. *Astronomers have tried to synchronize the atomic clocks with the Earth's spin... The rhythm was not synchronized with the steps.*

synonym a synonym **for** a word. *'Totalitarian' is not always a synonym for 'communist'.*

synonymous be synonymous **with** another word, idea, or thing. *To some economists, 'development' seems to be synonymous with 'growth'... Fashion is no longer synonymous with youth.*

T

tackle to tackle someone **over** something or **about** something. *Mrs Thatcher will tackle President Bush over repatriation... Employers are to be tackled about their approach to working women.*

tainted be tainted **with** or **by** something undesirable or unpleasant. *This Government is demoralised, incoherent, and tainted with corruption... Many Hungarians consider him to be tainted by his years of service in the Communist Party.*

take 1 to take something **from** a person or place. *You are not allowed to take food from the dining room... The most wonderful thing she had ever possessed was being taken from her.* **2** to take **after** a member of your family. *He took after his grandfather where character was concerned.* **3** to take **against** someone or something. *The Producer started taking against Dan and the whole script.* **4** to take **to** someone or something. *It was impossible to tell whether he'd take to Rose or not... He took to visiting her each week.* **5** to take a duty or task **upon** yourself. *Its two leaders took it upon themselves to solve the problem.* **6** to take something out **on** someone. *They must realize they cannot take their anxieties out on others.* **7** to take someone up **on** something. *Weatherby took me up on my offer.*

taken be taken **with** someone or something. *Michael was particularly taken with the clotted cream.*

talk 1 to talk **about, on,** or **of** something. *I've got lots of plans but I can't talk about them yet... Dr Pickering will talk on 'Life at a Higher Education Institution'. ...men who had talked of perfection.* **2** to talk **to** someone. *There'll be no decision until I've talked to Charlie.* **3** to talk down **to** someone. *She is no longer being criticized for talking down to her juniors.* **4** to talk someone **into** doing something. *He talked the leaders into ending the uprising.* **5** to talk someone **out of** doing something. *He allowed himself to be talked out of giving a speech.*

tally to tally **with** something. *The confessions and statements do not tally with each other... The initials tallied with those of the missing man.*

tamper to tamper **with** something. *The best advice is to avoid tampering with your diet.*

tandem in tandem; in tandem **with** something. *He claimed that violence and diplomacy would be used in tandem... It was operated in tandem with a small conventional power station.*

tantamount be tantamount **to** something. *The act was tantamount to unconditional surrender.*

tap on tap. *We've got all the information permanently on tap.*

target 1 a target **for** something or **of** something. *Ormondroyd's height made him an easy target for unkind remarks... Students were the prime targets of attack.* **2** on **target**. *This puts him on target for the world record.*

taste 1 a taste **of** something. *...recruits who give up after a taste of army life.* **2** a taste **for** something *She acquired a taste for wearing baseball caps.*

tax to tax someone **with** something they have done. *I taxed her with wilfully embracing feminism.*

taxi by taxi. *I suggest you come by taxi to my friend's house.*

team to team up **with** someone. *The singer first teamed up with the ensemble five years ago.*

tear 1 to tear **at** something. *A pet cat was tearing at his leg during the interview.* **2** to tear **into**

someone. *He really tore into me about my work.* **3** to tear someone away **from** a place or activity. *What a shame it was to tear Dolly away from the play.*

tears in tears. *He did not resist arrest and was led away in tears.*

tease to tease information **out of** someone. *On tour, everyone will be trying to tease the name of the man out of her.*

technique a technique **of** or **for** a particular activity or skill. *I am fascinated by the technique of electro-forming metals... The technique for this kind of television is quite simple.*

teem to teem **with** animals or people. *Those gleaming surfaces are teeming with bacteria.*

telephone **1** by telephone. *The threat was made on Thursday by telephone.* **2** be **on the telephone:** be speaking to someone by telephone. *Some said it was not wise to talk on the telephone.* **3** be **on the telephone:** have a telephone in your home or office. *I'm not on the telephone at home, but you can contact me at work.*

television on television. *Mr Voican was interviewed on television.*

tell **1** to tell someone **about** something. *Teachers are encouraged to tell pupils about occasions when they took the wrong decision.* **2** to tell one thing **from** another. *All cows look the same to me. I can never tell one from another.* **3** to tell something **from** evidence or facts. *You could tell from the crowd's reaction that she was popular.*

tend to tend **towards** a particular feature or characteristic. *The first half of the game tended towards the tentative.*

term **1** in particular **terms; in terms of** something. *In archaeological terms, this is a spectacular find... We think constantly in terms of people and*

their needs. **2** **on** someone's **terms.** *He eventually forced her to negotiate on his own terms.*

test **1** to test **for** something. *The eggs came from birds which had not been tested for salmonella.* **2** to test someone **on** something. *I will test you on your knowledge of French.* **3** to test a substance **on** a person or animal. *The vaccine has been tested on gorillas... We only test on volunteers.*

testament a testament **to** a particular characteristic, fact, or achievement. *Every millimetre of this car is a testament to the skills of the panel beaters.*

testify **1** to testify **against** someone. *Most of the surviving witnesses could testify against the suspects.* **2** to testify **for** someone. *She will be asked to testify for the defence.* **3** to testify **to** a particular fact or achievement. *An archaeologist testified to its probable authenticity... Fresh shells testified to the recent murder of four peasants.*

testimony a testimony **to** the quality of a thing or person. *The successful breeding record is a testimony to the contentment of the animals in the zoo.*

theorize to theorize **about** something or **on** something. *He refuses to theorize about his music. ...theorizing on the psychology of the fox.*

theory in theory. *In theory, all schools should by now be integrated.*

thick be thick **with** something. *The air was thick with black smoke.*

think **1** to think **of** or **about** someone or something. *It had to be done. Think of all we learned from it... He should take some time off and think about his next move.* **2** to think back **over** something in the past; to think back **to** something in the past. *It gives you an opportunity to think back over the year... No-one would ever* know how often he thought back to that balcony in the South of France.

thirst 1 a thirst **for** something. *In the rougher parts of Kingston, the thirst for revenge is intense.* **2** to thirst **for** something. *They are thirsting for success.*

thirsty be thirsty **for** something. *...wolves, thirsty for blood.*

thrall in thrall. *Her singing always held the audience in thrall.*

threat 1 under threat. *Rubberwood is one of the few tropical hardwoods not under threat.* **2** a threat **to** someone or something. *Tourism is not the worst threat to the Alps.* **3** a threat **of** something. *...the threat of increased European competition.*

threaten to threaten someone **with** something. *The school was threatened with closure.*

threshold on the threshold of something. *Nick Faldo is on the threshold of winning the Championship.*

thrill to thrill **to** something. *The audience thrilled to the composer's wilful disruption of rhythm.*

thrive to thrive **on** something. *He seems to thrive on controversy.*

throw 1 to throw something **at** someone or something you want to hit. *I threw a boot at him.* **2** to throw something **to** someone, for them to catch. *I threw the script across to Beaumont and said 'I must do this play.'* **3** to throw money, energy, or resources **into** something. *Many women throw all of their energies into a career.* **4** be thrown back **on** your own power or resources. *They were thrown back on their own diminished resources.*

throwback a throwback **to** something that existed in the past. *...a throwback to the days when heavy metal was dubbed 'dinosaur rock'.*

thrust to thrust something **upon** someone or **on** someone. *Institutions respond to the responsibilities thrust upon them... It was not for me to thrust my views on them.*

thumb 1 to thumb **through** a book or magazine. *He chose a book and thumbed through it quickly.* **2 under** someone's **thumb:** controlled by them. *Some teachers are very good at keeping pupils under their thumbs.*

tie 1 to tie **with** someone in a competition. *Kasparov tied with his old enemy in the World Cup tournament.* **2** to tie up **with** something. *Questions about the nature of masculinity are tied up with sport.*

tied be tied **to** a particular subject or opinion. *One should never be tied to dogma.*

time 1 in time: not late. *A lorry came round the corner and could not stop in time.* **2 in time:** eventually. *The amount of credit the customer gets will in time be less than the amount invested.* **3 on time:** at the correct time. *...customers who are not paying their bills on time.*

tinged be tinged **with** a particular feeling or colour. *He was a man with a great sense of humour tinged with a hint of mischievousness. ...young leaves tinged with brown and pink.*

tingle to tingle **with** a particular emotion. *He could feel himself tingling with excitement.*

tinker to tinker **with** something. *He thinks that no one should tinker with a product that actually works.*

tiptoe on tiptoe. *They stretched their arms and stood on tiptoe.*

tire to tire **of** something or someone. *We soon began to tire of swordfish with caper sauce.*

tired be tired **of** something or someone. *I'm tired of coming home to an empty house.*

title the title **of** something such as a book, article, or talk. *...the ironic* *title of his last album 'Middle Class White Boy'.*

tolerant be tolerant **of** someone or something. *Britain is becoming less tolerant of violence.*

tone to tone **with** something; to tone in **with** something. *That carpet doesn't really tone in with the curtains.*

topped be topped **with** something or **by** something. *...a steel wall topped with spikes... His six foot frame was topped by freckled features and a tuft of red hair.*

total in total. *The animal is about an inch long in total.*

touch 1 in touch; in touch **with** someone or something. *National television networks have been in touch... Executives need to be in touch with the office constantly.* **2** out of touch; out of touch **with** someone or something. *He will be a little out of touch, although he's a rapid learner... He seems quite out of touch with English life.* **3** to touch **on** a subject. *The talks concentrated on security, but also touched on arms control.*

tour on tour. *...the close fellowship that comes from being on tour together.*

tout to tout **for** business or custom. *There are more than 60 companies touting for the contract.*

tow in tow. *Our firm had the job of taking the vessel in tow... He arrived on Sunday with his children in tow.*

toy to toy **with** something. *He had quickly downed his first drink and was toying with the second... I am toying with the idea of entering him in the Gold Cup.*

trace without trace. *Ships were wrecked, sunk, or lost without trace.*

trade 1 trade **in** a particular kind of goods. *...the international trade in counterfeit drugs.* **2** to trade one thing **for** another. *He traded his goats for a Mercedes car.* **3** to trade **with** someone. *They have ceased to trade with the offending countries.* **4** to trade **on** an advantage that you have. *He's always been able to trade on his name.* **5** by trade. *Previously a saddler by trade, he now concentrates on horses.*

tradition a tradition **of** something. *There is a long tradition of health research in Bath.*

traffic to traffic **in** something, especially drugs, weapons, or stolen goods. *...gangs that traffic in cocaine and crack.*

trailer a trailer **for** a film or television programme. *...an extended trailer for his forthcoming movie on Van Gogh.*

train 1 by train. *Bob travelled across Europe by train.* **2** to train **as** something or **for** something. *Some students had opted to train as actors or musicians... She returned home to train for an attempt on the world record.* **3** to train a gun, camera, or light **on** someone or something. *Eight remote control cameras were trained on her as she spoke.*

training in training. *Tax rebates were extended to all nurses in training.*

traitor a traitor **to** a country, group of people, or particular belief. *Anyone using violence would be seen as a traitor to the cause.*

trample to trample **on** someone, their rights, beliefs, or hopes. *They have trampled on every political nicety to get their policies through.*

transcript a transcript **of** a piece of writing, music, or speech. *The cost of a transcript of the proceedings is prohibitive.*

transfer to transfer **from** one place, job, or method **to** a different one. *Dr Higgs transferred from Middlesbrough to a neo-natal unit in Newcastle.*

transform be transformed **from** one thing **into** another. *It's about a twelve-year-old boy who wakes up* to find he's been transformed into a thirty-year-old man.

transit in transit. *The contents had fallen out in transit.*

transition the transition **from** one thing **to** another. *...the transition from rates to poll tax.*

translate 1 to translate writing or speech **from** one language **into** another. *Her diaries have been translated into English... It is yet to be translated from the original Urdu.* 2 to translate an idea or desire **into** another form. *I arrived with a burning ambition to translate fiction into reality.*

translation 1 a translation **from** one state or form **to** or **into** another. *...practice in translation from the ancient Greek. ...marketing strategies and their translation into profit... There had previously been no reliable translation into French.* 2 **in translation.** *...contemporary and classic plays in translation.*

travesty a travesty **of** something. *It is surely a travesty of the principles on which privatization is based.*

trespass 1 to trespass **on** property which belongs to someone else. *Supporters trespassed on the pitch to join in.* 2 to trespass **upon** someone's generosity, friendship, helpfulness, and so on. *May I venture to trespass upon your sense of justice?*

trial on trial. *They might prefer to deport them than put them on trial... It is the whole system of interrogation that is on trial.*

tribute a tribute **to** someone or something. *Everything Anna did was a tribute to him. ...an ambitious tribute to the ideals of the French Revolution.*

trick to trick someone **into** doing something. *They have tricked the public into believing their promises.*

trifle to trifle **with** someone or something. *Neither side should*

speak for Europe, or appear to trifle with its interests.

trim be in trim. *All the principle contenders are said to be in fine trim.*

triumph to triumph **over** someone or something. *He predicted that the people would triumph over their despotic rulers.*

trouble 1 in trouble. *The boy had been in trouble at home.* 2 the trouble **with** someone or something. *The trouble with Ludo's argument is that he ignores the dangers... The trouble with Jane is she never knows when to stop.*

truce a truce **with** someone or **between** two people or groups. *Rebels had made a truce with the regime. ...provided the truce between the Chancellor and the Prime Minister can be maintained.*

truck by truck. *We travelled by truck to the nearest petrol station.*

true 1 be true **of** or **for** something or someone. *This is true of other institutions as well... Pretending to be someone else was good for my shyness—the same is true for many people.* 2 be true **to** someone or something. *Mr McGregor remains true to the revolution.*

trust 1 to trust **in** someone or something. *There is always a future for those who trust in Him.* 2 to trust someone **with** something valuable. *Can he be trusted with matters of national security?* 3 **in trust.** *Nature and life have been given to us in trust.*

try 1 to try **for** something. *He tried for a third win.* 2 be tried **for** a crime. *In a few weeks he will be tried for rape.*

tube by tube: travelling on the London Underground Railway. *It'll be quicker by tube.*

tug to tug **at** something. *He tugged at the metal handle. and it came off in his hand.*

tumble

tumble to tumble **to** something. *I soon tumbled to the fact that I was wasting my time.*

tune 1 to tune **to** a particular radio station or television channel. *The ratings have dropped since people started tuning to CNN for news.* 2 **in tune:** producing the right notes. *Not everyone sang in tune.* 3 **out of tune:** producing the wrong notes. *It's a tiny bit out of tune, but it's a lovely piano.* 4 be **in tune with** something: be consistent with it or close to it. *We think this is more in tune with what people receive at home.* 5 be **out of tune with** something: be inconsistent with it or not close to it. *Mr Ashdown said Thatcherism was out of tune with the times.*

turn 1 to turn **to** someone for help or advice. *Poor and uninformed women will turn to illegal abortionists.* 2 to turn **against** someone: to stop supporting them and oppose them. *Public opinion turned against Hearst.* 3 to turn **from** one method, system, or situation **to** another. *Most farmers had turned from crops to cattle... There is no excuse for turning to violence.* 4 to turn something **from** one state or condition **into** another. *He turned Barnham from a company worth £500,000 to one worth £98 million.* 5 to turn **into** something different or **to** something different. *He is concerned that the celebrations could turn into riots... In another month, the snow will turn to mud.* 6 to turn **on** someone: to attack them. *Amir's dogs turned on their master and tore him to pieces.* 7 to turn **on** a particular thing: to depend on it. *The case turned on the confession of a mentally handicapped boy.* 8 **in turn:** following a particular sequence. *Five ministers in turn were cornered and forced to listen.* 9 **in turn:** used to introduce something connected with the previous thing.

The improvement in relations has led in turn to a reduction in arms sales. 10 **out of turn:** when something happens at an inappropriate time. *There's no penalty for playing a stroke out of turn.*

tussle to tussle **with** someone or something. *Don't leave him tussling with the longer sentences.*

twiddle to twiddle **with** something. *Do you fidget, or twiddle with your hair?*

type a type **of** something. *This type of accommodation is always in short supply.*

typical be typical **of** a person, situation, or thing. *It is made from wood and corrugated iron typical of a Russian country church... It was typical of him to place Henry Moore statues on his estate.*

U

unacceptable be unacceptable **to** someone. *Nothing in that statement is unacceptable to me.*

unaccustomed be unaccustomed **to** something. *...birds which are unaccustomed to predators.*

unacquainted be unacquainted **with** something. *...people unacquainted with the facts.*

unaffected be unaffected **by** something. *...jobs which have been largely unaffected by the advance of automation.*

unafraid be unafraid **of** something. *The children were strangely unafraid of sharks.*

unattractive be unattractive **to** someone. *He had long known he was not unattractive to women.*

unavailable be unavailable **for** something. *Hearn was unavailable for comment last night.*

unaware be unaware **of** something. *The President and his* *guests were apparently unaware of the shooting.*

unbeknown unbeknown **to** someone. *Unbeknown to the rest of the members, they had sold the premises to the Ancasta Group.*

unburden to unburden yourself **to** someone. *Let her unburden herself to you.*

uncertain be uncertain **of** something or **about** something. *...people uncertain of their goals... Gower has been uncertain about his future in the game since his dismissal as captain.*

uncharacteristic be uncharacteristic **of** someone. *...a gesture uncharacteristic of the gentle Frenchman.*

unclear be unclear **about** something. *I'm still unclear about what he has actually done.*

uncommitted be uncommitted **to** something. *Wendy, at this stage, was uncommitted to any one area.*

unconcerned be unconcerned **about** something or **with** something. *He was quite unconcerned about worldly success... Her complaint was that the meeting had been boring and unconcerned with issues.*

unconnected be unconnected **with** something else. *The sale was completely unconnected with my retirement.*

unconscious be unconscious **of** something. *They may be quite unconscious of this need.*

undecided be undecided **about** something. *Nigel Mansell is still undecided about his future in motor racing.*

understanding 1 an understanding **of** a subject. *I already had a fair understanding of business practice.*
2 understanding **between** two or more people or groups. *...a project to encourage understanding between the races.*

uneasy be uneasy **about** something. *Companies are growing uneasy about the delay.*

unequal 1 be unequal **to** an action or task. *...international law being unequal to the demands of modern conflict.* 2 be unequal **to** someone. *They cannot love women because they have made women unequal to themselves.*

unfair 1 be unfair **to** someone or **on** someone. *This is very bad for the game, and unfair to the players... To ban this horse would be most unfair on the owners.* 2 be unfair **to** another person. *I used to be very unfair to him.*

unfaithful be unfaithful **to** your partner. *Is he the one who was unfaithful to his wife?*

unfamiliar 1 be unfamiliar **to** someone. *The sounds of traffic and the telephone are unfamiliar to them.* 2 be unfamiliar **with** something. *...those unfamiliar with modern Germany.*

unfit be unfit **for** a purpose, thing, or person. *This place is quite unfit for food preparation... Women are still considered unfit for priesthood amongst most Protestants and all Catholics.*

unhappy be unhappy **about, with,** or **at** something. *Both the Government and the profession are deeply unhappy about this report... They were clearly unhappy with the situation... Senior officers are equally unhappy at the costs.*

unimpressed be unimpressed **by** something or **with** something. *Bill Rodgers had been unimpressed by their performance... He pronounced himself unimpressed with the operation.*

uninterested be uninterested **in** something. *His prospective employers seemed uninterested in his academic background.*

unique be unique **to** a particular thing, person, or place. *...that blend of pity and comedy that is unique to Irish writers.*

unison

unison in unison: together. *The crowd groaned in unison.*

united 1 be united **in** an activity or opinion. *Both parties were united in opposition to the scheme.* **2** be united **with** something. *Young Herschel spent some months in England, then united with Hanover under King George the Third.*

unkind be unkind **to** someone. *Sometimes they were very unkind to me.*

unknown be unknown **to** someone. *His identity was unknown to anyone else.*

unload to unload something unwelcome **onto** someone else. *To unload all the blame onto Spaniards would be wrong.*

unprepared be unprepared **for** something. *She was quite unprepared for the scope of the problem.*

unrelated be unrelated **to** something else. *Doctors said his condition was unrelated to his riding career.*

unresponsive be unresponsive **to** something or someone. *...a government unresponsive to their needs.*

unsatisfied be unsatisfied **with** something. *...if you are unsatisfied with your doctor's advice.*

unsuitable be unsuitable **for** something; an unsuitable thing **for** something. *Goats will eat vegetation unsuitable for sheep... This made the hall an unsuitable room for meals.*

unsuited be unsuited **to** something. *I was totally unsuited to the profession.*

unsure 1 be unsure **of** yourself. *Then I thought about my 'plan' and no longer felt unsure of myself.* **2** be unsure **of** something or **about** something. *People were unsure of what was happening... Woodward was unsure about the rules on disclosing sources to the executive editor.*

untroubled be untroubled **by** something. *But Hunter appeared untroubled by doubts of any kind.*

unused /ʌnjuːst/ be unused **to** something. *Mr Folland is unused to publicity.*

unwelcome be unwelcome **to** someone. *Yesterday's declaration will be unwelcome to Mr Gorbachev.*

unworthy be unworthy **of** something or someone. *...a story which Stevenson himself evidently considered unworthy of publication... Let us stifle all thought of hypocrisy, which would be unworthy of us.*

upholstered be upholstered **in** a particular material. *The seats were upholstered in soft leather.*

uproot to uproot someone **from** their home. *It is a much bigger decision for someone to uproot himself from his native land.*

upset be upset **by**, **about**, or **at** something. *They were upset by the poverty they saw... She seems upset about something... Residents are upset at the prospect of losing their library.*

upshot the upshot **of** a series of events. *The upshot of this episode was that we had to make a choice between Ari and Liz.*

upsurge an upsurge **in** something or **of** something. *...an upsurge in medical negligence cases. ...the latest upsurge of violence.*

urge 1 an urge **for** something. *This issue indicates the underlying urge for conformity amongst youngsters.* **2** to urge something **on** or **upon** someone. *Frank had another reason for urging caution on them both.*

use 1 /juːz/ to use something **as** a particular thing. *...leaders who use citizens as pawns.* **2** /juːs/ the use **of** something. *...the excessive use of force by the police.* **3** a use **for** something: a way in which it can be used. *A proper use for the site might well be as a library.* **4** be of

victory

use: be useful. *As in golf, general coaching would be of some use.*
5 in use: being used. *...the variety of different aircraft in use in NATO air forces.*
used /juːst/ be used **to** something. *Mature politicians are used to dealing with these issues.*
useful be useful **for** doing something; be useful **to** someone. *Bleach is useful for cleaning any surface that it will not damage. ...a college where they will meet people who will be useful to them later on.*

V

vacancy a vacancy **in** a particular organization **for** a particular job. *...an unexpected vacancy in the department. ...advertising a vacancy for the post of information officer.*
vacation on vacation. *I'm here on vacation.*
vaccinate to vaccinate someone **against** a disease. *Most of them were vaccinated against hepatitis.*
vague be vague **about** something. *Even the best artists tended to be vague about the details.*
vain in vain. *But his efforts were in vain; England lost.*
value of value. *Nurseries are only of value for women with pre-school children.*
variance be at variance **with** something. *...views totally at variance with the contemporary climate of opinion.*
variant a variant **of** something or **on** something. *Each of these countries has evolved its own variant of democracy. ...this variant on medieval practice.*
variation 1 a variation **of** something or **on** something: a different form. *Snakes that live in sandy desert have developed a*

variation of this technique... They can be regarded as variations on two extreme world views. **2** a variation **in** something or **of** something: a change. *...short-term variations in temperature. ...a novelist's instinctive variation of mood and tempo.*
variety 1 a variety **of** things. *The college library had a wide variety of books.* **2** a variety **of** something: a particular type of it. *...a new variety of potato.*
vary to vary **with** or **according to** changing factors. *The colour of the fruit varies with age... Charges for most telephone calls vary according to distance and time of day.*
vehicle a vehicle **for** something. *The orchestra should be a vehicle for the music, not vice versa.*
vent to vent your feelings **on** someone. *...so that the audience could not vent their anger on individuals.*
verdict someone's verdict **on** something. *My verdict on the series: splendid.*
verge 1 on the verge of something. *The club was on the verge of bankruptcy.* **2** to verge **on** or **upon** something. *...an atmosphere of indiscipline verging on lawlessness.*
versed be versed **in** something. *She was not well versed in labour relations.*
version a version **of** something. *...a far more amusing version of the game.*
vested be vested **in** a person or group. *Hitherto, responsibility had been vested in professional administrators.*
vicinity in the vicinity of a place. *...a man who had seen them in the vicinity of the wrecked offices.*
victory a victory **for** someone or something, **over** or **against** an opponent. *The outcome of the dispute has been seen as a victory for the employers. ...his 6-4 victory*

over Steve Davis. ...their comprehensive victory against the faded champions.

vie to vie **with** someone **for** something desirable. *Three people are vying for the post of chairman.*

view 1 in someone's **view:** used when giving someone's opinion. *In my view, Jefferson wrote rather less well than he talked.* **2 in view of** something: taking it into consideration. *He could hardly be expected to do more in view of the resistance he faces.* **3** be **in view:** be visible. *Our hands are more often in view than our feet.* **4** be **on view:** be displayed. *His aim was to put the entire collection on view to the public.* **5 with a view to** doing something: used when stating a purpose. *She had rented a huge house with a view to giving lessons there.*

viewpoint from a particular **viewpoint.** *From the spectator's viewpoint it is a tedious strategy.*

virtue by virtue of something: because of it. *Adolescents now, by virtue of their new-found economic power, dictated fashions in everything.*

visible be visible **to** someone. *They sit in a circle, from which the blackboard is visible to everyone.*

vision someone's vision **of** something. *...an outsider's vision of the West.*

visit 1 a visit **from** someone. *I soon received my second visit from the police.* **2** to visit **with** someone: used in American English. *He had not visited with the rascal since 1946.*

visitor a visitor **to** a place or **from** a place. *...Czechoslovak visitors to Hungary and Poland... Each year, 500,000 visitors from all over the world flock there.*

vital be vital **to** or **for** something or someone. *...those students most vital to our economic future. ...a new trade agreement vital for the country's ailing economy.*

vogue be **in vogue:** be popular. *...the grotesque style which was then in vogue.*

voice a voice **in** a matter. *It is unacceptable that I should have no voice in the political affairs of my own country.*

volition of your **own volition.** *She didn't go down there of her own volition.*

volunteer to volunteer **for** something. *He was always volunteering for the more dangerous daytime patrols.*

vote 1 to vote **for** a candidate or proposal you like or **against** one you do not like. *Only 21 per cent said they would vote for Mrs Thatcher... The people had voted against change.* **2** to vote **on** an issue. *They have until 23 November to vote on the proposal.*

vouch to vouch **for** someone or something. *Having played alongside him at Rochdale, I can vouch for his ability.*

voucher a voucher **for** something. *...a voucher for air travel.*

vulnerable be vulnerable **to** attack, damage, or something unwanted. *Commercial television, they claimed, would be less vulnerable to political pressure.*

W, X, Y, Z

wade to wade **through** lots of writing. *...wading through the inevitable mass of paper-work.*

wait 1 to wait **for** someone or something. *I'm waiting for a friend... He said that they were still waiting for a reply from Mr Waddington.* **2** to wait **on** people in a restaurant: to serve them their food. *Lord Derby had twenty four people to wait on him at table.*

wake to wake up **to** a fact. *Politicians should wake up to the implication of this.*

walk 1 to walk away **from** a situation or agreement. *They are prepared to walk away from the deal if they are faced with extra demands.* 2 to walk away **with** a prize. *He walked away with $1,200 in cash.* 3 to walk in **on** someone: to interrupt them. *She was carrying out his orders when her mother walked in on her.* 4 to walk off **with** something. *My companion had walked off with my suitcase.* 5 to walk out **on** someone: to abandon them. *She walked out on Henry last Friday.*

wallow to wallow **in** a feeling or situation. *...an actor who wallows in the undeserved praise of his colleagues.*

want 1 to want something **from** someone or **of** someone. *Adolescents want guidance from their parents... What do you two want of me?* 2 someone's want **of** something: their lack of it. *He blamed himself for his want of foresight.* 3 **for want of** something: because it is lacking. *He began to read, for want of anything else to do.* 4 be **in want of** something: need it. *The night I first saw him he was badly in want of a meal.*

war 1 a war **with** or **against** another country. *...in the event of an American war with a foreign power. ...the war against Germany and Italy.* 2 a war **against** something bad. *...the war against starvation and disease.* 3 be **at war**; be **at war with** another country or group. *It's nearly 200 years since France was at war with England.*

warm to warm **to** someone or something. *Mr MacSharry warmed to the idea.*

warn 1 to warn someone **of** something or **about** something. *I had been warned about the stunt... He warned of revenge attacks by residents.* 2 to warn someone **against** doing something. *But*

doctors have warned me against stairs... Phillips warned against complacency.*

wary be wary **of** something or someone or **about** something. *They have good reason to be wary of the media... Demmy said he was wary about the proposal.*

waste to waste something such as money or time **on** something or someone. *...fear of wasting money on a new idea.*

wasted be wasted **on** someone. *Advice is wasted on someone who will not heed it.*

watch 1 to watch **for** or watch out **for** something you might see. *He began to read the papers, watching for an announcement of the Volkov concert. ...a growing need to watch out for industrial pollution.* 2 to watch **over** someone or something. *The wives took turns to watch over the children.*

wave to wave **to** someone or **at** someone. *Hanna waved to him and he waved back... He smiled and waved at them.*

way 1 a way **of** doing something. *...the fairest way of dealing with the problem.* 2 a way **round** a problem. *Such a move would seem to be a sensible way round the problem.* 3 **by way of** something: used when explaining the purpose of a statement. 'Gascoigne is a competitor,' Terry Venables said afterwards by way of explanation.* 4 be **in the way:** be obstructing someone. *Our job is not to get in the way.* 5 **in the way of** something: used to specify what you are talking about. *His stalls bring in little in the way of profits.* 6 **on the way;** on your **way:** in the course of a journey. *He was stopped for speeding on the way back from the ground... On my way to the parked car, I was set upon by a gang of youths.* 7 be **out of the way:** be finished or dealt with. *The announcement could have been delayed until the by-election*

weak

was out of the way. **8** be **under
way:** be happening. *The digging
was well under way.*

weak be weak **on** a particular
element. *The book was weak on
fact and documentation.*

weakness a weakness **for**
something. *She had a weakness for
garlic.*

wean to wean someone **off** or **from**
something. *After four months,
wean him off milk altogether.
...trying to wean people from
cigarettes.*

weary 1 be weary **of** something.
*...a financial journalist who one
day grew weary of writing about
the economy.* **2** to weary **of**
something. *He wearied of picking
her clothes up off the floor and
washing them.*

wedded be wedded **to** a particular
idea. *...a party genuinely wedded
to unrestricted free enterprise.*

weigh to weigh **on** or **upon**
someone. *I could still sleep at
night, however serious the
problems weighing on me were.*

welcome 1 welcome **to**
somewhere: used to greet someone
as they arrive somewhere or at the
beginning of an event. *Welcome to
Texas... Good evening, and
welcome to the programme.* **2** be
welcome **to** something. *We've got
eight hundred dollars between us
and you're welcome to it.*

west west **of** a place. *Membury is
close to the M4, three miles west of
Hungerford.*

what 1 what **about** someone or
something: used to ask a question
or make a suggestion. *What about
a spot of lunch, Colonel?* **2** what **of**
someone or something: used to ask
a question. *But what of the
possible consequences?*

wheedle 1 to wheedle something
out of someone. *She flattered
Seery and wheedled money out of
him.* **2** to wheedle someone **into**
doing something. *He tried to*
wheedle her into leaving the
house.

whine to whine **about** something.
*My father never complained or
whined about his work.*

whip to whip a person or group of
people **into** a particular state.
*Speeches, slogans, posters and
chants whipped the crowd into a
warlike fever.*

wink to wink **at** someone. *On my
way back in the Underground, a
man winked at me.*

wish to wish **for** something. *He
wished for death.*

withdraw to withdraw **from** a
place or activity. *Steven Jones has
withdrawn from next weekend's
Great North Run in Newcastle.*

withhold to withhold something
from someone. *The President has
a legal duty not to withhold
material evidence from a grand
jury.*

witness 1 a witness **to** an event.
*In some extraordinary way he had
been a witness to a tragedy.* **2** be
witness **to** something. *This was
the first time I was witness to one
of his rages.*

wonder 1 to wonder **about**
someone or something that is not
fully known. *I'd always wondered
about my father.* **2** to wonder **at**
something surprising. *One can
only wonder at children's nerves
and strength when this kind of
thing happens.*

word a word **with** someone. *Have
you had the chance of a word with
Lonnie yet?*

work 1 to work **for** an employer or
at a place or organization. *He has
moved to Worcester, where he
works for a medical firm... Mr
Cooper now works at the
Oklahoma Transplant Institute.*
2 to work **as** a type of worker.
*...the hospital where she works as
a nursing sister.* **3** to work **for** or
towards a particular thing. *They
also work for international peace...
They have been working towards*

the long term development of their oil sector. 4 to work **with** a person or group of people. *I enjoyed working with Hitchcock, he was a great joker.* 5 to work **on** or **at** something. *We are working on new drugs for the treatment of Parkinson's disease... Someone must have worked at it with a crowbar.* 6 to work **with** or **in** a particular substance. *People who have never worked with steel have trouble understanding this... He always works in oil paints.* 7 to work **through** a problem or difficulty. *They work through a series of issues and problems with key employees.* 8 to work yourself **into** a particular state. *She was working herself into a rage about his attitude.* 9 to work yourself up **to** doing something. *A group of girls excitedly work themselves up to going on some wild diet.* 10 to work up **to** a particular amount or level. *She recommends starting with a teaspoonful or less and working up gradually to 2 or 3 tablespoonfuls.*

worm to worm information out **of** someone. *The truth had been wormed out of him by his lawyers.*

worried be worried **about** someone or something. *He is worried about his reputation.*

worry to worry **about** someone or something. *I used to sit and worry about my future.*

worth a particular amount of money's worth **of** something. *They stole fifty thousand dollars' worth of equipment.*

worthy be worthy **of** someone or something. *I've proved myself worthy of you... The party had reformed itself and was now worthy of support.*

wrangle to wrangle **with** someone **over** something. *Negotiators were wrangling with the Coal Board in an effort to raise wages... They wrangled over whose turn it was to do the washing up.*

wrap 1 to wrap something **in** a covering or to wrap something up **in** a covering. *I tiptoed across the yard with the book wrapped in a plastic bag... My hair is wrapped up in a towel, because I've just washed it.* 2 to wrap a covering **round** or **around** something. *He had a paper napkin wrapped round his glass.*

wrapped up be wrapped up **in** a particular person or thing. *Like many isolated people, they are wrapped up in themselves.*

wreathed be wreathed **in** something or **with** something. *The dawn was pale, the sun wreathed in mist. ...a cross wreathed with roses.*

wrestle to wrestle **with** someone or something. *...the biggest problems the world's car manufacturers have had to wrestle with since their pioneering days.*

wriggle to wriggle **out of** a task or duty. *I can't manage to wriggle out of accompanying my parents to Europe.*

wring to wring something **out of** or **from** someone or something. *...the last possible advantage to be wrung out of this meeting... Nor could he wring from her any information as to where she had been.*

write 1 to write **to** someone. *Ken Morgan wrote to me this month and I shall be replying soon.* 2 to write something **into** a contract or agreement. *The new arrangements have been written into the agreement.* 3 to write off **to** a person or organization. *Why don't you write off to Sussex University and ask for their prospectus?* 4 to write someone or something off **as** a particular thing. *He was written off as a wet liberal.*

wrong be wrong **with** someone or something. *What's wrong with being popular?*

yearn

yearn to yearn **for** something. *We yearned for beauty, truth, and meaning in our lives.*

yell to yell **at** someone. *Look—let's stop yelling at each other.*

yield to yield **to** someone or something. *Radio has long been under pressure to yield to television.*

zero to zero in **on** something. *The missile then zeros in on the target.*

zest a zest **for** something. *They have nothing in common except for an invincible zest for survival.*